WILD ADVENTURE

The author in action

WILD ADVENTURE

HOWARD HILL

FOREWORD BY
ERROL FLYNN

WITH A NEW PREFACE BY JERRY HILL

THE DERRYDALE PRESS
LANHAM AND NEW YORK

THE DERRYDALE PRESS

Published in the United States of America
by The Derrydale Press
An imprint of The Rowman & Littlefield Publishing Group, Inc.
4501 Forbes Boulevard, Suite 200, Lanham, Maryland 20706

Distributed by NATIONAL BOOK NETWORK, INC.

ISBN 978-1-58667-033-7

The paper used in this publication meets the minimum requirements of
American National Standard for Information Sciences—Permanence of
Paper for Printed Library Materials, ANSI/NISO Z39.48-1992.
Manufactured in the United States of America.

DEDICATION

To my wife, Elizabeth, a truly great
sportswoman, who also likes to see
beyond the next range of mountains

CONTENTS

LIST OF ILLUSTRATIONS

ACKNOWLEDGEMENTS

The frontispiece and illustrations numbered 2, 13, 14, 16, 17, 18, 19, 20, 21, 24, 25, 27, 28, 29, 30, 31, 33, and 34 are reproduced from photographs from RKO's Release Tembo; *the remaining fifteen illustrations have been supplied by the author.*

PREFACE

W*ILD Adventure* is the second book that my uncle wrote. Like his first book titled *Hunting the Hard Way*, it is filled with bowhunting experiences unequaled by other bowhunter stories written. He continues to hold the reader's attention from cover to cover. Howard Hill lived somewhat of a storybook life. His beginning as a southern farmer's youngest son, being raised along the Coosa River, provided him at an early age exposure to wild animals and the surroundings. He began shooting the bow and arrow at the early age of four years old, with a bow and set of arrows that his father made for him out of a white oak strip and river cane for his arrows. It is amazing that these early teachings would lead him to all parts of the world, and at the same time introduce him to many famous people who took a liking to his easy way of living. These same people pushed aside their livelihoods, choosing to follow in his footsteps and be a part of a life that many during this period thought to be foolish and dangerous. During his lifetime, Howard Hill proved to the world that the bow and arrow was equal to the gun, when the arrow was well placed. He did things that others said could not be done with the bow and arrow. He was known in Hollywood as "Mr. Archery," and when he was called upon to make many of the shots before the movie cameras, no one disputed this title placed upon him. He split nine arrows for the cameras during the making of the movie *The Adventures of Robin Hood* starring Errol Flynn in 1938. Flynn, watching Howard Hill make this shot for him as his personal double, remarked to the director, "I sure am good, aren't I?" Many upon many stories have been told about this man and his archery prowess that even today after all these years (he passed away in 1975) many still consider him to be "The World's Greatest Archer."

Good hunting and good reading,

Jerry Hill

FOREWORD

WHEN you meet Howard Hill you know darn well you've met him before, but you can't remember where or when.

Let me solve your problem. If, like myself, you sometimes find yourself hanging on a bar rail and staring over the head of the bar-tender, behind those character-destroying bottles of Four Posies or Old Step-Mother, you'll spot Hill. There you will see a reproduction of a painting, the cultural contribution of some beer cartel like Somebody and Rusch, depicting *Custer's Last Stand*. That American aborigine, that Indian on the piebald pony is Hill. Yes, the guy giving out with the blood-curdling war whoop, drawing a bead on the heroic general (if a bead can be drawn with a bow and arrow Hill is the one who can do it) is our boy. This is no quaint flight of fancy. It *has* to be Hill. God knows, I've stared at both Hill and his weapon often enough, chilled to the marrow.

When Hill goes after any living creature with his bow for whatever reason, whether for food, motion pictures or sport, he has the same intensity, the same piercing black eyes, the same unmistakable snarl, leering with the triumph of the Indian about to wade up to his navel in the gore of the Paleface. He may be stalking only a rabbit, but it's still Hill.

He calls himself a Creek, I think, and is inordinately proud of it. But he is a real Indian, make no mistake, as this Paleface knows. Confronted by Hill bearing down upon me over the bar on that pinto pony charging over countless hordes of Four Posies, I have always felt a keen sympathy for the unlucky Custer.

It is only our long and enduring friendship (based upon a mutual love for hunting and the Great Outdoors) that has induced me to write this foreword to his book, a thing I would do for no one else. As yet, being on a different continent from him at the moment, I have not had a gander at Howard's tome, but I am sure it is a work calculated to bring out the best kind of savagery in American youth. The book is a cinch to stir many a nervous pulse as Hill has stirred mine in the past. It has to be filled with wild adventure.

In it, naturally, he will not tell you of the time we were out hunting mountain lion, and having just lassoed one, he had the frenzied brute screeching and turning somersaults at the end of a rope snubbed around a tree. Suddenly Howard yelled: "Here, hold this!" And I did, only to find out that I had hold of the tail of the enraged cat instead of the rope. Nor, I suppose, will this savage recount another incident that occurred while we were hunting wild boar on Santa Cruz Island when he left me hanging on the side of a cliff several hundred feet above the rocky sea-shore. While he sat in safety fifty yards away, eating boiled eggs and going into sporadic gales of laughter, he watched me suffer the terrors of chronic vertigo, too petrified to move an inch. Yes, Hill is an Indian.

Although no Indian myself, and laying no claim to being perhaps even an exceptional hunter, yet I do have much in common with Hill. The wailing note of the loon floating across a placid lake, the distant high-pitched cry of the timber wolf, the guttural roar of the jaguar and the blood-curdling cough of the charging wild boar, call to some deep inner response within us both that is not acquainted with modern civilization.

"Cupid" Hill, as I have called Howard ever since we first met while making the picture *Robin Hood*, has done things with a bow and arrow that few have essayed with the rifle, and I for one am going to read his book with great nostalgia, for some of the truly wonderful moments of my life have been spent tagging along at Howard's heels on our hunting trips in many strange corners of the world.

Rome, Italy

Errol Flynn

CHAPTER ONE

BY WAY OF INTRODUCTION

Iт is not my intention to set forth in this volume any concise or technical set of rules concerning the fine points relative to the photography of game or hunting with the bow, nor will I give in detail any exact method to be followed when shooting wild game with camera or bow. Rather, I shall tell some of the procedures I have found successful for the stalking of most of the animals on the continents of North America and of Africa, in order to gain a close position to them. Also, it is my plan to give more or less in detail, some of the thrills and the dangers I have met with, and how those experiences were enjoyed or overcome, according to the circumstances under which they were met.

Reading this book, one must remember that because all birds, animals, and reptiles are individuals, the incidents recounted might not happen again in the same way, even if experienced by the same person with the same wild creature, and under the same circumstances. For that reason it would be unwise even to suggest a set of rules to be used by the hunter or the cameraman when facing wild creatures.

Naturally, when a man goes into the wilds to photograph animals in their natural surroundings or to hunt them at close range with the bow, he needs all the scientific knowledge he has attained in perhaps many years of study, but he will speedily find that the purely scientific approach needs to be tempered by a certain amount of good common horse sense, in order to get the best results and survive the experiences unscathed. I think it is safe to say that in no other field of endeavour is the happy combination of technical and scientific knowledge, together with common horse sense, more rewarding than when studying the wild denizens of the fields, the streams, the forests, and jungles.

In studying wild creatures, one should be scientific enough to take nothing for granted, yet he should be sensible enough to realize that all animals, even in the same family, are individuals and seldom, indeed, or never, do any two of them possess identical characteristics. Especially is this statement true of the highly courageous (and therefore to man, highly dangerous) beasts.

There are in most cases basic characteristics inherent in all animals of the same genus, but each animal has enough individuality to set him apart from every other creature in the world. For this reason, it is unwise to become dogmatic as to how any wild animal will react under any given set of circumstances. While the scientist is likely to minimize or discredit the outstanding differences to be found in individual animals, the animal lover and ordinary hunter may be prone to exaggerate such distinctions.

However, I am convinced that the more personal experience one subjects himself to in studying and observing wild creatures, the more respect he has for them and the less dogmatic he becomes with regard to their characteristics. Most of us hunters who have spent the greater part of our lives in the bush realize how foolish it is to accept any definite set of rules for the rabbit or the lion, the bobcat or the elephant. Invariably, just as a man becomes convinced that a certain animal will do a certain thing under a given set of circumstances, he will meet an individual that will react in an exactly opposite way from others of his family.

There is an Indian in the Florida Everglades named Charlie Snow, a most intelligent fellow and a marvellous hunter, tracker, and woodsman. Any time Charlie is asked, for instance, will a deer do this or will a deer not do that, he has a stock answer, no matter what wild creature is in question. The answer is always the same. "Maybe yes! Maybe no! Don't know."

The fact that Charlie refuses to become dogmatic does not minimize the wonderful store of knowledge which he has of all the wild animals of South Florida. He knows too much about them to make any flat statements. Yet he can call a rabbit out of the scrub palmetto, lure a wild turkey gobbler to his death, coax the bobcat from the briar patch, entice the bull alligator to leave the murky depths of the 'Glades pool, or bring the hog bear (Florida black bear) on the run to within easy bow-and-arrow range.

Ned Frost, of Cody, Wyoming, is one of America's greatest

naturalists, according to both the late Dr. Osborne (long time head of the Museum of Natural History in New York City) and to Vernon Bailey (for many years Chief of the Biological Survey for the United States Government) and when asked a direct question about any wild creature, Ned will usually give an answer very much like that of Charlie Snow. It will go something like this:

"Well, yes; then again, no. It's hard to say for sure."

A famous Algonquin Indian hunter, Dave Coleman, of Quebec, will only say quietly: "I don't know."

The answer to any direct query about a wild creature asked of Wally Gravett, an exceptional woodsman and hunter of North British Columbia, would be: "No man can tell what any animal will do."

Frank Colcord, of Payson, Arizona, the world's champion hunter of mountain lions and one of the most capable woodsmen in America, would reply more to the point. His look of scorn would squelch the questioner and his words would leave no doubt in his mind. "Nobody knows what any wild critter will or won't do. He's got a head of his own!"

Antonio Lopez, of the Yaqui River country in Old Mexico, a famous jaguar hunter and expert roper, would only grin and say: "Me no say, Señor."

If the same question were asked of Casumway, an African Ruanguba native, who has spent thirty years in the Belgian Congo, in Tanganyika, Kenya, and Uganda as guide and tracker for all manner of big game hunting, he would only say: "*W-a-p-i!*" which means "Are you kidding?"

No matter how many hundreds of other great woodsmen might be queried as to what to expect from wild game, the answers of all would be about the same.

I have hunted many times with all the fellows mentioned above, and with some of them for months at a time, yet not once have I ever heard one of them make any broad statement that could cover any one species of bird, animal, or reptile. The answer of Charlie Snow sums up the attitude of them all: "Maybe yes! Maybe no! Don't know!"

When writing about any type of wild creature, it is necessary to set down a number of characteristics of the species, of course, but the careful writer should emphasize the fact that not only will two animals of the same family react differently when encountered by man but that even the same individual creature is liable to react differently under the same set of circumstances at different times.

The readers of books about wild animals, too, should remember that what is generally true of members of a given species, by no means implies that there are no exceptions to the general statements made. Keeping this fact in mind would save a lot of criticism that is heaped upon authors. Sometimes, it would actually seem that a few people read articles or books about wild game for one specific reason, to see what they can find wrong. Such persons will sometimes use the statements of one writer to disprove what is written by another, when the truth is, that often both writers are correct in what they have said.

To prove how differently the same animals react at different times, one has only to read the experiences of some of the world's most famous hunters in the past. When Colonel Theodore Roosevelt, with his son, Kermit, and Edmund Heller went to Africa in 1909, they met several very famous sportsmen and professional hunters. In his splendid book, *African Game Trails,* Col. Roosevelt gives more or less in detail an account of the discussions he had with a number of these famous men. Even though all of them had faced over and over again all the dangerous beasts of the Dark Continent, their ideas as to which of these creatures was really *the most dangerous* varied widely.

Some thought the lion the most deadly; others feared the buffalo the most; two or three classed the rhino at the top of the list, while still others had more dread of the elephant or the leopard.

Although there are other African big game animals that will fight desperately when cornered, the five just mentioned are the ones classified as dangerous. The leopard and the lion as a rule will seldom attack man except when wounded or when they believe themselves to be cornered, yet many have been the exceptions to this rule. There have been numerous man-eating lions and leopards that were true man-killers. It is interesting in passing to note, also, that whereas most writers refer to the leopard as hunting only at night, yet in many instances where that cat has become a man-killer, he has attacked his victims in broad daylight.

In speaking of an animal's charging or attacking when he is cornered, it is not meant that he is necessarily hemmed in with literally no way of escape. Actually, there have been few instances where any man has had a beast so cornered that there was no way out for the creature except to attack the hunter. What is meant, really, is that when man comes upon such a beast, the creature becomes so frightened that he thinks himself cornered and will attack, even though he might be able to run away in any direction he cared. One of the hazards the hunter of big game has to run, is that he never knows just when an animal will consider himself cornered and decide to fight it out.

In Africa there are perhaps more rogue elephants that will attack on sight than members of any other species, except the rhinoceros. While making the motion picture, *Tembo,* in Africa a few years ago, we kept a record of the charges made by all the animals during our ten-month safari. We found the rhino by far the most aggressive of all the dangerous creatures with the elephant second, the lion third, the buffalo fourth, and the leopard last. We saw very few leopards, only five in fact.

However, the leopard is a night prowler and seldom travels in the daylight hours unless driven by extreme hunger or when he has acquired a taste for human flesh and turned to man-killing. We learned of three man-eating leopards, and all of them caught their unfortunate victims during the daylight hours, which many persons would find almost incredible, having always read that leopards are entirely nocturnal in their habits.

We saw hundreds of buffalo but for the most part they were anxious to get out of sight as soon as possible. However, several individual bulls showed fight and once four of the black brutes ran my cameraman, Arthur Phelps, and me for a quarter of a mile. We were in a jeep and had little trouble in getting away from them. Had we been on foot, the story might have been much different. There were two natives killed by buffalo near our camp while we were in Africa, one in Tanganyika near Lake Manyara, and one in the Belgian Congo near Lake Albert. In each instance, the victim was travelling through the forest and was attacked and tossed by the bull buffalo without provocation.

We learned of six or eight natives that were killed by rogue elephants during our stay. Most of these people lost their lives

B

while trying to drive the marauding creatures out of their gardens.

One of the reasons that many experienced hunters get killed by animals is that they become over-confident in their weapons and in their ability to stop charging wild beasts. A second reason is that after having escaped from close places a good many times, still unharmed, they become careless.

It is usually the beginner, however, who takes too many chances. He simply does not know enough about the wild creatures to have any definite idea as to what can happen, and many times the novice gets killed, not realizing he is in danger until it is too late. Even avoiding all unnecessary risks and taking every possible precaution for safety, the man who is either hunting or photographing wild beasts will find that it can be a very dangerous business. Few professional hunters in Africa live long without being tossed by a buffalo or mauled by either a leopard or a lion. Those unfortunate enough to be struck down by an elephant or horned by a rhinoceros seldom escape with their lives.

I talked with one young Englishman named Reginald Montgomery. He was about thirty-five years old and had been for a while an elephant hunter for the British Government. His job had been to kill not only rogue elephants but also any old bulls that had exceptional ivory. According to the records, he had killed 197 elephants in three years of hunting. When I saw him, he no longer held this job for the Government, but was what is known in Central Africa as a white hunter and outfitter. In other words, he guided hunting parties and furnished all the necessary equipment for their safaris.

His reason for quitting the job as a British Government hunter was because of an experience that he had with a wounded elephant. He had hit the bull and it had charged him. He then hit the beast twice in the head at very close range with two slugs from a ·470 double elephant rifle, but failed to stop the enraged bull. The elephant got hold of him and slung him high into the air so that he landed up in the fork of a tree, where he held on without making a sound, while the maddened beast screamed and ran in circles, looking for him. Within a short time the animal died from his wounds, without having been able to find the hunter in the tree where he had been thrown. Mr. Montgomery said it was while he was holding on to that tree trunk and praying that the beast would not discover him that he decided he had had all the rogue elephant hunting he wanted. He knew that he was very fortunate to be alive.

Every now and then one reads an article by a sportsman who says it is no more dangerous to hunt African game than it is to shoot rabbits. The way some of the white hunters organize and carry out hunts for some sportsmen the author of such an article is correct, because the white hunter spots the game and drives the visitor to it in a car, then stands by with a small cannon while the "sportsman" takes a shot, or three, four, or five shots, maybe. If the would-be Nimrod wounds the game the white hunter, not the sportsman, goes after it and finishes the job. If the animal charges, the white hunter stops it.

However, any one who doubts that hunting African big game is dangerous has only to go to Nairobi, and read the epitaphs written on the gravestones in the cemetery there, and then jot down all those that read something like this:

CLARENCE SMITH
KILLED BY AN ELEPHANT

———————

TOMMY PRATHER
GORED TO DEATH BY A BUFFALO

———————

WILLIAM WATKINS
KILLED BY A LION

Better yet, let the doubtful fellow go into the back country and spend a couple of months, alone, or with a native guide, and bring back his own elephant's tusks, his lion and leopard hides, and his buffalo and rhinoceros horns. He will then, I am sure, not feel that he has been merely jack-rabbit hunting. If he wants a real thrill and some extra excitement let him leave his gun behind and tackle these same beasts with the bow and arrow or shoot them with a camera. I do not care what method he uses to hunt them or whether or not he shoots these beasts from blinds or out of trees, I guarantee that he will get more thrills and excitement than he really requires, before the feat is accomplished.

Naturally, many hunters exaggerate the ferocity of the animals, and in some cases over-emphasize the danger, but when you hear any man say there is no danger involved in hunting African big game, *don't you believe it!*

In some localities we visited in Africa we sometimes had as many as a dozen different animals charge us in one week, and sometimes we were charged three or four times in one day. I will acknowledge that so many charges in so short a time are unusual, but these things do happen. It can be readily understood that game which is being photographed is much more likely to charge than at other times, for the simple fact that the beasts get tired of being disturbed so often.

Several times when we came on to a rhinoceros the first time he would run away; after we followed him up two or three times he would get tired of being bothered and would attack. We had fewer attacks when we were afoot than while we were in jeeps, especially where rhinos were involved. They just seemed to work up in short order a violent dislike for jeeps. However, our party had no less than a dozen rhino charges while we were on foot. Fortunately, most of the beasts turned aside at a distance of fifteen to twenty feet.

If a fellow can keep his head at such a time he can side-step a rhino, but it is a dangerous pastime. We found that the best way to bluff a rhino was to charge towards him as he came forward. If we did this he usually veered off before reaching us but here, again, one could not depend fully on such action by the rhino, at best a truculent beast. It is amazing how fast a fellow can get up a tree or behind one when a rhino lets out a snort and dashes forward. Out of all the rhinos we photographed we had to kill only two and both those incidents occurred while we were on foot. We were able to outrun or outmanoeuvre them at every crisis when we were working them from jeeps. Not once did a rhino hit a jeep squarely, though one tough old individual brushed the bumper and another clipped the back end of the little car with his shoulder. Usually, however, we avoided the whole charge by a foot or two.

Once a mother rhino charged Arthur, my cameraman, and he and I had trouble in getting the motor started. The cow had been wallowing in the mud and had it all over her body, especially her head and horns. The motor took hold just as she lowered her head and made a blind rush. The jeep almost left the ground as I gave it all the gas and let out quickly on the clutch. The mama rhino was so sure she had us that she made a terrific swing with her head, intending to toss us, but we were not there. She came so close, however, that she threw mud on Arthur and the camera, and we figured that was close enough.

CHAPTER TWO

A NIGHT IN THE EVERGLADES

Racing like a mad bunch of Cossacks after a Mongolian for a good half-mile, we came to a large grass-covered meadow partly surrounded by a thick stand of scrub palmetto. We slid our lathered mounts to a stop beside the palmetto and listened for the foxhounds. No more than two hundred yards away we could hear the pack of dogs coming directly towards us and driving for all they were worth.

In the bright moonlight we saw a silver flash as a fox broke out of the dense cover, passed under the belly of Buddy Weidensee's horse and headed for a big hammock at the lower end of the meadow. A jumble of horses ensued as the whole group, yelling like a Comanche war party, tried to get into the lead after the fox.

Of course, riding without pink coats on horseback at night after a fox that is being chased by dogs is not proper hunting etiquette, but ours was a wild bunch that enjoyed excitement and adventure, and never stopped to consider the finer points of riding to the hounds. The Florida grey fox has no rules of etiquette when he goes after quail, duck, rabbit, young pig and barnyard fowl. It was our intention to give him a rough time.

This hunt took place some years ago near Brighton, Florida. In the party besides my wife and me were three young fellows, Glenn H. Curtiss, Jr. (son of the late Glenn H. Curtiss of aeroplane fame), Buddy Weidensee and Freddy Sutterlin, friends of young Curtiss. Others in the party were Sam Leverett, in charge of the pack of dogs and Charlie Snow, a full-blooded Seminole Indian, who was guiding the party.

Florida fox-hunting, the kind we were enjoying, has little resemblance to riding to the hounds the way it is done in Orange County, Virginia, for example. We followed the hounds at night over footing that well-bred horses, trained as hunters and jumpers, would hardly be able to walk over in the daytime without spraining a fetlock.

I do not mean to imply that there is not considerable danger in riding to the hounds in any fashion, especially over some of the well-laid-out courses. I had ridden to the hounds in Alabama with my father since the age of ten, and the sportsmen he associated with did not hunt merely for a day or two, but many times, six or eight of them would gather at a spot and set up camp and stay for a week or ten days and hunt every single night. Each of them would bring a full pack of well-trained hounds, so that a fresh group was ready for every hunt. It was not unusual for these men to carry four or five good horses to use on such an outing. Two or three hunters were just not enough to stand the steady grind.

After I grew up I had an opportunity to ride over a few well-laid-out courses, where a drag rather than a wild fox was used. I don't mind saying that I had taken more than one spill, but I never knew how wild fox-hunting could be until I went to Florida in 1925 and started hunting at night over that terrain.

Glenn H. Curtiss, Sr. had considerable real estate holdings in south and central Florida at the time. At a little hamlet called Brighton, on State Road 8, between Okechobee City and Sebring, Florida, he built a charming and well-appointed hotel as part of a real estate development programme. To help attract guests for the hotel he secured a pack of registered Walker foxhounds, several of which had been national champions, and a stable of horses.

Much of the country around Brighton is hard sand prairie, covered with short switch grass, which is ideal footing for any type of riding-horse. However, interspersed in various sizes and patterns over much of these sandy prairies are scrub palmetto, shallow lakes and ponds, "hammocks" (as the natives call the hummocks of trees), sloughs and muck pockets that combine to make the terrain quite treacherous to ride over at a canter. Most of the riders who visited the hotel would not follow the hounds at night.

The fact was that much of the ground in the vicinity was unsuited for high-bred jumpers and hunters. The Floridians, however, in that section used (and I presume they still do) a local strain of horse of their own breed that had been developed by the cattlemen. This horse was called a muck pony, and his blood lines were an admixture of American Five Gaited Saddle

Horse, Plantation Walking Horse, Mustang and a touch of Thoroughbred. Out of the crosses and from selective breeding had been developed an animal that was tough as sinew, strong as a bull and that did not know the meaning of the word "quit." They were not usually large horses, but fairly rangy, exceptionally fast, fair jumpers and so clever on their feet that they could run over ground where practically any other breed would find the going very hard if not impossible.

One particular characteristic of this muck pony, and perhaps the chief factor that made him so wonderful for that territory, was his very large, light, thin, tough hoof that enabled him to go through soft muck and quicksand at a full canter. Where an ordinary hunter or jumper would mire up to his knees on the first leap, the muck pony would have no trouble at all. His large thin foot had a very small frog which left a deep hollow underneath the foot, and this hollow seemed to pull the mud inward and cause it to pack tight enough to hold the weight of the horse. Of course the large size of the foot in proportion to the light weight of the pony was also a factor.

In that part of Florida, early morning hunting for really wild foxes was not too successful, because of the fact that as soon as the sun rose it began to get hot, and the fox and dogs could not last long enough to make a worthwhile race. At night, however, it was not unusual for a mature dog fox to run three and a half or four hours before being caught and "treed." One smart trick of the Florida grey fox was that, when he realized he could not shake the hounds and was about to be caught, he would either climb a leaning tree or go into a gopher hole. We therefore seldom caught one on the ground, and once they "treed", either in a gopher hole or up a tree, we left them unharmed. By practising this method, we had no trouble in finding plenty of foxes to chase.

Glenn H. Curtiss, Sr., called "G.H." by his friends, was quite interested in still photography, and, although he was a versatile sportsman, he did not like horseback riding. He seldom rode a horse at all, and never went fox-hunting with us. In order to secure some good pictures of fox and bobcat, both of which we often were able to tree, he encouraged me in the art of photography and whenever we went hunting I carried in a saddle bag a still camera, complete with flash bulb attachments. My early association with Mr. Curtiss had much to do with my becoming an outdoor motion picture photographer and producer in later life. In fact, it was only seven years later that I made my first motion picture expedition into the Rocky Mountains of Wyoming with Ned Frost.

We had arrived at Brighton from Miami early in the fall of 1926 for a few days' hunting. The first couple of days we spent quail shooting. It was the third afternoon after our arrival that the seven people already mentioned left Brighton a couple of hours before sundown and rode northwest some ten or twelve miles to a section known as Indian Prairie. Some of us had already enjoyed several successful hunts in this particular area. When we reached the edge of Indian Prairie we unsaddled our horses and leashed the dogs, then settled down around a camp-fire for a light snack and a few hours' of rest before beginning the night's hunt.

Slowly the full moon rose from behind a grove of royal and cabbage palms. Their trunks shone dim and ghostlike in the early rays. An interesting pattern of fluffy clouds billowed over our heads almost at the meridian. The Seven Sisters (Pleiades) played hide-and-seek among the swiftly moving thunder heads. From deep within the tropical swamp to our right, the resounding voice of the great horned owl could be heard above the croak of the bullfrogs. Insect noises from a thousand quarters floated on the gentle breeze. The night hawks zoomed around us as they dived and banked.

Here and there the leather-winged bat darted in a crazy pattern of flight, unceasing in his efforts to catch the black gnats and other flying insects that drifted about in swarms. Once the belly grunt of a bull alligator sounded along the edge of the marshy water-course nearby. A night heron glided above the treetops and flashed his golden eye at the dying camp-fire, then vanished in the night.

As always, the variety and prodigality of living creatures in South Florida was amazing and in fact almost unbelievable. Once I caught a fleeting glimpse of a Wilson snipe as he shot past our camp and only a few feet above the grass tops. The lonesome twitter of a screech owl sent a chill down my spine, as it always did, although I had been hearing the cry all my life in the Deep South. The whole scene was lighted in an eerie fashion by myriads of fireflies.

The peacefulness was broken by a loud snort from Cornstalk,

my stallion muck pony, as he gazed northward into the night. Skipper, prized strike dog, uncoiled from his sleeping position in the short grass and rose to his feet, his sensitive nose sniffing the night breeze. Charlie Snow eyed Skipper, then looked towards Cornstalk. He motioned with his head in the direction the alert stallion was looking and spoke quietly.

"Bull horse smell 'em dog fox, maybe bobcat."

Again he looked at Skipper. "Man dog catch 'em scent," he said. While he yet spoke, the sharp bark of a fox came downwind.

At the sound Skipper leaped forward and let out a bawl that brought every dog in camp to his feet. He hit the end of his leash and turned a complete flip, but came up yelling and making every effort to rid himself of the leash. Every one of our party was standing up, except Charlie.

Leverett slipped the collars of all the dogs and they were away with the speed of a frightened antelope. We hurriedly saddled our horses. By the time the last rider was up, Cap, our lead dog, barked a good half-mile away. Skipper, Fly, Winnie, Gert. Mae and all the rest of the pack soon joined in.

Charlie slowly rose from beside the fire and walked to his bare-backed Indian pony, a lean rawboned gelding. He gracefully leaped astride and was off, seemingly all in one motion. The gaunt gelding had surprising speed for such an ungainly creature. The rest of us followed Charlie across the switch grass flat at a fast clip. Wherever possible, we rode more or less abreast, rather than in single file. We had found that by following such a practice there was less chance of getting hurt. In case someone's mount lost his footing and went down, there would be no horse following that might step on the downed rider or become entangled with the fallen horse. Experience had taught us to allow each horse plenty of running room when at all possible.

We pulled up our horses and stopped a good two hundred yards away from the spot where the pack was busy trying to get the track lined out. They were working a large hammock of thick cover. Cabbage palms, water oaks, a mixture of several scrub hardwoods and a variety of vines made it hard for the dogs to get the fox moving in a straight line. The scent was fresh and the anxious dogs tore through the heavy cover like mad. For a minute or two there was considerable confusion as the dogs bawled and rushed here and there. Then Cap opened north of the hammock and the rest of the pack literally tore holes through the tangled vines inside the hammock as they raced towards the lead dog. They knew that the masterly Cap had picked up the fox's trail where they could follow at top speed.

We cut around the hammock and no sooner had we come in on the north side of it than the pack jumped the fox and the chase was on in earnest. Our horses had been on many such hunts and they seemed to enjoy the chase and the music of the pack as well as we did.

Cornstalk all but got out from under me as he leaped forward to the chase. He was a well-built, strong and powerful animal. He did not want to delay and allow the dogs too much start. I was able to keep my seat and soon had him under perfect control. My wife, riding a coal black filly, was almost abreast of me a few yards on my left. Young Curtiss, astride a Roman-nosed strawberry roan, was immediately to my right.

All the rest of the party were scattered to the right and left, and not one was more than a few yards back of the lead. We had plenty of open space and we let our horses have their heads. Our first ride of a half-mile had been sufficient to warm them up and they could run without danger of pulling a tendon.

I have hunted with a good many packs of foxhounds, but I have never seen any other pack that had the speed of these champion Walkers. Even our best strike dogs and slow trailers were extremely fast in a hot race. We had no worry about running in too close to the pack, for no horse living could catch that pack if they were allowed a few hundred yards start. They had been a quarter of a mile in front of us when they jumped the fox, so we knew that it would not be long before they would be lost in the distance. A horse can go at a faster clip than most foxhounds for a mile or so, but after that it is all in the dog's favour.

Young Glenn Curtiss, a capable and daring rider, had pulled out a couple of strides in front of Cornstalk and me. It was always a question which of the two horses was the faster, the stallion, Cornstalk, on which I rode or the strawberry gelding, Saint Cloud, on which Glenn was mounted. I was sure the stallion was just as fast as the roan, if not faster, and I knew he could outlast the gelding. At any\rate, all our horses were giving about the best they had.

Out of the moonlight I saw the ragged tops of a narrow strip of scrub palmetto loom up only a few yards in front of us. I pulled my mount down to half-speed before we hit the treacherous footing and he managed to keep his feet. Glenn Curtiss had not seen the palmetto, and he and Saint Cloud hit it at top speed. The roan went down, his feet flew from under him and his tail pointed skyward. As he started over, Curtiss quit the saddle and sailed spread-eagle through the air a good fifteen feet in front of the upturned horse.

Young Glenn landed flat on his belly in a shallow slough of muck and water beyond the narrow strip of palmetto, and he skidded for a couple of yards. He was not hurt at all, as it turned out, but his eyes were full of mud and water, and he looked as though he had lain belly first in a hog wallow.

I was sure the unfortunate horse had broken his own neck. It looked as if his head had been doubled back under him when he went over, but he had no more than landed on his back, after turning over in a forward somersault, then he was on his feet again. It seemed a miracle that he was entirely unhurt. Young Curtiss, a grand sportsman, took only time enough to wash the mud out of his eyes and we were riding again. We could barely hear the dogs a mile or more ahead of us, still going straight north.

We eased our horses down to a medium canter for a couple of miles, then pulled them up to listen to the dogs. I rode a few yards away from the rest, slid off the horse and walked a few yards farther, so that the noise of the horses' breathing would not interfere with my listening. At first I could hear nothing, but soon I could faintly detect the deep, resonant voice of Skipper. With the passing seconds it grew louder. Before long I could hear the entire pack. They were heading back, not coming directly towards us, but a considerable way east, to our right.

Our horses had had a good chance to catch their breath and were anxious to go. Back in the saddle I told the others what I deduced from having listened for the dogs. We turned east and ran as fast as our mounts could go for a good half-mile. Then we came to a wide, open, grass-covered meadow, partly surrounded by scrub palmetto. We stopped our horses just short of the dense cover in the upper end. From the sounds, we could tell that the hounds were no more than two hundred yards north of us and they were coming directly towards us. Cap, the leader, was out in front, but Winnie, a well-set Walker bitch, was close on his heels. Cap was a born front runner, but Winnie liked it up there too.

There was a silver flash as the dog fox came out of the palmetto right among us. He shot under the belly of the horse Buddy Weidensee was riding, as I said at the beginning of this story, and headed across the meadow without losing a stride.

There was a jumble of horses as everyone tried to be the first under way. Buddy and Freddy had stopped a few yards behind the rest of us and they got into the clear before the others of the party could turn and free themselves of each other for the chase. Buddy was in the lead, Freddy, a couple of strides back of him, with my wife, Libba, and me almost perfectly abreast of each other next. Leverett was several yards behind us. Glenn Curtiss and Charlie Snow had got so much in each other's way in the scramble that they were both left at the post. We were yelling like a party of Comanches on the warpath.

The fox, of course, having a running start, was well out in front before any of us could get under way. Our yelling had not helped to slow him down any, but we were determined to overtake him if possible. Such a chase is thrilling—beyond description. When we finally got straightened out, the real race began.

Buddy and Freddy were well mounted, but I felt confident that Cornstalk would outlast them. All of us were fanning our horses, except Libba. Her little black filly needed no coaxing. She was a sensitive, willing little creature and, oh boy, how she could run! She was breathing down my neck as I came abreast of Freddy. By the time we had come up close in back of Buddy she had pulled up head-and-head with Cornstalk. It looked as though she was going on out in front. I leaned low over Cornstalk's neck, patted him gently and spoke encouragingly: "Come on boy! Come on! You're not going to let that girl beat you. Come on!"

I believe to this day he understood me, because he tucked his ears back, raised his chin up a little and I could feel him flatten out. He had slipped into over-drive and tramped down on the throttle. I have never before or since ridden a faster horse.

I was halfway alongside Buddy and could see the fox only five or six feet in front of his horse. There was a loud crash and I found myself sailing through space, head first.

"Hold up, Libba! Hold up!" I yelled.

Something came in contact with my grasping hands, and I gripped tight and held on. I turned over in the air, a forward somersault, and landed on my feet, ran a couple of strides, lost my balance and plunged into a tangle of vines and small brush.

I got to my feet and ran back where I could dimly see three horses down in one pile, and one standing beside the jumbled heap. I saw that the horse standing was the black filly and that Libba was still in the saddle. How she had managed to stop so quickly I will never know.

"Buddy! Freddy!" I yelled a couple of times as loud as I could. Buddy answered several yards back of where I had landed in the vines, and Freddy yelled "Okay!" from a considerable distance off to the left. None of us was badly hurt. Fred had a few lacerations about the neck and face where the palmetto fronds had cut him; Buddy had a lump on his head where he sideswiped a tree, and I had a wrenched right shoulder, which I had twisted when I caught and held on to something with my hand while in the air. In my hand I still held the bridle off Cornstalk.

What had actually happened was that Buddy was so intent on the fox, he had not seen the hammock. I was so intent on passing Buddy I had not thought of a hammock, and Freddy had seen it too late to stop his tough-mouthed pony, but Libba, an excellent rider from having ridden all her life, had literally slid her mount to a stop in time. As I went over Cornstalk's head, my right hand had touched the top of the bridle back of his ears and I had grabbed it and held on, slipping it right off his head.

Long before we got the horses untangled and on their feet, the dogs had passed and continued after the fox. They "treed" him in a gopher hole inside the hammock.

Buddy's mount had sprained an ankle, but not badly, and had sustained several body bruises caused from the pounding feet of the other two horses that had tripped and fallen on top of him. Cornstalk had a couple of front teeth knocked loose, but nothing serious, and Freddy's blaze-faced gelding never had a scratch.

This was one of the worst spills I was ever tangled up with during my seven years of hunting in Florida. By the time we reached the hotel, after getting the dogs away from the gopher hole, it was two o'clock in the morning. However, the exciting night had been something to remember.

CHAPTER THREE

MY FIRST MOTION PICTURE
EXPEDITION

In 1933 I went on my first motion picture expedition. Since I was six-years old I had hunted with the shot-gun, rifle and the bow and arrow, but this trip into the Rocky Mountains of Wyoming was my first hunt in the big game country armed only with the camera. In those days coloured motion pictures had not been perfected; black and white film, however, had been developed to a point where it was possible to take fairly good pictures in ordinary light. I had done some work with a motion picture camera, but was by no means an expert. Fortunately, I was not the head cameraman. My main job was to shoot the bow and arrow, but secondarily I was to secure motion pictures of wild animals when I was not using the bow.

As it turned out, I spent about ninety per cent. of the ten-month expedition, crawling on my hands and knees, wading up and down streams, ploughing through snow with or without snowshoes, and sliding on my belly like a lizard in all manner of places, armed with a De Vry one hundred foot spring-wind motion picture camera, shooting pictures of all kinds of animals and birds found in that wild section of our country. The bow and arrow work was easy and required very little of my time. It did not take long for me to realize that camera hunting was the toughest kind of hunting and I still think so to-day.

As my companion, guide, outfitter and head cameraman, I had Ned Frost, of Cody, Wyoming. Ned was not only one of the best naturalists in America, but among his other experiences he had been a hunter of mountain lions and grizzly bear for the Government and a trapper of Lobo wolf. His skill in the use of the heavy rifle was even then legendary in that section of the country, and to me his knowledge of all the denizens of the woods was a revelation. He seemed to know the thoughts of the birds and the animals, and at times I felt sure that he could actually read their minds. Often he would anticipate the

Mike Osceola in a dug-out in Big Cypress,
the southern Florida Everglades

An alligator in Florida, caught on the surface of the water

A bull-elk in Wyoming, with antlers still in the velvet stage

A cougar, or mountain lion, cornered on the ground, in Arizona

next move of some wild creature long enough in advance of its occurrence that he would be able to take advantage of the next incident. It was almost uncanny to me, although I had spent a great deal of my life in the woods.

Merely by observing animal spoor, Ned could give a fairly accurate account of what had taken place at any given time. By reading the tracks alone, he could tell whether it was a male, female, a half-grown or a baby animal involved, whether the creature had been feeding or travelling, and whether he was scared or quietly content when the tracks were made.

At first when Ned would read this wood-lore as though from a printed volume of actual happenings, I could not believe it possible for one to understand so clearly, merely by looking at a few tracks, what had transpired. After I had spent some months in the bush with Ned, however, I came to know that when he did a bit of what seemed to the ordinary woodsman to be surmising, Ned was not guessing at all. His knowledge of the wild creatures in that mountain area was so great that he definitely knew what had taken place.

To give just one instance of how well Ned Frost could read signs, one day he and I were riding through the forest on the North Fork of the Shoshone River and were crossing a high ridge. Without warning to me, he stopped his horse and began laughing. There had been a small snowfall a couple of days before and a few drifts of snow still lay in spots underneath the pine trees. When I drew up beside Ned as he sat there on his horse laughing, I was curious to know what he had seen that struck him as being so amusing.

He could see that I did not understand his amusement, so (not realizing that what he was about to say was anything out of the ordinary) he explained: "I was just laughing at the coyote that tried to catch a snowshoe rabbit here." He pointed to where there were some coyote tracks in a patch of snow.

A little beyond the coyote tracks I could see those of a snow-shoe rabbit. I knew what coyote and what rabbit tracks he was talking about, but I could see nothing funny about it, as I often saw coyote and rabbit tracks very close together. Ned, however, went on with his story. "See that log back there, Howard? That coyote sneaked up behind it while the snowshoe was feeding on that dry grass over there in that patch of snow. When the coyote reached the log he figured he could catch that

c

rabbit before he made it to his hiding place, but one thing the coyote never figured was that that particular snowshoe was a very smart rabbit.

"When the coyote made a run for the rabbit he was so close before the snowshoe saw him that the rabbit knew he didn't have time to get to his den over there in that pile of rocks before the coyote caught him, so he played it smart. Instead of going straight towards the rockpile, he headed directly down the hill, sideways to his hole. Then he ran straight towards that big pine you see down there a little way."

As Ned talked he pointed out to me the rockpile where the rabbit lived and the pine towards which he had run. I could see the tracks and knew that what he said was correct, but I was at a loss as to what he had seen beyond the point of the pine tree. Ned went on with his story, exactly as though he had been an eye witness to the encounter.

"Well, sir," he said, as he rolled a cigarette, "that coyote was about to catch himself a snowshoe three feet this side of that pine tree. He was so sure he was going to get him that he was looking at nothing but the rabbit.

"Now, what makes me laugh is that the rabbit sure played a dirty trick on that coyote. You see, he knew that the coyote just about had him, so he made a right angle turn towards the rockpile. The coyote tried to make the turn with him, but the pine needles were too slippery and the coyote was not expecting such a quick change of direction.

"When he failed to make the turn he was so close to the tree he side-swiped it with his rear end. I'll bet he came near breaking his back."

He licked his cigarette, lit it, then rode over to the pine tree in question, stepped down off his horse and reached out and removed a bunch of coyote hair from the rough bark of the pine and said, as he held the fur in his hand: "I'll bet you that coyote has a sore fanny!"

Ned climbed back in the saddle and rode on down the trail. As he rode away, I fell in behind him, and, realizing that here was a man who knew wild creatures as few men ever come to know them, I counted myself fortunate to have him as a teacher and made up my mind to listen when he talked about animals.

Ned was also an excellent cameraman and had a feeling for pictorial setting and attractive backgrounds, an asset that means much in securing beautiful and at the same time authentic film of outdoor subjects.

For the first six or seven weeks in the bush we rose at four every morning, wrangled our horses, had breakfast, loaded the cameras on our horses in two saddle bags, took our glasses and hit the forest. Ned was using an Akeley camera and it was necessary to carry it along on an extra pack horse.

We would climb some mountain to a point he knew of, from which we could get a good view of all the surrounding country. There we would leave our horses in the shelter of a cliff or heavy timber, then we would get out on the point with our field-glasses and watch all the open country for miles around until we spotted some type of animal. It might be a bear, a moose, an elk, a deer or a timber wolf. After Ned had watched for a few minutes whatever we had found, he would then decide the best way to go after the creature. Sometimes it would be a family or other group that we discovered, rather than a lone individual.

The vast knowledge Ned had of animals and their habits made it possible to know just where to go and how to intercept or approach the creature or the group which we wanted to photograph. As he made the plans for our stalk, I plied him with questions as to why, how he knew, and so on. He was a wonderful and patient teacher, and he knew that I was not asking questions merely to satisfy idle curiosity, but that I was eager to learn from each experience. Invariably, his hunches worked out perfectly and we got some wonderful motion pictures.

After about three weeks of work together, he started sending me out alone, following the spotting of some animal from a vantage point. He would give me instructions as to how to work the creature I was going after, and it was surprising how lucky I was at getting good close shots of some of the most wary animals.

Occasionally I would deviate somewhat from the plans Ned had laid out for me, and in almost every instance when I did so, I failed to get any decent shots. However, I must have asked a thousand questions about what I should do when an animal did this or that, and Ned was constantly patient and told me clearly and concisely what he thought. Nearly always, though, he would end by saying that no animal will always follow a given pattern. He assured me that all wild creatures had different personalities and that often any one of them would react contrary to the rule. I have always remembered this tenet of Ned's, and I still find it to be true, in no matter what part of the world the creature in question may be found.

One morning after we had been working together for several weeks, Ned said: "Well, Howard, you've been a good student and I think you know enough about animals to go out on your own. We'll have twice the chance to get pictures if we go in different directions. You're an excellent stalker," he went on, "and I just feel that we'll have better luck working separately." I was elated to realize that he thought I knew enough to go after pictures alone.

By this time I had become familiar with many of the lookout points and knew by name many of the different areas. Our camp was located quite a way up from the mouth of Jones Creek, where it joins the North Fork of the Shoshone River. In the high country, there was still snow ten or twelve feet deep in protected canyons. The exposed sides of hills, however, were fairly clear of snow.

I had rigged my De Vry camera on what we called a Jacob's staff. Instead of a tripod I used one straight shaft about four feet long, with a flat metal plate on top to which the camera was attached. On the bottom end I had a ferrule with a sharp spike about three inches long which could be stuck in the ground. On top of the camera box I rigged a level, so that I could quickly see when I had my camera parallel to the ground. A camera mounted in this way can be carried easily and can be brought into shooting position almost instantly. By sticking the spike in the ground and resting the back of the camera box against one's forehead, the cameraman can hold the box steady. I had arranged a short stud about one half-inch long with square coarse threads, so that the camera could be taken off or placed on the Jacob's staff quickly and easily.

There are many times in the bush when one must crawl on his belly like an alligator to get close to the quarry. At such times, even a straight Jacob's staff is not desirable. It is too unhandy and clumsy to carry while using the alligator type of locomotion. Hence, I rigged a strap with a single belt harness, so that when I had to crawl or go on hands and knees, I could fasten the camera on my back. In that way I had both hands and legs free. As soon as I could work into close proximity to the game I wanted to photograph, I could quickly remove the camera from my back and hold it by hand to make a shot. At times, I used a convenient log or boulder for a base. Such precarious camera positions are not conductive to steady pictures, it is true, yet often one will find it the only way he can get a picture.

Anyone attempting to shoot animal pictures in the open will find it absolutely essential to learn how to take a light reading, make the proper calculations and set the lens and diaphragm positions quickly; otherwise, the cameraman will often lose too much time in getting set, and the animal he is trying to photograph will be gone. If the light is bright and constant, one can merely check his light every half-hour or so, and be ready to shoot without too much bother.

The background of a location, of course, has a great deal to do with how much light must be allowed. It is a very good plan to study the various wooded backgrounds and then remember about how much difference there is in them. If one knows just about how much more light a dark background requires than does a light one, it will only be necessary to change stops instead of taking a light reading and going through the other calculations every time.

Often when I am in the bush and have a little spare time I take various light readings with different backgrounds and put them down in my field note-book, together with a short description of each scene, and in the notes I designate from what quarter the source of light came for each particular scene. Later, in camp in the evenings, I study these field notes. It is really surprising how, with a little study, one will soon be able to calculate accurately the proper camera settings by taking a quick light reading. On days when the sun has been shining brightly I have made perfect settings of the camera without taking any light readings or making calculations, simply by remembering my field notes.

During those first weeks with Ned, I had taken many field notes and had studied them diligently. I did not even have a light meter with me when I set out alone, but I was able to guess pretty close as to what the light would be at certain times of the day with the various backgrounds to be encountered. Naturally, one has a much greater latitude with fast black-and-white film than he does with the slow colour film. Although the latest colour film is much faster than the older film was, yet it is even now far less than half as fast as the black-and-white.

In camp during the evenings I learned to load my camera correctly and quickly, always working beneath a blanket to shut out any light. In the field we used the daylight-loading film rolls. However, in those days one could easily light-strike a considerable portion of a roll if not extremely careful. We, therefore, made it a practice to use a coat or a small blanket over the camera while loading.

When I hit the woods my first day out, alone with my De Vry, I was more than anxious to get good pictures for several reasons, but as I look back now, I realize that my strongest motive was my desire not to disappoint Ned.

CHAPTER FOUR

PHOTOGRAPHING GRIZZLY
AND ELK ON MY OWN

FROM my position high up on the side of Old Baldy Peak I could see for miles north, south and west. Only towards the east where the high range behind me rose in majestic splendour was my view limited. There was a cold wind sweeping down the north fork of Jones Creek canyon. I had taken cover behind a giant black spruce and had my heavy jacket, which was lined with sheepskin, pulled up tight around me to keep out the unpleasant wind. A hundred yards below in a narrow rock-lined draw I had tied my horse under good cover.

With the aid of ten-power glasses I carefully combed the vast expanse of timber, open meadows and the side hills of the ridge that formed the west boundary of Jones Creek Valley. This was my first day out alone with the camera and despite my eagerness to find an interesting subject to photograph, the beast I picked up in my glasses, a mile or so across the canyon on an open side hill in bright sunlight, sent a chill up my spine.

I could not believe my eyes. Yet when I had a second and closer look I had to accept the fact that I had spotted one of the largest male grizzly bears I would ever see. He weighed a good seven hundred pounds, I estimated, and because I had only a camera to shoot him, he looked much larger than that. Ned and I had watched these side hills several times on previous occasions for just such a sight, but without reward. In fact, we had not seen a grizzly all spring, but on my first day out alone, my first camera assignment had to be this big brute that is by all odds one of the strongest, toughest and most courageous beasts in the world. The grizzly can give the lion, so-called King of Beasts, three chews and half a dozen claws, then slap half his head off with a single stroke of his powerful paw.

I was sorely tempted to sit tight against the friendly spruce and let the silver tip rustle his breakfast of worms, lizards, crickets and other bugs without any interruption, but I knew

39

I could not lie to Ned and be pleased with myself, so I watched the monster of a bear for several minutes and saw that he was working his way south along the mountain side.

Then I slid off the tall peak, got aboard my horse and made a fast ride under cover of the forest to a point a half-mile below where I had last seen the big bear. As I cantered my horse slowly through the forest, I had a lot of time to think, and every thought had to do with grizzly bear. I recalled seeing the long red scars on both Ned's knees where he had once been bitten by one. The big brute had crushed both Ned's legs in the knee joints. Not only that, but the same grizzly had also killed Ned's cook in a one-night visit to their camp.

Then I remembered the pine saplings Ned had shown me, the size of my leg, that a grizzly had bitten off eight feet above the ground as though they had been matchsticks. I knew that grizzly bears had been known to break the neck of a 1500-pound steer with one mighty blow of a front paw. I recalled dozens of stories the old-timers of Wyoming had told me about brushes they had had with angry silver tips, and all of them had been most unpleasant incidents. I could imagine all kinds of things that might happen to me and my camera, if this grizzly chanced to smell or to see me at close range. Yet there was no way for me to secure a good picture unless I got fairly close. I was using only a two-inch lens. I felt nervous, not to say downright scared, and very much alone.

I had spotted a ledge of rock on the side hill which I hoped to reach before the big silver tip moved that far south. There was a good chance that he might not work along the mountain side as far down as the rocks, in which I had planned to hide and wait for him, but someway I had a feeling I had not seen the last of that bear.

My mustang was strong and powerful and he made good time climbing the side canyon that wound fairly close to the rock out-cropping. I let him catch his wind only twice going up the rugged mountain side. Finally, I pulled in a hundred yards above the pile of rocks, tied the lathered and puffing mustang in a shallow draw out of the wind, got my camera out of one of the saddle bags and made my way as fast as I could down to the hiding place I had selected.

When a bear is feeding he seems not to be moving very fast, but he will cover a lot more ground than appears to be the case.

When I got into the rock out-cropping, there were several big boulders that had broken off from the cliff above and fallen into a great heap. I came out first atop the cliff and I could see a quarter of a mile along the open mountain side in the direction in which the grizzly had last been observed.

The cliff was narrow and so much in the open that it offered no place for me to hide; then too, the cold north wind had a perfect shake at a fellow on top of it. I hurried down and around the cliff and took cover in the pile of big boulders beneath it. There I found I could hide perfectly and get entirely out of the cold wind, but the spot offered little protection should the bear decide to charge. There was not a tree big enough to climb within two hundred yards in any direction. I realized that I would really be trapped if the big grizzly came after me, but it was there or no place at all, so I decided to chance it, a very foolish business.

I got my camera set up on top of one of the big rocks, then I lifted two heavy boulders the size of nail kegs on top of the same rock and placed one on either side of the camera so I could turn it at almost any angle necessary to make a shot, yet there would not be enough room for the bear to see through if he should hear the camera running and look towards it. The two boulders were about eight inches higher than my camera, so I finally found a long flat rock that I could lift and I laid it over the top of the camera and let the ends rest on the other two rocks, thus forming a sort of bridge.

By raising my head just high enough to look through the eyepiece, I could avoid being seen, except through the narrow openings between the three rocks and around the sides and top of the camera. There was a convenient place for me to sit between two large boulders, and from which I could see the side of the mountain for a hundred yards or so towards the north, and it was from that direction the bear could be expected to appear.

I had been so busy arranging my camera position I had more or less forgotten the danger of the silver tip, but now when that was over I had nothing to do but wait and think. Needless to say, again I thought an awful lot about bear.

After perhaps twenty or thirty minutes I heard a blue jay set up a screaming from the top of a clump of jack pines up the canyon. Then a big golden eagle came sailing across the canyon and when he got almost over the spot where the blue jay was raising so much noise, he banked and turned in a tight circle. As he circled he rose, and doing a couple of fast flaps with his wings, glided right towards the cliff above where I sat. I saw that he was going to light on the cliff and if I had had the camera in my hands I could have secured a wonderful picture as he came in over my head no more than thirty feet above me. He settled on the cliff and turned around to face the creek far below. As he directed his keen gaze towards the stream he saw me. The great bird let out one angry scream and took wing. This time he circled above the cliff and was lost from sight.

I watched him disappear and as I turned my gaze downwards I saw the big grizzly about a hundred yards away, ambling along the side of the mountain. If he kept his course he would come about thirty-five or forty yards below me. This was considerably closer than I had hoped he would come.

My heart did a couple of buck-in-wings, then took off like a drumming grouse. I sat frozen for a moment, then I moved in behind my camera. It was all set and ready to roll. I found that my hands were shaking so badly I was afraid I would not be able to keep from jiggling the camera when I held the release button. I kept reminding myself over and over that a man had only one time to die, but I was unable to convince myself that this was as good a time as any other I might find later.

I took my field-glasses and raised up just high enough above the rocks to have one look at the huge grizzly. I had known all along that this was a big bear, but when I had a good look at him at close range through the ten-power glasses, he was bigger than I had first thought. His fur was prime and he was very fat, yet I could see the ripple of his powerful muscles as he walked. The manner in which a grizzly walks shows plainly what powerful brutes they are. They move with grace and agility that are surprising in an animal so large and so compactly built.

The old silver tip moved from rock to rock, flipping each one over with his strong, powerful front claws as he came to it. Occasionally he found a worm, a grub, a lizard or a cricket and his long tongue would flick out and scoop up the unfortunate little creature. Once or twice he came to a tender clump of rhubarb that had popped up where the snow had melted, and this he ate with gusto.

About sixty yards away from me he reached a fallen log that was a couple of feet in diameter and ten or twelve feet long. First he rolled the log and it broke in two near the middle. It was pretty well decayed and was evidently full of ants and grubs, because the grizzly spent a minute or two licking up some form of insect he found beneath it, then he walked over to one of the pieces of the log, picked it up, and crashed it to the ground. It burst into several pieces. The section of wet rotten timber must have weighed several hundred pounds, but the grizzly handled it as if it had been a log of balsa. Within a couple of minutes he had completely torn all sections to pieces and had eaten the grubs contained therein.

When he had finished, he came along the slope, keeping to his original course that ran parallel to the mountain side. I lowered my glasses and made ready to take pictures. Soon the beast came into camera range about fifty yards from my position. I got him in the centre of the finder and pushed down on the release button.

The De Vry started to whine as it picked up speed. It seemed to me I had never heard a camera make so much noise. It sounded like a Model T Ford on a rough road. A bear has poor eyesight, but his nose and ears are exceptionally acute. Thank goodness, the wind was blowing considerably, for it kept the noise of the camera from carrying so far as it would have done otherwise. However, I had shot less than ten feet of film when the big grizzly stopped dead in his tracks.

I knew he had heard the camera and would soon locate it. I cut the switch and the camera stopped. By then the big bear was looking directly at the rock pile, and I never moved a muscle. I felt sure he would not be able to spot me through the small opening around the camera box if I kept perfectly still. At that moment I was living awfully fast. What would I do if he started towards the pile of rocks?

He stood up on his back legs and had a good look at my position, but he could not see me. As he stood there on his hind feet, his huge front legs and powerful paws hung down more than half-way to the ground. He looked a great deal like a giant gorilla. It required all the nerve I could muster to keep from ducking out of sight, but I felt sure if I moved at all he would spot me.

After about ten seconds he dropped back on all four feet and turned around and had a good look in the direction from which he had come. He could not make up his mind from what quarter the source of the sound had originated, but he definitely had heard it. He sniffed the air but it told him nothing. I was almost perfectly straight down wind from him.

Finally, he faced about and ambled on his course along the side of the hill. He gave his massive head a vicious shake and emitted a low growl, seeming to say: "There's something amiss here somewhere, but I can't seem to locate it. Whatever it is, though, I'm ready for action."

As he came abreast of me, about forty yards down the side of the mountain from my hiding place, I was afraid to turn on the camera, for fear he would hear it and come for me. I knew the beast was already perturbed if not actually angry. I kept still and waited until he got several yards farther away. There he turned over another rock and as it started to roll downhill I again pressed the release button.

Even before the camera reached maximum speed, the alert grizzly reared up on his back legs and let out a loud growl. The long fur on his neck and back stood on end. He was as mad as a wet hornet, and all he wanted was to be sure where this noise was coming from and he would do something about it.

The instant I saw the grizzly had heard the camera I stopped rolling. I knew he meant business, and if there was anything I did not want, it was to allow this bear to locate me. The big brute was entirely at a loss as to the source of the noise. He dropped back on all fours but made a couple of strides downhill, then turned and walked back in the direction from which he had come. Then he made a few strides towards my position. If he had spotted me he would have charged, of that I am sure.

He growled three or four times and kept the long fur on his back and neck roached. After a couple of minutes of this angry behaviour he made a series of vicious smacks with his mouth. At that instant the wind made a swirl and carried my scent towards the already aroused beast. Detecting the smell of man, he turned his nose into the wind. Luckily for me, the freak swirl that gave the bear my scent misled him. He headed back over the side of the hill along the route he had just traversed in a very fast walk, growling constantly. He was sure, now, that this noise had to do with man, his hated enemy, and he was anxious to come to grips with him.

A grizzly bear is deathly afraid of man, but when he is cornered or thinks himself to be, he becomes so angry he loses all sense of fear and will charge on sight of the foe. When the big silver tip had gone twenty or thirty yards along his back trail and failed to locate my position, he lost his nerve. Letting out one angry growl, he broke for the timber down towards the creek and was out of sight before I had time to get the camera going. Once he had decided to clear out, he lost no time in heading for cover.

Right there I made up my mind that never again would I intercept a grizzly bear without having a way out for myself. It was my opinion that I had used up all my luck on this first encounter and, besides, another experience like this and I would be old, long before my time.

After the bear disappeared into the timber I waited several minutes to make sure he was not coming back, then I slowly stood up and had a good look all along the mountain side. A couple of hundred yards below me and some three hundred to the north, I spotted two bull elk, feeding along the slope of the mountain. I eased back behind the boulders and waited as they gradually came forward.

Within a half-hour they were near enough for me to get a good long shot with the movie camera. They were feeding up hill, directly towards my position, and I took two medium shots as they approached me. This was more to my liking.

Bull elks, though large powerful animals, are docile and actually timid. They never show fight except among themselves during the mating season. The wind seemed to have become stronger, and when I made a shot of them at about thirty yards, they still did not hear the camera running. I was getting low on film and was afraid to try to reload, lest they should see me when I removed the camera box from on top of the rock.

Elk (wapiti) have the three senses that wild animals rely on almost entirely for protection, hearing, seeing, and smelling, all acutely developed. I knew the two bulls would surely detect any movement to change film when I was so near them. When they got within about twenty-five yards of me, I had twenty feet of film left.

I started to roll the De Vry. They heard it and both looked up at the same instant. They spotted the camera and made off at top speed, disappearing into the same thick forest which had hidden the grizzly.

I reloaded my camera and then ate my lunch. Afterwards, I watched the open side of the mountain till the light began to fail, but saw no other animal close enough to make any more pictures. It was about three-thirty when I made my way back to my horse and on to camp. I had some grand pictures of the elk, as it turned out later, and the first shot I took of the grizzly was marvellous, but it was barely long enough for one scene. As I rode towards camp, I wondered what Ned would say about the way I had handled the bear situation.

That evening, after we had eaten supper, I told him just what had happened and he waited without comment until I had finished.

Then he said: "Howard, pictures are not worth such a risk as you took to-day, no matter how good they might be. If that grizzly had been able to locate you he'd have torn you to doll rags. I don't mean to scold you for taking such a chance, because you don't know grizzly bear, but from here on out you let the grizzlies strictly alone unless we are together."

It caused me not the slightest bit of unhappiness to agree that I would steer clear of silver tips in the future.

CHAPTER FIVE

MOUNTAIN SHEEP

O F all the animals that inhabit the earth, none other can see quite so well as the bighorn sheep *(Ovis canadensis)*, which dwells in the Rocky Mountains of North America. The Rocky Mountain bighorn, as he is commonly called, can see as far and as clearly with his naked eye as the average person can see with the aid of ten-power binoculars. Besides his binocular vision, the bighorn sheep is extremely wary, and the fact that he lives for the most part in the highest peaks and most rugged cliffs, gives proof of his intelligence. His alert and wary disposition makes him so hard to approach that he is classed by many sportsmen as the number one trophy of the world.

Although not dangerous game, he is so adroit and agile in the rough and almost inaccessible haunts where he is found that he offers a challenge to the best woodsman. Only the chamois of Europe, the klipspringer of Africa, the Ovis poli (a sheep similar to him) of the Himalayas in Asia, and the North American mountain goat rival this king of the mountain peaks, and not one of the others mentioned is so versatile as he.

Despite the fact that bighorns were known to the Indians and were constantly hunted by them as an article of food for hundreds of years before the white man reached America, they still occurred in great numbers throughout the Rockies when the West was first settled. Among the first white men to discover the true bighorn were the noted American explorers, Lewis and Clark. The high-powered rifle and the scope rifle sights naturally have helped to diminish the number of this species remaining in their native habitat, but they may still be found in considerable numbers in some inaccessible sections.

To photograph these creatures at close range was an exceptionally tough assignment which I had set for myself, but together with the accomplished Ned Frost, in 1933, I set out

47

to undertake this task. On account of the rugged terrain in which the bighorn was to be found, we knew it was impossible to carry the heavy cameras that were suited to long microscopic lenses. Carrying even the light portable cameras with short lenses only added to our already Herculean task.

However, we equipped ourselves with two light 35 mm. portable cameras and moved into the Absaroka Range of the Rockies, south-east of the Yellowstone National Park boundary, and set up camp along the bank of Open Creek. I had selected a box type De Vry camera, while Ned had chosen to bring his Bell and Howell Eyemo. both of them 100-foot spring-wind-machines. No tripod of any kind was feasible in mountain sheep country. In order to get close to those wary creatures, we would have to climb jagged peaks and follow narrow trails where the use of both hands and feet would be needed to nego-tiate the devious and precipitous route. We each rigged a kind of gear or harness, by which we could fasten the cameras on our backs, leaving both our hands and our feet free.

According to the late Vernon Bailey, Ned Frost knew more about mountain sheep than any other man in America. With Ned's knowledge and experience, I felt that we had at least a remote chance to outwit the wary bighorn, though my own knowledge of that creature was *nil*. Ned spent many patient hours teaching me the habits and the characteristics of moun-tain sheep. He showed me the difference between the track of the ewe and the ram, and how to tell whether the animal that made a given track was young or old. He told me in detail about the feeding habits and the bedding grounds of the species, and where they would most likely be found at different times of the day. I shall never forget what he said when he came to the subject of the vision of the bighorn.

"There's one thing, Howard, that you must remember about a mountain sheep. He has the most wonderful eye of any animal in existence, and when you make a stalk on him be sure that you keep a solid rock between you and him at all times." As an afterthought, he added: "Now, make sure that the rock you take cover behind is at least a foot thick. Other-wise, he'll see you through it!"

Of course, he was joking at that point, but he wanted to impress on me the necessity of keeping completely out of sight.

Errol Flynn shows his father a wild boar killed by the
author with his bow

Pelicans waiting hopefully for some lunch in the Gulf of California

In the weeks that followed I learned many things first hand about our quarry. For instance, I found that a bighorn has no blind spots. His large eyes are so placed in his head (on the sides rather than in front) that he can see just as well behind him as from the sides and forward. The Rocky Mountain bighorn can actually see without moving his head the whole 360 degrees around him. If this clever creature had developed his senses of hearing and smelling as acutely as his vision, it would be utterly impossible to get near him without being detected.

However, in the jagged peaks which are the home of the bighorn, the wind is seldom still nor does it often blow from any one direction for a long time. The noise of the wind, of falling rocks dislodged by thaws and natural erosion is so constant that the sheep rarely pays much attention to noises of any kind. The fact that the wind is deflected by the various peaks and the abrupt canyons, makes it rarely possible to know from what quarter it will be moving at any given point. Should the scent of man be carried to the sheep and he should flee, he would be just as likely to run headlong into his enemy as to run away from him. One might think that the animal would be alerted by having caught the scent of man, but the truth is, the bighorn is *always* alert.

At any rate, I soon learned that I had little concern about his sense of smell or of hearing, but after a short time I began to take Ned's warning seriously about being sure the rock I took cover behind was at least a foot thick, so wonderful was his vision. I had hunted wild turkey and Canadian geese and I thought they could see extremely well, but I found that the mountain sheep could see so much farther than either of those birds, that there really was no comparison.

One day Ned and I left our horses in a jack pine thicket on the west side of a mountain peak and crawled up to the crest of the hill on our bellies, then allowed only our heads and shoulders to come into view over the top. On the next range across a wide valley we spotted with the glasses a lone ram feeding on top of the mountain. It was a good three miles by airline from us. He was grazing on the very crest and we could see him outlined perfectly against the blue sky.

After watching him for several minutes, Ned said: " Howard, do you think that sheep can see a man this far away? "

D

"No, Ned," I replied confidently. "I doubt that an eagle could see well enough at this distance to recognize a man, if he could see him at all."

"Well, you just keep your glasses on him and I'll stand up. Then we'll see how long it will take him to spot me."

He stood up and started to roll a cigarette. Before he had it half-finished, the big ram stopped his feeding and had one look towards us. He quickly turned so that he was facing in our direction. For ten seconds he never took his eyes off Ned, then he nervously moved over the crest of the hill out of sight.

In a few seconds he came back into sight and with him were two ewes. All three of them stood perfectly still, looking at Ned. I was keeping my glasses on them all the time.

Finally, Ned said: "Now you watch them when I go out of sight." He walked down behind the hill, and within half a minute the three sheep turned and ran over the crest of the mountain, and that was the last we saw of them.

They definitely had seen Ned and were alarmed, although they were a good three miles away. This experience convinced me they could see even better than the eagle.

There is one peculiar trait that we often observed in these animals. Any time they see a man any great distance away, they will stand and watch just as long as that person stays in sight. The moment, however, that one goes out of sight of the sheep, they leave the vicinity. Ned said he had had them watch him for as long as eight hours without feeding or going out of sight. Many times when they are holding such long vigils, watching, they will lie down so as to rest more comfortably, but they never for a moment lose sight of the person they are watching. Once a mountain sheep spots a person there is no use to hide and try to wait him out. As promptly as he catches a glimpse of a man, he is sure he sees him and the moment such a person takes cover, the wary bighorn is off on the run.

The average animal, like the deer, elk, moose, and bear may be frightened by the appearance of man and take flight as a result, but unless the hunter tries to harm or to follow the game, any one of the varieties just named may go only a short distance before stopping his flight and beginning to feed again, or the animal may lie down and rest within a short distance from the spot where he was disturbed. Not so the mountain sheep. When he is frightened by a human being he takes no chances, but quits the entire vicinity for several days. Ned told me that he had on several occasions followed bighorns after they had taken flight, just to see how far they would go before settling down to normal feeding again, and he had found that some of them went twenty miles or more. In no case did they go less than five or six.

Not only is the bighorn wild, he is also most cunning, and when surprised, will act with wisdom. Despite the fact that he is thoroughly scared, he does not lose his head or perform any foolish deeds. He thinks fast and correctly and acts even faster.

Once I spotted a lone ram feeding, and I watched him until he quit grazing and went in behind a large rock near the top of the mountain, where he lay down out of the wind. I had worked my way up a steep narrow canyon and had got within five or six hundred yards of him without being seen. I knew that normally the bighorn feeds and rests in rotation. On a cold day in a spot where the feed is plentiful he may feed for a half-hour or so, then lie down for an hour, then feed for another period. If the feed is scarce and it is not too cold, he may browse around for an hour or two before resting.

The day in question was quite cold and windy and the feeding ground of the bighorns offered an abundance of bunch grass. After I had spotted the big ram, I had to wait only a few moments until he quit feeding and went in behind the boulder to rest. As soon as he lay down I made a fast detour and came up on him from behind the rock. It was a good hundred yards from the boulder where the sheep lay to some jagged cliffs down the mountain side, and I was confident that the instant the ram was disturbed he would head for the cliffs. Between him and the boulder was a carpet of bunch grass. It was far above timber line and there were no obstructions of any kind that would afford the ram cover until he could reach the cliffs.

I had my camera all set and ready, figuring I would sneak up to the large rock, then work my way around it until I came into view of the ram. The boulder was as big as a five-room house and about sixty feet high. Ned and I had wanted to get a moving picture of a sheep in full flight on smooth ground to show just how fast they can travel, and had I staged a setting,

I could not have picked a better spot than this. The light was excellent from my position, coming in over my shoulder from the right quarter. I reasoned that when the sheep ran towards the cliff, the light would be perfect to bring out the gloss of his fine coat.

At the last second I checked my camera and eased very slowly around the boulder, which was not round but almost square. When I came into view on the side where the ram lay, he instantly saw me and was up and away. I was no more than thirty or forty feet from him when he got up and he was plenty scared, but he never lost his head.

Instead of making a break for the cliffs down the mountainside as I had expected, he dived uphill around the corner of the boulder. My camera had not had time to get up to speed before he was out of sight behind the rock. I knew that in any direction this ram ran off that mountain top, he would have to cross over a lot of open ground. In fact, there was no cover except the cliff within half a mile. I felt sure he intended going over the top of the hill and down the opposite side.

I retraced my steps on the double and when I reached a spot on the opposite side of the rock, I saw no ram. He had not had time to reach the crest of the hill, I knew, but where had he gone?

At that instant I heard a loud snort from directly above me on top of the rock. I looked up in time to catch a glimpse of the old ram's white rump as he leaped off the rock on the same side where he had been resting. I realized now that the cunning bighorn had given me the double cross. He intended to go for the cliffs all the time, but had made the false break uphill to fool me, and I must say, I had taken the bait—hook, line and sinker.

I scrambled back around the boulder recklessly, realizing just what a stupid idiot I had been, but by the time the camera came up to speed the ram made a long leap and went out of sight among the cliffs. What I actually got on film was one leap of a ram at long range. I had completely missed the shot, but in spite of my chagrin I could only laugh and admire the bighorn for his quick thinking.

Later, when I told Ned in camp about the episode, he had a good laugh, but he told me not to feel too badly about it, because mountain sheep had more sense than people. I had to agree, they at least had more sense than some people, especially Howard Hill.

It was not long after this exasperating experience, however, that I had a chance to execute a piece of skulduggery that enabled me to get a real close-up picture of a surprised and bewildered bighorn ram. Ned and I had left camp one morning before daylight and made a long tiresome climb up to the top of the Wapiti Ridge Range of the Rocky Mountains. At that particular spot along the range, it was wide and flat on the crest with three or four stringers or high ridges running out from the east side of the main body of the mountain itself. The side ridges were nearly the same height as the main one and each extended for a mile or more.

Just under the crest of one of these ridges we spotted a lone ram quietly feeding. There was little chance to make a stalk around and behind the sheep before he should quit feeding and bed down for a rest. Also there were so many rough, jagged cliffs around him that we knew once he bedded down among them we would lose sight of him, and it would be a miracle if we were able to get near enough to take a good picture. His position was a ridge to our right, and almost a half mile away.

We decided for Ned to walk boldly out in plain sight of the sheep and move along the crest of the next ridge parallel to the one where the bighorn was feeding. I reasoned that as soon as the old ram saw Ned he would stop grazing and watch him. As long as the distance between them was great, the wise creature would not run away, I was sure. While he was thus busy watching Ned, I planned to hurry along the offside of the main ridge until I got in back of him, then I would come over the top and work my way down the opposite side of the ridge he was on until I could come in almost on top of him.

Ned thought our plan might work and he immediately came out from among the boulders where we had been concealed and started walking away from the feeding sheep. The instant Ned came into the open the alert ram saw him and raised his head. When I observed that the bighorn did not immediately head for cover, I started on my way to come in back of him.

On the ridge just above where the ram was feeding I had spotted a high outcropping of rocks, so I had little trouble in identifying the exact position of the sheep when I came near the crest of the ridge back of him about an hour later.

The moment I came near enough to see the next ridge north of the one the ram and I were on, I spotted Ned with my glasses, and I knew that the bighorn had not taken flight. Ned was busy making a pile of rocks in plain sight, but was paying apparently not the slightest attention to the ram.

I worked my way carefully through the boulders until I could see over the crest of the ridge and down along the side of it. I had my camera set and ready for action any second. Easing one eye around the corner of a big rock, I saw no more than twenty yards below me the old ram staring across the canyon at Ned.

Aside from the broken cliffs which concealed me, there was no other cover closer than a hundred yards to the sheep. Without waiting, I leaped out from behind the rock and ran towards the surprised and badly frightened mountain sheep, giving the old Rebel yell as I went. I had released the camera switch the moment I started forward.

The poor sheep was so astonished he never had a chance to think, but he started going places. He headed back towards the main range of mountains, but there was no cover in that direction for half a mile. Quickly realizing this fact, he cut downhill and away from the main ridge.

In the meantime I had slid to a stop and held him right in the centre of my finder. Though the mountain side at this point was very steep, that bighorn was pushing so hard with his hind legs he was throwing back gravel as he ran down the side of the steep ridge. I kept yelling as loud as I could and the terrified bighorn concentrated on running. Never before or since have I seen any creature make such a reckless sprint. How he stayed on his feet over such steep, insecure footing I will never know, but not once did he stumble or slow down.

Finally he made the bottom of the canyon and kept right on mushing until he went out of sight in the forest.

I had a wonderful shot and it turned out to be a very sharp and clear picture. The expression of astonishment on the ram's face when I leaped out from behind the boulder, I shall never forget. He showed that he simply could not believe I was so close to him. This one could have been shot with the bow. Once again we had proved that it pays to understand the instincts and habits of wild creatures, if a person hopes to make good close-up pictures of them in their native habitat.

Often I have wondered what that sheep must have thought about Ned's rock piling, up there on the top of the mountain. Whatever his thoughts may have been, he was so intrigued in watching Ned that he forgot everything else, and that made me happy, because for once I had not been made the goat.

CHAPTER SIX

SURPRISED BY A BLACK BEAR

It was around the latter part of May when Ned and I set up camp near a small lake in the Two Ocean Plateau country some ten or twelve miles below the south boundary of Yellowstone Park. It was near the end of the calving season for elk and we had not yet secured any satisfactory pictures of baby elk. A greater part of the Jackson Hole elk herd go to this region to drop their calves. It is a high, flat-topped mountain with considerable areas of virgin pine and black spruce. Interspersed with the timbered sections, however, are innumerable open parks and small meadows.

Soon after the winter snow has melted away, usually about the latter part of April or the first of May, these parks are covered with lush buffalo and bunch grass. The fact that there is an abundance of food, combined with good cover, makes it an ideal spot for early spring feeding and a perfect place for elk mothers to raise their calves. The heavy timber offers splendid protection for the young animals from the strong cold winds that often prevail in the high Rockies in the springtime, while the tender, nutritious grass furnishes adequate food for both the mother elk and their offspring.

Two Ocean Pass derives its name from the fact that it is a natural watershed. From its western slope all waters drain into the Pacific Ocean, while on the eastern side all rain and melting snow drain into the Gulf of Mexico and finally reach the Atlantic Ocean. Besides this phenomenon this one flat-topped mountain has the distinction of being the source of the head waters of four different rivers: the Yellowstone, the Wind, the Snake and the Colorado. The Yellowstone and the Wind Rivers, after joining other streams and finally becoming a part of the Mississippi, eventually reach the Gulf of Mexico, while the Colorado flows into the Gulf of California, and the Snake into the Pacific Ocean.

The Two Ocean Plateau country is as beautiful as it is unique.

The green rolling meadows, the great spruce and pine trees, the fast running brooks, the wildflowers and the abundance of wild-life are blended by nature in a fashion that is fairly breath-taking.

When we arrived and set up our camp, there were still a few small snow banks unmelted in protected places, but everywhere in the open glades the grass was already several inches high. It grew right up to the very edges of the remaining banks of snow. We observed considerable elk spoor near the streams and the lake shores.

On our way in we had seen several cow elks with their young calves, already big enough to follow their mothers as they bounded away, and we were afraid that we were too late to find a newly-born calf, but Ned reminded me: "Not all elk calves are dropped very close together. The entire calving season actually covers several weeks."

The first couple of days after we made camp we walked many miles with our cameras, looking for an elk calf young enough that he would be unable to run. To find such a one was going to be quite a chore, because a baby elk can go like the wind by the time he is two days old. By the third night in camp we realized it was impossible to cover enough territory on foot to locate a baby easily, so we decided to go back to the same method we had used to find bear and mountain sheep.

The next morning we were up before daylight and on our horses. We climbed the highest peak on top of the mountain, from which we could search the open meadows that stretched out below with our field-glasses. The sun had just risen when we discovered an elk mother with a calf only a few hours old in a small meadow a mile or so away. The little fellow was so new he had a hard job to stand on his wobbly legs.

It would require a considerable bit of stalking to get close to them, as the big timber was scarce. Only a few black spruce grew in the area. Underneath them were dense patches of thousands of young seedlings of the same variety as the mother tree. It would be necessary to cover the last several hundred yards mostly on hands and knees in order to keep out of sight of our quarry.

The mother elk soon caused the calf to lie down in the open, where the warmth of the sun would help dry him off and would put strength into his sappy little body. When the youngster had coiled up like a tired puppy into a tight ball, the mother began grazing near him. We knew that she was hungry and would perhaps graze for a couple of hours if not disturbed. Now was the time to get a picture.

To my surprise, Ned said: "Howard, you're a much better stalker than I am, because you've hunted so long with your bow and arrow. Why don't you ride down there and make a sneak on her? I'll stay up here and see if I can't spot another calf. That way, we'll have two chances if I'm able to find one."

I was not too flattered by Ned's telling me I was a better stalker than he, for the simple reason that I knew better, but I was pleased that he had gained enough confidence in me as a cameraman to be willing to let me take over such an important assignment. I knew that the cold damp ground, the wet grass and the sharp shale rocks would not be pleasant to my hands and knees, to say nothing of my belly, provided I had to do some sliding on my stomach to get close to the quarry. This last fact, I felt sure, had been conducive to Ned's decision.

So elated was I, however, at the prospect of getting some good pictures when it had begun to look as though we would be unable to find a baby elk, that I hurriedly mounted my horse, made my way off the point and headed for the animals.

When it became necessary, I left my horse concealed in a patch of young pines and then went forward on foot. Within a quarter of a mile I spotted the elk still hungrily grazing. She seldom got more than a few yards away from her calf. She would munch the grass a moment or so, then raise her head and have a good look in all directions. I realised at once that this elk mother was extremely alert and wary. The least false move on my part and she would manage to get her offspring into the dense thicket only a few yards away from where they now were. Once she had the little fellow out of sight, she would hide him and I would never be able to find him. It is amazing how quickly most baby animals can be hidden by their mothers, and how obediently they will lie perfectly still for hours, not moving a muscle. Among the brown pine needles and small saplings a man could not hope to find a baby elk, half buried beneath this protective covering.

I spent the greater part of two hours on hands and knees,

cautiously working from one black spruce tree and its surrounding clump of seedlings to the next. Once or twice it was necessary to advance several yards flat on my belly, in order to cross
an open space between spruce clumps. I would carry my camera
forward as far as I could reach in front of me, rest it on the wet
grass, then by placing my hands on either side of me I would
slide on top of the grass a foot or so, then push the camera forward again.

This was a slow, tedious process, but it is surprising how little
cover is needed to make a successful stalk on game, if one is
experienced. Not once did I move a muscle except while the
mother elk had her head down, grazing. I kept a sharp eye on
her at all times and the instant her head came up I stuck tight
against the ground. There was practically no breeze, at all, but
what little wind was blowing was in my favour. The sun was
now high in the heavens and the bright rays were coming in
from the left quarter back of me. Finally I reached next to the
last clump of spruce saplings before I would be in a perfect spot
and at a good distance to get an excellent picture. My hopes
were high.

This particular bunch of spruce was almost square in shape
and covered a space measuring roughly thirty feet on each side.
It was necessary to crawl only six feet between the clump I was
then hiding behind and the last one. The elk had turned her
rump towards me and it was going to be an easy matter to make
the distance between the two pieces of cover as soon as she
lowered her head.

While I cautiously made the last check to see that my camera
was ready for a shot, another personality that I was unaware of
at the time had entered the setting. Neither was the newcomer
aware of my presence, but the fact was that a huge black bear,
weighing all of four hundred pounds, had fed in from the south
and was at that very moment coming along the other side
of the same clump of spruce seedlings that I was hiding
behind.

I was on my knees and by raising as high as I could I was
able to watch the elk through the openings among the tops of
the little saplings. It was not possible to see the bear, however,
as his back did not stand high enough above the seedlings to be
visible.

The bear continued to feed and had no idea there was a man

within miles. His soft-padded feet as he ambled along on top of the wet grass made no sound.

I had eased right up to the corner of the spruce patch and was ready to step quickly across the narrow opening between the two clumps the very instant the elk mother next lowered her head to feed. In front of me I held my camera with both hands and was half squatting, with my feet in a position to make a quick advance. I was carefully keeping my eyes on the elk cow through the top of the seedlings.

In the meantime, the black bear was coming along the other side, just around the corner from where I anxiously waited. I saw the cow's head go down and I rose a little higher and started to move forward. As my head came past the corner of the spruce, my left cheek literally touched the end of the nose of that bear. My eyes and his were staring into each other's. How we both stopped so abruptly I will never be able to say, but there we were, almost nose-to-nose, frozen stiff with fear.

I cannot for the life of me remember who moved first, but 1 think I did. I suppose we stared at each other for only a small portion of a second, but a thousand things happened within my brain and body; my mouth went dry as powder, a chill penetrated the very marrow of my bones. Without thinking, I let out a yell that could have been heard a mile or more. I had no volition in the matter. The yell was just there, coming out of my mouth.

As I yelled I shoved the camera right into the face of the bear and leaped backward, breaking any record ever attained in a single backward leap. My second leap carried me another record distance, but a fallen log about two feet through, lying on top of the ground, caught my heels as I came down, and I did a clean somersault backward.

As I rolled up on my feet but still facing the spot of the encounter, I saw the astonished and bewildered bruin in full flight, already more than halfway across the little meadow where the elk and her calf had been. No mother elk nor baby was in sight. I cannot say how she had got the calf up and away so quickly, but perhaps my yell had aroused strength inside the little fellow that he had not known he possessed.

Neither do I know what the bear did when I shoved the camera into his face. I faintly remember that he, too, made a terrific noise, not exactly a growl or a scream. In my condition, I thought it a sort of combination loud snort and a bellow.

As I went backward and lit on my shoulders, head and back, the impact must have partially shaken the fright out of me, because as I watched that big bear running like the Devil himself was after him, I realized that I was laughing. Although still shaking like a disturbed bowl of jelly, I think I would have laughed at him, regardless of what had happened to me. I did not know yet whether I had been bitten, clawed, hit or kicked by the bear. I just hadn't had time to take stock to see whether or not I was all in one piece, but even then I knew that what I had just experienced could not fail to be one of the most amusing scenes that ever took place between a wild bear and a human being.

It could have been fatal to me. Had the bear been given a split second's warning of my presence, the chances are he would have torn me to pieces, but before he had time to think I had shattered all chance of thought by my terrifying yell in his ears. The entire episode lasted only a few seconds and the bear never stopped as long as he was in sight, nor did he show any signs of slowing down as he plunged into the timber on the far side of the meadow.

It was some time before I had the strength to go forward and retrieve my camera, which lay near the corner of the clump of spruce. I sat down on a log and tried to smoke a cigarette, but it had no taste, and besides, I could not for the life of me get any saliva in my mouth. It was as dry as dust.

After a bit I got my camera and found it was uninjured. Then I made my way to a little ravine not far away and got a drink of water. Soon I began to feel better, but the shock to my nerves had left me still jittery. When I reached my horse I put the camera inside the saddle bag, then tried another cigarette. This time it tasted all right and helped me to regain a measure of composure. Definitely, however, I felt that I had had enough for one day, so I made my way back to camp.

All the rest of the day I stayed in camp, trying to decide whether or not to tell Ned what had happened. Finally I came to the conclusion that it would be just as well to tell him only that I failed to get a picture. I just hated to admit to him what a coward I felt I had been.

By the time Ned reached camp shortly before sundown I had cooked a good supper. We ate it, talking casually about various things and finally, moving outside the cook tent, we sat down in a couple of comfortable camp chairs and were enjoying an extra cup of coffee. It was our custom every evening after supper to discuss the happenings of the day, while we were drinking this third and last cup of coffee for the night.

It seemed to me that for some reason Ned was quieter than usual, but I decided it was just my self-consciousness that made it seem he was a little different from his accustomed self.

Anyway, I finally asked: "Well, Ned, did you spot another elk and baby after I left?"

"Well, no. Not right away," he said, "but I found two this afternoon and I think I got some swell pictures."

Apparently as an afterthought, he said: "By the way, how did you make out?"

"Oh, no good."

"What went wrong?" he asked. point-blank.

"Nothing particular," I replied. "I guess she heard me and spooked out."

"Don't let it worry you, Howard. I think I got all the baby elk pictures we need."

I breathed a sigh of relief and felt much better inside, to know that he had been successful and that I had got by beautifully without having to tell him my experience.

He finished his cup and said: "You know, I've been in these mountains for almost sixty-five years and to-day I saw the most unusual incident I've ever witnessed."

"You did! What on earth did you see?" I knew that it must have been something really spectacular to impress Ned so much.

He took a long drag from his cigarette and blew the smoke in a thin stream skyward, then looked directly at me with the most devilish grin I had ever seen on his face and said: "I was looking through my glasses and I saw a cameraman kiss a big black bear." He burst out laughing, and there was nothing I could do but join him.

Then he told me how he had been watching me when he saw the bear feeding in from another direction, and that he had felt a premonition the bear and I were going to meet, so he just kept watching us both till it happened.

He said it was a thousand wonders the bear did not kill me. A black bear seldom attacks a man, Ned told me, but having a person come in so close to him as I had done would frighten any wild animal enough to cause him to attack. Then I told him about yelling right in the face of the bear.

"Yeah, I heard you," he said quietly. "That's what saved your life."

You know, he may have been right, because that was no ordinary yell.

CHAPTER SEVEN

PHOTOGRAPHING MOOSE

ORDINARILY, the moose is a docile creature that goes about his own business with little thought of other four-footed animals or of man. The largest antlered animal in the world, often weighing more than half a ton, he has little to fear from most of his neighbours in the forest. Wolves and cougar are his only natural enemies and the former hesitate to attack him unless a pack of them come upon him in a spot where he is at a disadvantage.

Often when a moose is stymied in deep snow he will walk continually over a small area and so keep the snow packed hard, forming what is known as a moose pit. Many times, when a moose is caught by an early snow, he has to spend the entire winter in a pit of this kind. Occasionally the walls of such a pit may be from ten to twelve feet high, making it impossible for the creature to get out until spring sun melts away the snow. In such confinement the trapped animal has little food, since only the bark and lower limbs of the trees inside the pit are available for him to eat. Such a meagre food supply sometimes is not enough to keep the unfortunate creature alive. When a pack of wolves find a moose in such a situation they wait till the animal grows weak from little food, then the pack attacks and kills the trapped creature.

In deep soft snow a moose cannot handle himself well enough to protect his rear quarters from a pack of wolves. They will attack from all sides, and while some go for his nose and throat others come in from behind and cut his hamstrings. Once the tendons are cut above the hock, the moose finds his powerful hind legs useless and the unfortunate bovine is soon killed and eaten. Even under such handicaps, however, the bull moose often kills two or three of the attacking wolves before he is himself brought down. The cow moose, having no antlers, falls an easy victim to the deadly wolf pack. She can fight, however, with her sharp front hooves and where one wolf only is involved,

Three blue marlin killed with the bow from the *Sirocco*
in the Gulf of California

The author takes a shot from the *Sirocco*, off the west coast of Mexico

The author in his
self-made diving
helmet on the way
down, near Key
Largo, Florida

Dolphins on the move
in the Gulf of California

she has been known to split the skull of the predator, killing him instantly.

The moose prefers to live near large bodies of water, and during the months when the surfaces are not frozen he uses the lake or stream in his vicinity as natural protection. He is an excellent swimmer and when danger from wolves threatens, will enter the water. No wolf or pack of wolves will follow a moose into water. The long powerful legs of that beast often enable him to walk on the bottom of the river or lake, while the wolf would have to swim to reach him. Under such conditions, one moose could kill a large pack of wolves without much danger of getting hurt.

The cougar, or mountain lion, is of course much larger than the average wolf and he uses an entirely different method of bringing down the antlered king. The big cat either stalks the victim or lies in wait on a rock cliff or the limb of a tree. At the opportune moment he leaps on the withers of the moose, fastens his teeth in the top of the neck muscles, and by the use of his wicked claws cuts the jugular vein of his victim. Then he leaps clear and waits for the quarry to bleed to death.

In some cases the cougar will break the neck of a moose by fastening himself atop the withers of the creature with his teeth and one front paw, while with the other front foot he reaches forward and obtains a hold with his claws in the nose of the moose. By forcing the head of the victim backward and sideways he is able to break the neck. I have never seen a moose killed in this latter manner, yet I believe this method has been used often enough to be accepted as an authentic one. Old time cougar hunters and Indians have given me detailed accounts of such kills.

In recent years the moose in Wyoming have had little to fear from either the wolves or the cougar. There have been no wolves in the Wyoming Rockies for some forty-five or fifty years, and the few cougar that still exist there find it much easier to bring down a deer, elk, or some smaller animal. Seldom do they attack the lordly moose these days. Government hunters and the high bounties paid for wolf and cougar skins by the cattle and sheep ranchers spelled doom for both these predatory enemies of the moose many years ago.

Although usually, as I have said, a moose pays little attention to man, there are two conditions under which one must be

E

extremely careful when photographing them. In the fall of the year when the rut begins, bull moose often become irritable and will attack man on sight. Particularly is it dangerous when a person happens to get between the bull and the cow at this season. A week or so before the rut begins, the bulls begin to follow the cows at a distance. They realize that the mating season is near and even though the cows are not yet ready for the rut, the bulls follow them. If a cameraman is unfortunate enough to happen along and finds himself between a cow and the attentive bull, he may be charged without warning. Once the bull is so aroused, he charges with great speed and courage. A man must be prepared either to shoot the beast or to get up a tree quickly, if he is not himself to be killed outright.

In the early spring it is the cow moose with a baby that is dangerous. When she has had a calf, she becomes very cautious and belligerent. It requires a week or ten days for the baby to get strong enough to follow her readily. During these few days the mother hides her young calf in the tall grass or in dense brush between feedings. The little fellow will lie quietly for hours just where his mother places him and will not move a muscle if approached by man. The mother seldom goes far from the spot where she has concealed her offspring and she watches with a jealous eye. Woe be unto him that disturbs the sleeping youngster or even draws near him!

During the early spring of 1933 Ned Frost and I had worked separately, photographing all manner of wild life, but when the deer, elk, and moose began dropping their calves in the latter part of May and the first of June, we decided we had better go out together for picture shots.

When we were lucky enough to find a young baby, one of us would handle the little fellow while the other ran the camera. We knew that we had little to fear from the elk and deer mothers, but the moose cow was a different matter. A baby deer, elk, or antelope only a couple of days old can run like the wind and in order to get good close-up pictures of them one must spot a mother with a youngster and watch until the cow or doe caches the baby for a nap. As soon as the mother feeds away a short distance, a person can steal in and catch the baby before the mother has time to give it warning. Deer, elk, and antelope mothers will temporarily leave their babies, but not the moose mother.

For several days we had been combing the high country around Moose Meadow, near the headwaters of Middle Creek in the Rockies, about thirty miles south-east of the Yellowstone National Park boundary, looking for baby moose. We were riding along a narrow animal trail beside the creek in heavy timber, when we spotted a mother moose and her new baby a short distance from the trail in a small opening.

Ned slapped the spurs to his horse and letting out a yell that would have scared a Comanche Indian, headed for the moose. The tearing of the horse through the underbrush and the yelling of Ned so frightened the mother that she gave her calf a quick nudge with her head that sent him flying through the air. He landed in some thick brush where he flattened out and lay still.

The cow dashed off into the forest with Ned in hot pursuit. As she broke away she gave a half groan that told the youngster to stay put. Strange that this baby only a few hours old should understand the meaning of that warning by its mother, but he never once stirred after being thrown into the brush.

I think I was about as much surprised as the cow moose at the apparent sudden hysteria of Ned, but I just sat steady on my horse and waited to see what would happen next. My gelding wanted to follow Ned and his mount, but I held him in. He reared on his back legs and tried to run but I managed to restrain him.

A considerable distance away I could hear Ned and the moose still crashing through the timber. Within a couple of minutes, however, Ned came back with the same speed he had gone. As he reached the clearing where we had first seen the moose, he slid his horse to a stop, leaped from the saddle, and diving into the brush, caught the baby moose. He had the little fellow by the nose and lower jaw, so he could not yell, but the calf was kicking and squirming like a snake in hot ashes. Ned yelled for me to come quickly.

Just as he called me the calf got his muzzle free and let out a frightened bleat. I was rushing through the underbrush and did not hear the baby cry for help, but his mother had heard it, and she was losing no time in coming to the rescue of her young, as I soon learned.

I made the clearing and, leaping out of the saddle, was in the act of getting my camera out of the saddle bag when Mother

Moose dashed into the open with every hair standing straight out like the bristles on a charging wild boar.

In the meantime, when Ned heard the baby yell, he knew that the mother would soon be back, so he had ducked behind the trunk of a huge pine tree, holding the baby well concealed beneath his coat, and keeping a firm grip on the youngster's muzzle so that he could not cry again.

Mother Moose took one quick look and came at me on the double. I let the camera slide back into the saddle bag and ducked under the neck of my horse on the side opposite to the cow. I had not time to mount my horse or to gather up the reins. He saw the angry moose charging down on him and he had no intention of being caught flat-footed.

The cow was almost on top of him before he had time to get moving. He made one leap forward as she came in, her front feet flying like pistons. One of her sharp hooves struck him just back of the hip bone along the top of his rump and cut a gash six or eight inches long. I had seen what was coming and was holding the horn of the saddle in a firm grip with both hands. As the horse leaped, trying to get out of the way, I was snatched off the ground but managed to hold on to the horn of the saddle.

The sudden attack so frightened my horse that he exploded into action. Kicking and bucking. he stampeded through the underbrush, with Mother Moose right on his heels. I have never been a bronc rider and under ordinary circumstances I would have wanted no part of a horse as reckless as this one was, but I had much less fear of this berserk mustang than of the infuriated cow.

I drew my feet up clear of the ground and clung desperately to the saddle horn. Most of my shirt and pants were torn off by the brush, but when the horse broke out of the forest into the open I was still clinging to the horn of the saddle.

The moose had followed us for only twenty or thirty yards, but evidently my horse overlooked that fact, because he ran a good hundred yards before he made the open country and was still going when I managed to let go with one hand and grab hold of one of the split reins.

As soon as I had the rein, I swung myself clear and hit the ground on my feet. Pulling back as hard as I could on the one rein, I was able to swing the frantic horse into a half circle.

However, I lost my footing and went down on my back. The scared mustang dragged me several yards before he stopped.

I got to my feet, secured the other rein, and leaped into the saddle. I could still hear a lot of noise back in the timber, and I was afraid Ned was having a tough go with Mother Moose. By using my spurs generously, I was able to force my mount back into the forest towards the clearing we had just left. Part way in, we saw Ned's riderless horse coming out of the timber with the moose cow right behind him.

The instant my horse spotted the moose he whirled on his hind legs and again started going places. I rode him out and when he finally quit plunging I headed him back into the forest towards the cow. There was no noise coming from the timber and I was afraid the moose had killed Ned. Neither he nor I had a weapon of any kind except a pocket knife, and that was a mere trinket under such circumstances.

I had a rough time getting my horse close enough to see whether or not the moose was still around and what had happened. Finally I yelled as loud as I could for Ned, but not a sound came from him. I yelled again three or four times. No answer. By then I just knew he had been worked over by the angry cow.

Driving my spurs into the scared, nervous horse, I made him go a bit closer so I could see the small clearing where I had had my last glimpse of Ned as he ducked back of a pine tree with the calf. There I saw Ned, standing with his back flat against the pine, as still as a stone.

On the opposite side of the tree no more than ten feet away, I could dimly see the outline of the mother moose, and on the ground between her front feet lay the baby coiled up in a comfortable ball. The hair along his mama's back and neck still stood on end. She was eyeing me with deadly intent.

Boy, what a spot Ned was in! If that moose ever realized he was back of the tree he would be cut to ribbons. No wonder he had not answered when I called. I was trying to figure some way to rescue him when I saw he was motioning with his head for me to leave.

In an instant I was gone. My horse needed no coaxing to get out of the swamp. Although I hated to leave Ned in such a spot, I felt sure he knew what was best. I rode out and picked up his horse which had stopped out on the meadow a hundred yards or so from the edge of the woods. I could see that he had three cuts on his rump and one along his side just back of the saddle blanket, but none of them was much more than a bad scratch. He had managed to avoid the full force of the blows as the cow had struck with her hooves.

Back near the edge of the swamp I waited, not knowing what to expect next. After a few minutes that seemed hours Ned came walking slowly out of the forest with the silliest grin on his face I have ever seen. He had a good look at me with most of my clothes gone. Then he examined the horses.

Finally, he asked: "Are you hurt, Howard?"

"Nothing but my clothes and my feelings," I said, grinning back at him. Without further comment he climbed aboard his horse and we headed back to camp a couple of miles up the creek.

When we reached camp and I had dressed again, Art, our cook, served us with some hot coffee. While we relaxed and enjoyed the hot beverage Ned broke the silence.

"You know, Howard, it's a wonder somebody didn't get badly hurt by that moose. I thought when I spotted her," he went on, "that she was a young heifer with her first calf, and that we could scare her off and make some pictures, but she turned out to be an old gal with lots of experience and plenty of nerve."

I could only agree that the mother, whether young or old, had no intention of allowing her youngster to become a movie star.

Ned told me that when the moose returned after the baby yelled for help, he knew that things were going to happen. He said he ducked back of the tree, thinking maybe the mother would chase me far enough away to allow him to run with the baby and hide, but he did not have a chance to go any place except behind the tree. When the cow went after Ned's horse, he said he put the calf down and hid behind the pine tree where I discovered him when I was finally able to make my horse go in the forest.

Ned said that the instant the cow saw her calf she ran to meet it and stood over it for protection. As soon as I had ridden away, she thought all her enemies had vanished, so taking the baby with her, she went deeper into the forest. She had never seen Ned after he got off his horse. Naturally, after the two had gone, Ned had nothing further to fear.

From that first encounter I learned that a cow moose with a young calf is not easy to deal with.

A couple of days later we took Nedward, Ned's son, and Art, our cook, with us, and set out again, looking for a mother moose with a baby. Art and Nedward carried switches ten or twelve feet long with them which they would have a use for later, I learned.

Just before we reached the upper end of Moose Meadow, we worked up the mountain side where we could get a good view of the open glade. With the aid of field-glasses, Ned soon spotted a moose cow and a calf in a small clump of scattered bush near the centre of the meadow. By taking cover in the timber that grew along Middle Creek, which ran right through the centre of the meadow, we were able to get within a couple of hundred yards of our quarry without being seen.

We hurried down to a position opposite the moose and here we made ready for the task ahead. Nedward and Art were to ride out slowly and give the mother moose time to hide her baby. As soon as this was done they were to charge her and give her a good going-over with the long switches until they forced her to take to the forest. As soon as the mother was out of sight, Nedward was to drop his handkerchief near the calf so that Ned and I could easily spot it. Ned reasoned that if the cow saw only Nedward and Art, and that if both of them chased her, she would leave the baby hidden without worrying about his safety, believing she had lured the two enemies away from the calf.

Ned had figured perfectly, because we made it out to the calf and I caught him and held on to his muzzle until he quietened down. The little fellow lost his fear of me in a couple of minutes and we had an easy time getting some lovely pictures of him. In fact, he got so friendly that he began to play. He would run up to me, then dash off and kick up his heels as a domesticated baby calf will often do when in a playful mood. After two or three such dashes he came running towards me, stopped short and for some unknown reason he bleated, again much like a calf in a barnlot.

We could see Nedward and Art a couple of hundred yards away near the edge of the forest and we knew they were between us and the mother of the calf. But a couple of seconds after the calf bleated, the cow came out of the trees right past the two

men on the dead run and made straight for us. Art and Nedward gave chase, but she had a good start on them and it was
doubtful whether or not they would be able to overtake her
before she reached us. I was holding the little fellow and Ned
was grinding away with the camera when I saw her coming.

I yelled: "Here comes Big Mama, Ned. I won't be around
here long, so you'd better work fast!"

"You won't be leaving alone," he said, running for his horse.

I dropped the little moose like a hot potato and got aboard
my horse. As we headed for cover we looked back and that
little old calf was coming along right behind us. Art and Nedward saw we were leaving, so they broke off the chase. We
yelled at the moose baby, but he kept coming right along behind
our horses.

His mother was gaining at every jump and she could see that
her child was following us. This, of course, made her madder
than ever; in fact, she must have been scandalized. When she
was only about twenty yards behind us, Ned and I put spurs to
our horses and left her and the youngster far behind. She
promptly overtook the little fellow and they stopped. Two or
three times he walked around her and tried to follow Ned and
me, but each time the cow got in front of him. Finally she convinced him that she, instead of us, was responsible for him. I
always wondered if she gave him a piece of her mind. Anyway,
we left them standing in the meadow and the little guy surely
seemed to be enjoying his lunch. His short nub of a tail was
going a mile a minute.

"That," I said to Ned on our way back to camp, "is what I
call out-smarting a mama moose."

"At least, it's a safer way than the one we tried before," he
said, grinning.

CHAPTER EIGHT

SUGGESTIONS FOR OUTDOOR CAMERAMEN

Anyone who desires to shoot either still or motion pictures of wildlife should first of all give considerable thought to the kind of cameras that are best suited for such work. Naturally, almost every camera enthusiast likes some particular make of camera better than any other. However, the mere fact that one likes a certain camera does not mean that his favourite is best suited for this particular type of photography. In some cases of course, his choice might just happen to be the very machine needed, but this is not necessarily true.

There are a few requirements that should be considered most seriously before a person selects a still camera for shooting wildlife pictures. Especially is this true if he contemplates the shooting of dangerous game animals. I shall give these requirements briefly in the order of what I consider their importance. They are:

1. A good fast coated lens.
2. A fast quiet shutter.
3. A ground glass focusing plate.
4. A simple and easy-to-set shutter.
5. Lightness for ease of carrying.
6. Rugged construction.
7. Ease of repair.
8. Size such that an 8 x 10 can be made from the negative without losing too much quality.

Almost every good make of camera has some of these qualifications but few, indeed, have them all. Any camera that does not have a good fast coated lens will lack quality when negatives are shot under any other than ideal conditions, and one must remember that seldom will he be able to stalk really wild animals in their natural surroundings so that such conditions will prevail. So many other factors are involved, which will be discussed later in this chapter, in order to get close enough to wild game, that one may not be able to secure the most desired position from which to shoot a picture. For that reason, alone, it is worth while to have a lens that will make the best possible picture under ordinary conditions.

The proper shutter is in some ways even more indispensable than is a good lens. A noisy shutter may provoke a charge by ferocious game, and it is sure to frighten many creatures away that might otherwise loiter and give the cameraman opportunity to take several shots. The faster the shutter, the better the man behind the camera can stop moving animals. I seldom use a shutter speed of less than 1/100, and in most cases if the light will allow, I shoot at from 1/200 to 1/250. Naturally, I am speaking of hand held cameras; anyone who tries to use a tripod in the bush is adding a lot of grief to his already many problems and is cutting his chances in half, so far as being able to stalk is concerned.

There are a few animals that may become very angry when they hear a noisy shutter. When one sneaks up very close to a lion, Cape buffalo, elephant, rhinoceros, bull moose (in the rutting season), grizzly bear or even a hippopotamus, there is a twenty per cent. chance that he will be charged if the animal is suddenly disturbed. I know of few things that perturb wild creatures more than a noisy shutter on a still camera. For some reason the steady hum of a motion picture camera does not make them nearly so angry as does the metallic click of the shutter of a still camera. There are many natural buzzing sounds in the bush, but I have not heard anything there to match the click of a still camera, unless it be the snap of a dead twig usually made by some creature that is making a quiet, deadly stalk. An animal that is walking naturally through the forests makes many different kinds of noises and several of them may be made at the same time, but a creature making a sneak endeavours to cause no noise at all. He may happen to have a dry twig or stick snap beneath his feet. It is possible that the reason why nearly any animal becomes so agitated at the click of a shutter is the fact that he thinks it is another animal making a stalk on him. Take my serious advice; do not use a noisy shutter in the brush, if you hope to live long when photographing at close range any of the animals mentioned above.

If one has a ground glass focusing plate it takes little time to adjust the camera to the proper distance, leaving only the matter of setting the diaphragm to the proper opening, assuming of course, that the speed of the shutter has already been decided upon and the proper adjustment made. Being able to estimate the proper amount of light needed and to set the stops quickly is of prime importance, as time in many cases is limited to a few seconds when making close shots. Besides, if the ground glass focusing device is accurate, the chance for error is very small, whereas if one has to guess the distance, the margin of error is appreciably increased.

The ability to make the proper shutter adjustments is important, for the same reasons as given concerning the focusing. Remember, once the cameraman is in the proper position to do so, speed in taking a picture is most essential. Especially does this statement hold when the animal involved is an alert, wary creature, such as the mountain sheep, black bear, coyote, wolf, deer, jaguar, mountain goat, impala, klipspringer, kob, waterbuck, kudu, and many other types of antelope. In fact, any animal that is usually the hunted rather than the hunter may be exceptionally wary and easy to frighten. Most of the bovine creatures are being constantly hunted by the feline species and live only so long as they keep alert and vigilant. It is natural for them to take flight at the least sign of danger. Many times the least bit of noise will cause them to explode into action, without waiting to see what caused the disturbance.

It is often necessary to walk considerable distances to find and stalk an animal-subject for the camera. Then after the quarry has been located, it may be necessary to crawl on hands and knees or to slide forward on one's belly in order to get within camera range. Again, one may need to use both hands as well as both feet to negotiate certain areas, so it is most helpful to have a camera that is easy to carry. I usually rig a light camera harness so that I can carry my camera on my back, on the side, or in front, as circumstances require. Such a harness should be light in weight and simple to adjust, and should have no more straps and buckles than absolutely necessary. Even a very light object will become heavy after one packs it for several hours at a stretch.

Many times it may be necessary to drop a camera and take to a tree or to dodge behind a rock or a big tree trunk, and again in rough, rocky country one may lose his footing and fall; for these reasons a camera should be rugged and hard to jar out of kilter.

Some cameras are so made that they can be taken apart, cleaned and put back together fairly easily, and many of their parts can be improvised with simple tools while in the field. Naturally, one must take as good care as possible of his equipment, but at best there will be times when a certain amount of abuse will be unavoidable.

I have never cared for the smaller camera made by several of the leading manufacturers. Besides being hard to focus and more or less troublesome to set properly, the negatives for this type are so small they do not lend themselves too well for blow-ups. There are several cameras that will qualify for this kind of work, and I do not wish to impose my preferences on any one, but from personal experience in getting animal pictures in really rugged country, under everyday conditions, I like the Rolliflex best for all outdoor animal photography. For shooting landscapes, waterfalls, and large group pictures, however, I generally prefer a 4 x 5 Graflex.

The cameras I have found best suited for 35 mm. motion pictures of wild animals are the Akeley, Sinclair, DeBrie High Speed and the hand-carried Eyemo. There are many other makes that have been successfully used and are perhaps just as good; however, these are my preferences above any others I have tried.

The Akeley was designed and built by the late Carl Akeley, an explorer unequalled in outdoor motion picture photography. There are a few refinements built into this camera that are not found in any other make. It is light, fast to operate, sturdy; it can be cranked by hand or operated by a synchronous motor. It has a parallex finder suitable for all long lenses up to 24 inches, as well as a quick-change lens device. The Akeley carries a 400-foot roll of film and has a panning gear device which is superior to that of any other make. Easy to repair, simple to operate, this camera, in my opinion, will take more abuse than any other motion picture camera ever built.

The Sinclair is an English make, double-spring wind camera that takes a 200-foot roll of film and will shoot 180 feet without re-winding. This is an exceptionally steady and rugged machine, unusually quiet, is easy to set and shoots pictures of superior quality.

The French DeBrie, especially built for high-speed work, has no real competition in this field. It can also be used at normal speed but its most useful function is doing excellent work in high speed. I have one such camera that can be driven up to nine or ten times normal speed. At eight times normal I have run a complete 400-foot roll of film through it without a scratch, a film buckle or an aperture abrasion. Not once, but hundreds of times I have used this dependable camera and the results are always the same, clear, steady pictures of exceptional quality. There may be other cameras that will compare favourably with the DeBrie High Speed, but I have never seen or used one. Before I owned the DeBrie, I tried many other high speed machines and some of them performed fairly well up to four times normal speed, but above that rate they just would not do a good job.

The DeBrie, like the Akeley, can be hand cranked or motor driven. I prefer to hand crank this machine, as one can reach a maximum speed much quicker when using the hand crank. Over a period of years I have run perhaps more than fifty thousand feet of film through this particular camera at a speed above seven times normal, and a great portion of this film was run at more than nine times normal, but up to this writing, the camera has never broken down nor failed to make first quality pictures.

The Eyemo is not an expensive camera. The quality of the pictures shot with this machine does not equal that of film shot with either of the other machines I have just discussed, but many times, one is able to grab a shot with an Eyemo that could not have been secured with any other camera. It carries only a hundred feet of film, but the whole thing is so light and versatile that one can hand hold it and take fairly good quality pictures, and do so quicker than with any other machine yet invented. I never use the Eyemo on a tripod for the simple reason that the other cameras mentioned usually shoot better pictures, but for quick pick-up shots that must be got in a hurry or not at all, in unexpected moments, it has no equal. I therefore consider it indispensable for the kind of pictures I make.

My experience with 16 mm. cameras is limited, compared to that with the 35. However, I prefer the Bolex or Cine Special for 16 mm. work. All the professional cameramen I have had work with me on outdoor pictures prefer to use either one or both of these two machines for 16 mm. film. Mitchell makes perhaps the finest camera for this size film, but it is not compact enough to use in the field when taking action pictures of wild-life where conditions may be rugged.

Any standard light meter will suffice, but I personally prefer the Norwood Director. All lenses should be colour corrected (coated), especially for outdoor work. As to filters, I shall not discuss the different types, as much depends on the kind and the speed of the film being used, and on what effect the camera-man is trying to obtain in any given shot. Moreover, in the field, one seldom has time to experiment with too many filters when securing animal pictures. In shooting coloured film, I use whatever kind of filter the manufacturer of the film recommends. Be sure to study the written instructions furnished by the makers of the particular film you are using before shooting any new kind of colour film, or else be sure you are entirely familiar with the proper filters generally accepted for the coloured film of the older and better known brands.

In the matter of the subjects one is trying to photograph in the field, that is, the animals themselves, it is even more impor-tant to understand the fundamentals of stalking, the habits, senses, characteristics and the general psychology of wild creatures than it is to have the proper camera equipment. Not just any cameraman accustomed to work around studios, on sound stages or even in compounds, can go out and secure good shots of wild animals in their natural surroundings, no matter how wonderful the cameras and other appurtenances he may take along.

A cameraman is liable to get killed unless he is able to stalk and knows what reactions to expect from wild game. Many times it is much safer to sit idly by and allow an animal to walk out of camera range without moving a muscle or shooting even one picture. It requires constant study and more than a little experience to be able to photograph some species. Usually, how-ever, there is no need to worry about danger from wild creatures, unless they are wounded or cornered.

On the other hand, there are a few animals, that although as harmless as babes at most seasons of the year, are at other times and under certain conditions killers of the first water. As an illustration, during the winter, spring, and summer a bull moose will run like a turkey whenever he sees, hears, or smells man, but in the fall during the rutting season he may charge on sight and without warning. The cow moose is not dangerous during the rutting season, but look out for her when she has a very young calf in the early spring. (See chapter on Photographing Moose.) I do not mean to imply that all bull moose will charge on sight during the rut, but some of them will, and it takes only one charge to kill a man. I know of several instances in which these bulls have charged friends of mine, and only by shooting the moose dead or by climbing a tree were they able to save themselves.

Personally, I have had only one bull moose to charge me, and luckily, I was riding a good fast horse on the occasion and lost no time in clearing out of the vicinity. I had accidentally ridden between a cow moose and the bull that was following her. She was several yards ahead of him and crossed the trail I was following only a few yards in front of me. When she saw me, she took to heel, and I, unaware that a bull was anywhere near, rode on along the trail. The bull charged suddenly and with absolutely no warning.

The most dangerous animal in America is the grizzly bear, and incidentally, once he makes up his mind to charge, he is to my way of thinking one of the most vicious and determined beasts in the world. Even the lion, the Cape buffalo, or the elephant is no harder to stop. One of the reasons he is so dangerous is that he is totally unpredictable. Nine times out of ten or even more often, he may take flight from man, but there is always a good chance that he will put up a fight, and unless one has a good heavy rifle and knows how to use it—well, he'd better be prepared to meet his Maker, and I am not trying to be facetious.

My advice to any hunter with the camera is to let certain animals strictly alone, unless he is accompanied by a dead-shot armed with a good heavy rifle (no less than a ·375 Magnum), as well as having a calm, steady nerve and a maximum of guts. Be sure that the rifleman is an experienced hunter who is entirely familiar with the particular breed of animal being hunted. The beasts to be avoided, unless the cameraman is well protected as just advised, are: first, the elephant; second, the African buffalo; third, the grizzly bear; then the lion, jaguar, rhinoceros, leopard and the wild boar loosely more or less in the order named.

The chances are that few camera hunters will be able to find many jaguar or leopards in daylight, but it is entirely possible to do so. Most man-eating leopards are day-time hunters.

There is a chance to side-step a charging wild boar or a rhinoceros, but there is no certainty that either of these beasts will keep going after one charge. If they really mean business and make a second charge, the chances are they will do it so quickly that one has little time to avoid it. Especially is this statement true in the case of the wild boar, and the odds are too great to take chances with either of these beasts. Even when accompanied by a rifleman, as already suggested, the danger is great enough, particularly if the animal in question is in close quarters. No picture is so important to secure that it is worth the death of a cameraman.

Fortunately, the animals that are the hardest to stalk are usually the least dangerous, or even not at all dangerous. Different methods of stalking are employed in approaching different species of animals, for the simple reason that the development of the senses varies greatly among different families of wild creatures. For instance, the American moose and bear and the African elephant, rhinoceros and hippopotamus, all have extremely poor eyesight in comparison with most other wild animals. One may be able to approach within fairly close range of any of the creatures just named, even if in open ground, so long as he has the wind in his favour and makes his stalk quietly. If a man does not move forward while one of these animals is looking directly at him, he will seldom be distinguished by the beast until within fairly close range.

I have stood without any appreciable cover within twenty-five yards of a trail and watched a herd of more than a hundred and fifty elephants pass, without any of them having seen me. At that distance they would surely have detected me had I moved. I dared not even roll my motion picture camera for fear they would detect the movement. This particular herd consisted of cows, calves, and yearlings, with a few large but immature bulls. Elephant mothers with young calves are decidedly short tempered, especially when a large number of them are together. I had already shot some good close pictures of cows and calves, so I did not feel too badly at having to pass up this grand opportunity to add to the collection. I had only one native boy with me and neither of us had a weapon of any kind. Frankly, however, I would have taken no pictures of elephants under such

A blue marlin which went completely through a dinghy in the Gulf of California

Taking aim

circumstances, even if we had had an arsenal—the brutes were too close and there were too many of them. One might drop a couple of elephants before they could charge twenty yards, but not one hundred and fifty.

Had I known nothing about the temperament of African elephants, I would perhaps have tried to shoot some footage, and had I done so, the chances are that some one else would now be writing this book. If I had been well concealed, I would not have hesitated, because there was a strong wind in our favour and the noise of its blowing through the foliage of the small brush and grass would probably have drowned out the sound of the camera. We had been waiting for a herd of water-buck to come along the trail and had decided to leave the place and return to our jeep, which we had concealed in some heavy bush a couple of hundred yards away. No sooner had we left our bush blind than the herd of elephants appeared out of the forest. I had to fight myself to keep from running (as well as a man could run with a knee that had been crushed in a hunting accident a few months before), but Casumway, my hunter boy, happened to be with me and the second he saw the elephants, he exclaimed:

"*Simama, hapa! Simama hapa, upasi!*" ("Stop here! Stop here, quickly!")

This boy had been born and reared in the Rutshuru River country, in the Belgian Congo, which is right in the heart of elephant country, and he had been the gun bearer for a German ivory hunter in years past. Casumway knew elephants at first hand and understood them better than anyone else I met in Africa. The rhinoceros bush and grass around us was about four feet high, but was scattered. From some quarters we were fairly well concealed, but from others we had practically no cover between us and the beasts. While the herd was passing, neither of us looked directly at them, for fear they would see a reflection when we batted our eyes.

After they had gone past and were at a safe distance, I asked Casumway: "What would have happened had we run from the herd?"

He grinned as he always did at a naive question from me and said, as a matter of fact: "*Tembo Kinyu, Bwana.*" ("Elephants kill us, Master.") We shot many pictures of elephants within twenty-five or thirty yards, but believe me, we had plenty of cover to keep well concealed from them, as well as a good breeze in our favour.

I have found that the moose, bear, rhino, hippo and wild boar see little better than does the elephant. While the rhino has the best nose of any of these beasts, the elephant and the moose can hear better than the others. All these varieties can both smell and hear extremely well.

There are few wild creatures that do not depend a great deal on hearing and smelling; the bighorn sheep and the mountain goat, on the contrary, depend almost entirely on their sense of sight to give them warning of man's approach. Almost all other animal species which I have hunted, have all three of the senses mentioned fairly well and evenly developed, and do not rely on any one sense alone. Most birds and reptiles, as distinguished from the mammals, use chiefly only the senses of sight and hearing for protection. Personally, I do not know of a single bird or reptile that has a sense of smell sufficient on which to rely as a warning when man is near, yet apparent exceptions to this general rule are the facts that the vulture and some forms of snakes seem to locate much of their food by smelling it.

I once met a Georgia Cracker, as we of the south call a native of that State, who told me he was positive that a wise old turkey gobbler which he had hunted for many years, could smell like a bloodhound. This Cracker knew the ways of wild turkey. He could tell some mighty tall tales to prove how he knew that particular gobbler could smell, but I have to admit I think he was just " giving me the business," as the boys in Alabama used to say. At any rate, I have done considerable turkey hunting and I have never worried about the sense of smell of that or any other bird. So far as I know, I have never spooked a wild turkey by having him scent me.

One of the best methods to learn about the ways of animals is to seek out the most successful hunter in the area where one intends to shoot a lot of pictures and, if possible, strike up a friendship. Usually, sooner or later, most of the typical local hunters thus met will begin talking about the peculiar habits and characteristics of the animals in the vicinity. Many times the newcomer can persuade a hunter to talk by not acting too smart and by asking a few leading questions. However, it does not pay to act too naive, for some old time hunters think it great sport to tell city folk wild yarns that may be entirely void of any real facts worth listening to. The real blanket Indian, and there are still a few, has a world of practical knowledge of wild game and a lot of common horsesense about animals. It pays to listen to him if one is lucky enough to be able to get him to talk. I am sure the Red Man knows more about animal psychology than anyone else, and fortunate, indeed, is the man who can gain the confidence of a real honest-to-goodness woods Indian and get him to tell what he knows about wood and animal lore.

Any observant person can learn a great deal about animals without any help, provided he applies himself diligently to the task. Nothing I have ever done gives me more enjoyment and satisfaction than to outsmart some wise old animal and get a good close-up picture of him. Not often have I been able to accomplish this, but the few times it has happened, it has given me a big lift.

If everything else in this chapter is forgotten or ignored, there is one thing that every camera hunter should remember: be extremely careful to take nothing for granted where a dangerous beast is concerned. Play your hand for all it is worth, but *play it safe*. Even when taking every precaution for safety, it is still a game of chance. One does not have to look for thrills when shooting animal pictures with a camera; many times the thrills just walk right up and take hold of you.

CHAPTER NINE

ADVENTURE WITH COUGAR

H IGH above the Tonto Canyon we slid our quarter-horses to a stop on the very brink of the Tonto Rim in Central Arizona. A mile or so to the east and more than two thousand feet below, we could hear the barking pack of Blue Tick and Walker hound dogs driving up the valley at surprising speed. They had jumped the big Tom cougar, and the chase was on.

We could hardly restrain our anxious mounts as the barking of the dogs grew louder. The horses knew as well as we did that the hounds were coming towards us. They had carried riders on many such hunts and it was in their blood to want to be in on the chase. Frank Colcord, my companion and the owner of the dogs and horses, listened only a few seconds, then said: "Let's go, Howard! We'll have to move if we cut them off at Coyote Pass." Instantly he was off along the rimrock in a shower of gravel and loose dirt.

My gelding followed at such speed that he very nearly got out from under me. I could feel the ripple of his hard strong muscles beneath the saddle as he accelerated his pace. For a mile or more we raced along the top of the cliff at a dangerous speed. Around windfalls, over logs, through rock-strewn ditches and over the tops of mountain buckrush we dashed as fast as the willing steeds could go. I had been on many wild horseback rides before that time, chasing foxes, bobcat, and cougar in Florida, but never anything like this. At least, down on that southern peninsula the ground had offered more suitable footing for our horses.

My mount was so anxious to stay up with Frank and his horse that he was hard to manage. However, I was able to stay aboard and to duck the overhanging limbs and vines. No matter what the footing, he never faltered. I was wondering how long these horses could sustain such speed when I saw Frank neck-rein his mount towards the edge of the Rim.

In three strides they went over the side of the high cliff and for a split second were lost from my sight. My mount was heading for the same spot on the wall of the cliff, without any loss of speed. I pulled up on the reins but it was too late: we were already over the edge and sailing through space. I could see nothing but blue sky, but as my mount started to drop, his feet hit a shale rock slide that ran from a few feet beneath the top of the cliff to the floor of the canyon, a good two thousand feet below. The whole mountain slide of shale rock was moving in a sort of escalator effect.

As the feet of my horse hit the loose moving shale, he went in above his fetlocks, but was off on his next leap without a bobble. I could see Frank twenty yards ahead of me, and his horse was going down the steep mountain side as steadily as though running on level ground. I would have been afraid to walk down that rock slide on my own feet, not to mention riding down it at half a mile a minute, but Frank and the horses knew about shale slides and they were not in the least perturbed. All I could do was to stay in my saddle and pray that we would make the bottom, still right side up.

Before I realized it, we had come to the end of the slide and were off across the floor of the canyon. A quarter of a mile through the valley timber we came to a small knoll and shot up to the top of it, where Frank pulled in sharply. I had not expected such a sudden stop and I had passed him a couple of strides before I could skid my horse to a halt.

Above the loud breathing of our two quarter-horses we could hear the dogs driving towards us. Despite our head-start of a mile or more and the breakneck speed at which we had gone, the hounds had gained on us considerably.

In only a few seconds Frank had sensed the direction in which the Tom was headed and he was off again, with me following. I was amazed at the stamina of the horses. Even though they had made a dead run of a mile and a half with only eight or ten seconds to breathe, they were running with seemingly the same speed as when they had started. A few hundred yards along the ridge we were riding, we came to a huge boulder about the size of a three-storey office building. We skirted the right side of it, opposite the direction from which the dogs were approaching.

Just before we got past the big rock cliff, Frank reined in again and jumped out of his saddle, letting the split reins dangle on the ground. He yelled to me: "Hurry up and get your camera and follow me if you want to get a picture of that Tom cat when he comes through the pass!"

I soon had my Eyemo out of the saddle bag and was at his heels, running towards a narrow pass some sixty yards away. I was winding the camera as I hustled along, hoping against hope that the reckless ride had not fouled the film inside the camera so that it would not feed through the shutter gate. Now I understood why Frank had insisted that morning on tying down the saddle bags with an extra latigo. Had those saddle bags been loose on the bottom end, we would have torn them off half a dozen times before we finished the ride just completed.

There was no time to take a light-reading, but it was a bright, sunny day and the pass was directly in the open. My 35 mm. lens was at "infinity." I was using Super Pan black and white film, so I opened my stop between 11 and 16.

As we came out from behind the big rock I could hear the dogs and they were considerably less than a quarter of a mile away. We stopped behind a couple of large yellow pine trees, fairly close to the pass and waited. I held the camera against the trunk of the nearest tree to help steady it, as I was breathing hard from the run we had made on foot from the point where we had left our horses.

We had no more than settled behind the trees when the voice of old Keeno, the lead dog, bawled less than two hundred yards away. He was considerably ahead of the rest of the pack and I felt that the cougar must have already gone through the pass. Just as this thought entered my mind, there was a yellow flash as the big mountain lion broke out into the opening and came barrelling through the pass.

I caught him in the finder and rolled the camera, securing a wonderful shot of him as he passed. He was so intent on getting away from the dogs that he never even glanced towards us.

As he was lost from sight over the pass, Frank said: "It won't be long now, Howard. That cat will have to take a tree or Keeno will catch him."

In a few seconds Keeno came through the pass and I took a shot of him. He was everlastingly running. He had no time for barking, but was just letting out a whining grunt about every fifty yards. I could see he was making much better speed than the cougar and I knew if the hound could hold his speed, Frank was right. That cat would have to take to a tree or be caught on the ground.

After Keeno passed, it was a good half minute before the rest of the pack arrived. Frank really had a crush on Red Keeno, for he said to me while we waited for the other dogs: "There's never been a cat that can stay long in front of that flop-eared hound. No sir, he's not much on the cold trail, but once a cat is jumped there's not a lion dog in Arizona that can stay up there with him!"

Keeno was a long, lean, lanky hound of a peculiar mixed breed, one-half Blue Tick, one-quarter Walker foxhound and a quarter Red Bone. Ordinarily, dogs of such a cross are good tough fighters and have a good nose, but are not too speedy. Red Keeno, however, cared little about fighting and had a poor nose for cold trailing, but somewhere along the line through his Walker foxhound blood he had picked up speed to burn.

I have hunted foxes and cats since I was eight or nine years old, and down in Alabama where I was reared, people have the fastest Walker foxhounds in America. At several National Fox-Hunting Conventions which I have attended, I've seen some mighty fast dogs, but I don't think I've ever seen a faster one than this.

Whether or not he had the guts to stay with such speed over a long haul of five or six hours I do not know, but for a short race after a bear or a cat, he was tops. Frank said he could keep right on going for hours and I am inclined to believe him. The dog had the build and the disposition for a real sticker and probably was. At any rate, he had what it took to put a mountain lion up a tree. Even before the rest of the pack made the pass we heard Keeno bark "treed" a quarter of a mile beyond it.

As soon as I got a picture of the pack coming through the pass, we hurried back to our horses and rode over to where the big Tom cougar had climbed a huge yellow pine. It was located in a narrow rough canyon where there was little light. The canyon wall and the forest of pine almost entirely obscured the sunlight.

It had been my plan to photograph Frank and a couple of other fellows roping a cougar, but one of the cowboys that had planned to help with the roping had become sick the day before the hunt and had returned to the ranch. When we had found the cougar tracks that morning and had started the dogs off on the cold trail, Frank had sent the other boy on foot along with the dogs.

We were hunting on top of the Tonto Rim in Arizona, and there were very few places where the horses could get off the Rim and down into the valley below. For that reason Frank had decided to stay on top until the dogs trailed the track out and jumped the cougar before he rode off the Rim. He told me that most of the panthers came out of the canyon and up on top of the Rim to take a tree, but some did not. The one we had "treed" had, of course, followed along the Rim a way, then headed out over the foothill.

I made several pictures of the cat up in the pine tree while we waited for Red Wilkins, the boy who had gone with the dogs and who was going to help Frank rope the cougar. It was the better part of an hour before he arrived. The spot which the cat had chosen to take a tree was very disappointing to me, because there was no sunlight at all, and the rocks were dark. I knew that any pictures I took in that location would be of very poor quality. Besides the handicap of bad light, there were so many boulders and the side hill was so steep that I had few places from which to secure pictures of any kind. When I told Frank my troubles he made what I thought was a wonderful suggestion.

"I tell you what, Howard. We'll just rope this baby, tie him up, then take him out on top and away from the canyon into the big pine forest, then turn him loose and tree him again. Up there we'll have lots of light and the ground is not so rough."

I readily fell in with Frank's idea. I never stopped to wonder how we were going to get a hundred and seventy pounds of mountain lion out of the canyon, then up on top of the Tonto Rim, which was a good mile and a half away and more than two thousand feet above us.

Neither did I realize that Frank had already figured he would use me to help rope and tie up the cat, so long as I couldn't be taking pictures. I did not know it then, but it really takes three men to rope and tie up a big cougar, and this one was about as big as they grow. One man can rope a mountain lion easily, but to tie him for the purpose of transportation, is another matter. Frank had not mentioned this roping and tying of the cougar until after Red had arrived.

Within a very few moments Red had skinned up the big

pine in which the cougar was lying out on the first limb above the ground, which was about thirty-five or forty feet up. Frank tossed a lariat up to the cowboy and a stick about eight to ten feet long. Red fashioned a loop some two feet in diameter and hung it on the little end of the stick, then eased it out very slowly towards the cougar's head. The first time or two the cat slapped the loop off the stick then bit the end of the stick, but each time Red would make another loop and try again.

He was standing on the same limb that held the cougar, but was near the tree trunk, while the big Tom was out near the end, lying across the small limbs which branched out from the main one. I never have understood why a mountain lion will not attack a man in a tree, for the animal is definitely cornered at such a time, but during my years of hunting this creature since then, I have never seen one go for a man under such conditions.

A bobcat is a baby in size, compared to a cougar, but any time one of those cats is " treed," no man had better try going up to rope him. The fellow that ever tries it won't have to go all the way up to get him, for the gutty little cat will meet him more than half-way. If anybody starts up the tree, the bobcat comes down to meet him, and when he gets within springing distance, the foolhardy hunter will have a lot of bobcat right in the middle of him.

Well, Red got the loop over the cougar's head after about four attempts and he let the big cat gnaw on the end of the stick as he drew the lariat up around the neck of the Tom. Red dropped the rope to Frank, who caught it and waited for the roper to come down. In the meantime, I had got back out of the way.

As Red touched the ground, Frank said, exactly as though he were asking nothing out of the ordinary: "Howard, will you come down here and help us pull this cougar out of the tree?"

"Wait just a minute," I said. "I know *from nothing* about roping cougar and, brother, I have no desire to learn!"

"But you want to get him out where you can get a good picture, don't you?" Frank sounded as though he was disappointed that I did not jump at the chance to help rope the cat.

That was the first wild cougar I had ever seen in my life and if there was anything I wanted to do less than to help rope and tie up that one, it was to help tie up two cougars.

"No, Frank," I said. "I'm a cameraman and an archer, not a cowboy or a cougar-boy."

"Listen, Howard," he pleaded "All I want you to do is help us snake him out of the tree and when he hits the ground it will knock the wind out of him. Then Red and I will tie him up before he comes to."

"But what will happen if the fall fails to knock the wind out of him?" I wanted to know.

"If you don't help us pull this cougar out of the tree he may bite the lariat in two and. jump out and go for miles. It'll be dark in an hour or so and we could easily lose him."

We had been hunting cougar two weeks and this one was the first we had located, although we had covered several hundred miles in our search. I shuddered to think of losing him, yet I wanted no part of that yellow-eyed Tom-cat. I knew, however, that Frank was getting disgusted with me for not being willing to help with this "little job," as he put it.

After considerably more conversation I finally agreed to help pull the cougar down, but I made it plain that when he hit the ground my part was finished.

We got set and made a short run to take up the slack, then gave a mighty heave on the rope. The cougar was snatched off the end of the limb as slick as a whistle. He turned over a couple of times on his way down and all four of his feet were working like greased lightning.

The second that I saw the cougar was actually falling I dropped the rope and headed out of there in a hurry. I was looking back over my shoulder when the big cat hit the ground, right side up. He had no more than landed when he made a terrific leap down the mountain side.

All the dogs had been tied up and when they saw the cat on the ground they started bawling and trying to go after the Tom. The ungodly noise they made, only frightened the lion more. He seemingly was all over the side of the mountain, growling, scratching and trying to bite the lariat, but the hondo was on his neck, just back of his ears and he could not get the rope in his mouth.

Frank and Red had succeeded in snaffling the end of the lariat around a tree and Red was holding the rope while Frank was after the Tom, trying to catch him by the tail. I never saw such a mad, crazy scramble in all my life.

The rope was choking the cougar and for the amount of energy he was putting out he was not getting enough air. After a minute he choked down enough to lose his sense of balance. In a wild rush he side-swiped a big rock and the impact momentarily knocked him out.

Frank was on top of him like a bird after a grasshopper. He grabbed the cat by the tail and ran downhill until the rope came taut. About that time the cat came to, and if ever there was a mad cat, he was it. With all four feet he was striking out in every direction. At the same time he was trying to bite, but the boys had him stretched out and he could not reach either of them. At that juncture I heard Frank yell. "Howard, Howard, HOWARD! Come here, quick!"

"Nuts!" I yelled as loud as I could. "I'm not coming!"

"What's the matter with you? Ain't none of you durned dudes got no guts?" he yelled back. He was all excited and did not care what he said.

I was on top of a big rock, out of danger and out of the way. When he called me a dude, that made me pretty mad, but when he said I had no guts I really saw red. I leaped off the boulder and hurried down to where he had the cougar by the tail.

"What do you want?" I yelled right in his ear. With the dogs all barking and the cougar growling and us two screaming at each other, it must have sounded terrible, had there been an unbiased ear to hear the bedlam.

"Hold this cat by the tail while I tie him up!"

I grabbed the cougar by the tail and braced myself. Frank looked at me before he let go his hold and said: "If you let him get loose he'll tear me to pieces. You think you can hold him?"

"Tie up the cat," I yelled. "If the tail stays on I've got this end of him."

Frank let go his hold and whipped out two pigging strings (short tie ropes) and within a few seconds he had lassoed both the front feet and both the hind feet of the cat and had tied all four of them together.

He jumped back and said: "Let go his tail, Howard, and get out of the way!"

I didn't wait to be told a second time, but turned loose the tail and got out of the way. With all four feet tied together the cat was helpless except for his mouth.

Red threw Frank another tie rope; then Frank picked up a stick about the size of a man's wrist and stuck it in the cougar's mouth. The cat clamped down on it and closed his glazing eyes. He was just about choked stiff, and would never let go the stick until he came to. With the third rope Frank lassoed the upper and lower jaws in front of the stick towards the end of the nose, drew the loop tight and took a couple of half hitches so it could not work loose. Then he took out his jack-knife and cut the lariat that had finally choked the cougar unconscious.

He was not breathing at all and I thought he was dead, but Frank gave him a couple of mashes in the ribs and the big Tom started breathing again. In a moment or two he opened his eyes, but he was helpless as a kitten. All he could do was bite down on the stick to show how he felt.

As soon as the cat snapped out of his trance Frank looked up to where I was sitting on a boulder, still mad as a wet hen, and said: "Howard, you're better than a green hand at ropin' cougar. I think we'll put you on steady, humph, Red?" He looked at Red.

"Yeah," the cowpoke replied, "He's got a lotta guts for a dude."

They both laughed and I was amazed to hear myself laughing with them. Now that it was all over, I realized it had been a great thrill.

By the time we had carried the cougar on a pole a mile or so down the canyon to a ranch house that night, it was ten o'clock. There we borrowed a pick-up truck and carried the cat back up on top of the Rim where we had our camp.

Frank had brought along a steel cage that he used for live cougars. We placed the cat inside the cage and cut his bonds. In a couple of days he was as good as ever.

A few days after that we carried him into the forest and turned him loose. The dogs chased him up another big pine, this time in a spot where the light was good. The ranchers roped him, pulled him out and tied him up again, but this time I was the cameraman. They had another tail-holder to take my place.

This cougar roping is no child's play. Every once in a while a fellow gets badly clawed or bitten. One boy I knew had his arm broken in two places by a cougar while trying to tie up the beast. Frank has been scratched several times by the cats, but never hurt seriously.

Of all the reckless daredevils I have ever had the pleasure of seeing, Frank Colcord is by far the wildest. During the years that have followed the episode just told, I have been with him on several hunts so wild as to be crazy. I've seen him rope not only wild cattle and jaguar, but once he, with the same Red of this story and another boy called Trigger, lassoed a six hundred pound black bear. What's more, they tied him hard and fast.

CHAPTER TEN

ROPING BEAR UNDER THE
TONTO RIM

ONE spring in the late thirties, about a year after I had my first hunt for cougar with Frank Colcord in Arizona in the Tonto Rim country, I received a letter from him, which read, in part:

DEAR HOWARD,

Why don't you come down and help me round up and brand my calf crop? Then we will go after an out-lawed bear that is killing a lot of cattle and sheep here under the Tonto Rim. I can't go right away, but it would take us only a few weeks to brand my calves if you will help me and my son. Then we could go after the outlaw. I will pick up Red and Trigger and we will rope this bear for you. It ought to make a good picture. I promise I won't ask you to help rope the bear like I did the cougar, but we'll have some fun. Bear roping is a wild and woolly pastime and anything can happen, but if you're lucky you ought to get a swell picture.

Six weeks after I got this letter we had branded the last calf. Camped on top of the Tonto Rim were Red, Trigger, Frank, Al Wetzel and I. Al was an outdoor motion picture cameraman of long standing and had helped me with many other pictures. I figured that this bear roping episode was going to be quite an exciting event and I wanted to be sure we got it on film. With Al and me both operating a camera, I felt that we would be able to cover such an adventure adequately.

This time I had taken three cameras, an Eyemo for short pick-up shots, an Akeley for all the long, medium and close shots where quality was imperative and a high-speed DeBrie to get the slow motion. Of course, the Akeley and the high-speed DeBrie had to be operated from a tripod, but I planned to use the Eyemo free-hand, to grab action shots at close range.

I had left all the cameras behind when I went down to help Frank with his calf branding, but Al had arrived just as we completed that job, with all the requisites in a station wagon, and we were well equipped to make such a picture as we had in mind. We picked up a couple of extra local boys, whose names have slipped my mind, to help Al handle and set up the cameras and other equipment.

Up on top of the Tonto Rim there is a vast forest of virgin yellow pine timber, and, for the most part, the country is either flat or rolling hills. There are, however, two or three very deep and narrow rough canyons that cut through the region. The timbered area is traversed by several old wood roads which are used by hunters to get into the back country. These trails, or traces, run north at right angles to the Rim. We felt that if we were fortunate enough to catch the marauding bear above the Rim, we would have a fair chance of " treeing " or bringing him to bay before he could make it to the Tonto Rim. If, however, the bear should go under the Rim there were several ways by which we could get into the country with the station wagon, though it would be necessary to go a roundabout route and would take considerable time. Some of the old ranch trails over which salt was hauled to the cattle were blocked by fallen trees, but unless the outlaw bear chose the actual side of the Rim itself, or a rugged side canyon, we would be able to get fairly close to him by way of these old roads. We had studied carefully all the possibilities of the situation and were prepared to give it a try and see what happened.

Frank and the rest of the natives called the marauding black bear Butch, because of the way he slaughtered the cattle and sheep in the vicinity. The Butcher often killed several animals in one night.

Frank had his dogs so well trained to run only cougar and bear that they did not seem to care to go after any other wild animal. His pack of hounds of about fifteen consisted of a breed that had been developed as a cross between three good strains of hunting dogs, Blue Tick, Red Bone and Walker, in varying proportions. One or two individuals had a touch of bloodhound in them, but for the most part they were combinations of the first three breeds mentioned.

There is a good reason for not having a pack of dogs that are of any one strain of pure blood for the type of hunting Frank did. In the first place, a pure Red Bone is not husky enough to stand the gaff of fighting bear and cougar. Then while the speed of the Walker is desirable, and he has plenty of guts and a good nose, sometimes he is too fast for the rugged cliff country found in the mountains. Neither is he ideally built for rugged fighting. The Blue Tick lacks the speed and the nose of the Walker and the Red Bone, but he is heavily built, a rugged individual that has the grit of a bulldog and a stamina equal to that of the best Walker. This particular strain of Blue Tick had been brought into the Tonto Rim country more than a hundred years before by Frank's grandfather, and they had hunted the rugged terrain for so long that nature had developed in them just the right physical conformation to suit the particular type of work they did for Colcord.

Frank told me that he had seen one of this breed of dogs kill a full-grown mountain lion single-handed and live to fight again. Any one dog that can conquer this rugged cat is not only a great fighter, but he must be exceptionally strong in both jaw and body.

Besides the wonderful qualities of these Blue Ticks, they had one rather trying characteristic that was different from anything I had ever seen in any other breed of hounds. They had a mean, contrary streak in their disposition that caused them to dislike being touched by human hands. It was dangerous to try and pick up one of them to put him in a truck or car. He just resented being handled by any man. Once they were inside a truck or car, no one, not even Frank, could get into the vehicle without the aid of a good club. They would stand without trouble and allow one they knew to put a collar or a chain around their necks and could be led without offering resistance, but they did not like being petted or touched in any way. To pick up one was to be badly bitten.

If two of these dogs got into a fight and were separated they would have to be kept apart for several days, out of sight of each other, before they would forget their differences. Sometimes even this period of separation would not help and they would go for each other the moment the opportunity presented itself. Frank had long since learned that when two of them started fighting, the best thing to do was to keep the rest of the pack

The watchful lion

Angry lion

A lion killed by the author with bow and arrow, on an African safari

away and let the belligerents settle their differences for themselves. Sometimes he lost one or the other of the hounds, as
they often fought until one was killed.

Frank told me proudly that he had never seen any living
animal that his Blue Ticks were afraid of. They respected bear,
cougar and peccary (wild boar), but when roused they would,
at the most advantageous moment, attack even these three
species. They fought as a unit, much like a pack of Airedales.
They would surround a cornered animal and close in from all
sides, then the instant the bayed creature attacked a dog, the
rest of the pack set on him from the rear and sides. If a bear
got cornered in the cliffs or stood with his back against a cliff
or canyon wall where the dogs could not sneak up and bite him
when he was not looking, they would keep away from him, out
of harm's way, and harass him. However, if the bayed creature
started to run, they were at him in an instant.

This particular pack with which we were hunting, a mixture
of Blue Tick, Red Bone and Walker, as I have said, were
extremely strong and vicious and Frank assured me they had
actually killed several black bears, some of them full grown.
Some of the dogs had lost half an ear or carried long scars where
their bodies had been torn and lacerated in encounters with bear,
cougar and boar. Many of them were so individualistic and so
courageous that a book could be written concerning their personality and feats of daring, but I will only say that they are
a breed which deserves and commands respect. These are truly
hunting dogs of the first water.

We had with us a dozen good roping quarter-horses that were
clever and fast of foot, with plenty of grey matter between the
ears. They, too, had been bred in the high country and knew
how to handle themselves in the steep, rocky terrain. They
could not only go like the wind, but had no desire to quit or to
loaf. Anyone who climbed into the saddle atop one of them
had better know something about riding or he would not be
up long. On a frosty morning they just had to buck a little,
"to straighten out the kinks in their muscles," as Frank
explained their actions. Once on the trail or on a chase, however, these mounts buckled down to the job of work to be done,
but no rider could relax and get careless astride any of them.

They never failed to try out a new rider, and if he was not a
pretty fair horseman they soon knew it and the fellow was in

G

for a bad time. Ours was a happy, reckless outfit of fellows who thrived on excitement. All except Al Wetzel, my cameraman, had spent much of their lives in the forests, hunting and studying game.

Frank Colcord had been a Government hunter of mountain lion (cougar) and bear. Red and Trigger were born on ranches near Payson, Arizona, and were top ropers and riders. These two and Frank had all contested in rodeos and were tough, seasoned horsemen of no mean ability. After all is said, however, bear roping was a mighty tough assignment for anybody, no matter what his background.

It was the third morning after we had made camp that we awoke to find about two inches of snow atop the Rim country. A freak late spring fall of snow had covered the ground during the night. After we had saddled our mounts and " got the kinks out of them," we headed west, parallel to the Tonto Rim. Within a mile of camp we came on to the footprints of Butch, the outlaw bear. in the soft melting snow. He had passed since the snow had ceased falling—somewhere around midnight. The hounds had little trouble in moving along the wake of the outlaw. For an hour or so they cold trailed him through the virgin pine forest. At last his tracks led over the canyon wall and down towards the Tonto Basin below.

I had my Eyemo camera well tucked into a saddle bag and securely tied down, so that I would not lose it if we were required to make a fast run through the rugged countryside. Al and his two helpers had the rest of the cameras and equipment in the station wagon and they waited on the main road that ran parallel with the Rim along the top of the plateau. Their job was to stay within hearing distance of the dogs, if possible, and to stay on the main road, so that if and when we brought the bear to bay we would know where to find them.

The pack of hounds were followed by Red and Trigger on foot, after they had tracked the bear over the Rim. They had gone only a short way down the side of the steep wall when they jumped the outlaw from a mass of jagged rocks. Now the chase was on in earnest.

A black bear is not so fast of foot as a cougar, but he usually has better staying qualities. Then, too, the bear unlike the big cat, often refuses to take a tree when the dogs come up to him. Usually, when overtaken, a bear will fight off the dogs and then run again until overtaken a second time. In other words, a black bear often puts on a running fight that may carry on for miles.

We knew that Butch was going to make it rough on the hounds, for he was big, strong and a deadly killer. He would be too big for the dogs to manhandle; they would have to wear him down by nipping on his buttocks and then getting out of the way. It would take good foot-work, and any hound that closed with him or was careless enough to get caught by him with either teeth or claws would quickly be a dead canine.

The rugged black headed west along the steep side of the Rim wall. Frank and I cantered along the top of the Rim for a mile or so, more or less leisurely, until we came to a spot where we could ride off the Rim and down into the canyon.

Every so often we stopped to listen and each time we could hear the pack driving the bear along the Rim wall at a good clip. We made it to the bottom of the canyon well ahead of the dogs and the quarry. There we waited in a big opening in the forest. Frank told me that if the bear held his present course he would surely come across the clearing. He advised me to stay in the saddle and try to shoot my pictures from horseback.

"That bear is going to be a mighty aggravated critter by the time he gets here, Howard, and if he saw you afoot he might give you a good mauling," Frank told me. I knew that his advice was sound.

We could hear the big bear panting, long before he burst into the clearing. The dogs were close on his heels. In fact, Keeno, the lead dog, had caught up with the killer, but was too smart to attack alone.

We waited as the hot, angry beast came crashing towards us through the underbrush. The instant the big brute broke out into the opening, he spotted Frank and me. He let out one snort and kept right on coming. Frank had his lariat down, but he told me he would not try to rope the beast. He merely wanted his rope handy, "just in case."

Frank is such an unpredictable fellow that I was not sure what he might try. I had my camera ready and was determined to get a picture, if at all possible, of whatever happened.

As soon as the horses got a good look at the oncoming brute they wanted to go places, none of them in the direction of the bear, I assure you. I can't say that I blamed them. He was

huge, weighing close to six hundred pounds. Saliva dripped
from his jaws, which were wide open in order that he could
breathe more easily. There were great balls of white froth all
over his head and shoulders. The roach of hair along his neck
and back stood straight up about six inches. He looked meaner
than a drunken Sioux buck at a pow-wow.

For a minute or two I had my hands full, trying to control
my horse without losing the camera. I quickly saw there was
no chance of taking a picture from the back of that horse. As
soon as I got him under fair control I managed to get my camera
back into the saddle bag. With two hands on the reins I could
manage my bronc a little better, and I say bronc advisedly, for
he had changed in a couple of seconds from a well-trained cow-
horse into a wall-eyed frightened mustang. I have never been
a cowboy, and I would not claim to be able to ride a bucking
horse, but when I had a good look at that raging monster I had
no intention of letting the cayuse spill me.

About the time I got the camera back in the saddle bag and
had secured a good hold on each rein, Frank raked his horse in
the ribs with his long rowels and let out a blood-curdling
yell, at the same time heading straight for the oncoming
killer.

There were now half a dozen dogs that had come in close
behind the bear. and when Frank yelled and started forward as
though he was going to run right over the brute, two or three
of the dogs nailed Butch in the hams with their long teeth. For
a second the surprised black was at a loss as to his next move.
He thought the horse and rider were going to hit him for sure,
and he was afraid to take his eyes off them to get at the hounds.
Yet they were giving his stern-end a rough going over.

At about six feet from the bear Frank swerved to the right
and shot past the killer, who immediately lunged forward and
made a terrific swipe at Frank's horse that missed only by inches.
If he had not been dragging three dogs which hung on to his
back legs, I am sure he would have connected.

I had tried to follow Frank in towards the bear, but when we
were still fifty feet from him my horse swerved away, snorting
and bucking. He wanted no part of that animal. I finally got
his head up and went to work with my spurs, but I could not
get him near the beast.

By now the whole pack of dogs had come up and between the

hounds biting him and Frank's riding in and walloping him over the head with the end of his lariat, the old killer was taking a real beating. But not for long.

When Colcord had made three or four passes at him and failed to come to grips, the wise old black knew that he could forget the man. He went to work on the dogs. All the old hounds were smart and the instant the bear made for one of them they got out of his way on the double. One of the young dogs, however, failed to move in time, and the sharp front claws of Butch caught him dead centre. The one blow killed him instantly. The unfortunate hound was cuffed a double somer-sault. The rest of the pack gave ground and the bear headed up the trail, down which Frank and I had just come from the top of the Rim.

If I had only been able to get a picture of that first fracas between Frank, the bear and the dogs, it would have been terrific, but there was no way I could hold my horse enough to keep him sufficiently under control for such an acomplish-ment, and I would not have been on foot anywhere close to that wild melee for all the apples in the State of Washington. Believe me, that was no spot on which to be standing.

Old Butch made about the same speed up the steep mountain trail as he had been making on the level, yet the tenacious pack gave him no respite. They were behind and on both sides of him, yelling at the top of their lungs.

I pulled my horse up alongside Frank and shouted: " What do we do now? "

" Just hang on! " he yelled back. " He's headed for the top of the Rim rock and that's where we want him to go. When he gets up in the forest above the Rim we'll put a rope on him."

" Forget that *we* stuff! " I said. " Remember your promise. Besides, I've got no lariat." (I had seen to that.)

" Okay, Okay. I'll rope him," he said, grinning.

The bear was making good time going up the trail and I suggested we follow. " Not yet," Frank said. " He might decide he doesn't want to go all the way to the top and if he turns down the trail and comes on to a fellow a-horseback, well—" he stopped. I knew what the results would be.

In a few minutes Red and Trigger, who had been following the dogs on foot, arrived. We let them catch their breath a minute. Then Frank said: "Well, boys, it looks like Old Butch is going out on top, so catch on to our horses' tails and we'll get going." The boys caught hold of the long hair of the tails of our mounts and we started up the trail. It is amazing how easy it is to go uphill hanging on to the tail of a good strong horse.

We came out on top of the Rim to find Al and his two assistants waiting in the station wagon. They had heard the dogs coming up the steep wall of the Rim and had arrived in time to see the bear and the dogs cross the road a hundred yards or so in front of them.

Our horses were well winded, so we gave them a breather for a few minutes. There was a terrific noise of barking and fighting dogs a few hundred yards away in the forest. Then the clamour stopped.

Suddenly a couple of hounds began barking "treed." Frank popped the spurs to his horse and yelled over his shoulder: "Come on, fellows. The bear is up!"

At that particular spot the ground was fairly level and not too rocky. I let Red take my horse to fetch his and Trigger's mounts, while I drove the station wagon off the road, then worked my way through the forest to within twenty or thirty yards of the tree which the bear had climbed.

Old Butch had chosen a fair-sized oak with lots of limbs on it. He was so hot and tired that he had gone only twelve or fifteen feet up the tree and was sitting in a fork with a hind leg dangling on each side.

As soon as we arrived in the station wagon Frank said: "You boys had better work fast and get your cameras set up, because as soon as that bear is rested he'll come out of that small tree." There was a considerable opening in the forest in the immediate vicinity of the oak in which the bear was sitting.

I pulled the station wagon out about fifty yards from the tree and parked sideways to it. We soon had the Akeley camera mounted on a tripod and tied fast on a platform on top of the vehicle. From that position Al had an ideal spot to get pictures of any action that might take place. He put on a two-inch lens and had the longer lenses at hand, laid out on the platform alongside the tripod so that quick substitutions could be made.

I figured I would take the Eyemo and stay on the ground and

get some close shots, but when Frank learned of my intention he would allow no part of it. He told me that as soon as Old Butch got out of the tree he would come for me if I were on foot. I told him I could not handle the horse and take pictures at the same time, because my horse was afraid of the bear and would not stand still.

About that time Red came up with the other mounts and Frank told him to put my saddle on another horse. This time he was giving me a beautiful half American saddle and half mustang stallion. He told me that a stallion was not afraid of any animal and that I would be able to shoot pictures from this one which would stand until I wanted him to go.

Red and Trigger soon had all the horses saddled and we were up and ready for action. I rode my stallion in close to the tree where the big black bear sat. When he saw me coming towards him, he let out a growl and got himself squared away on the limb. Then he gave his jaws a couple of juicy smacks. I was ready for my mount to bolt, but he merely looked up at the bear and kept walking towards him.

I stopped him about fifteen feet from the oak and took a picture of Old Butch as he growled and snorted. The stallion just stood still in bold disrespect of the bear. As the camera ground away the big bear became so infuriated that he came hurrying down the tree backward.

Frank yelled: "Get out of there, Howard!" so I turned my horse sharply and headed away. Frank, Trigger and Red were well back away from the tree on the opposite side from me. They had their ropes ready.

As Old Butch hit the ground and started after my horse, already well on his way, all three of the men let out a war whoop and came after the bear. The killer looked back and saw three screaming horsemen charging towards him. He forgot me altogether and headed straight for the station wagon full speed.

Al was rolling as the bear went towards him. I felt sure the beast was going to leap right up on top of the station wagon with Al, so I pulled my horse up short and turned towards the vehicle. The bear was within thirty feet of the machine and running hard. Right on his heels were the three cowboys.

I saw Frank's loop go out and settle cleanly around the bear's neck, but before he could slide his horse to a stop and take up the slack, the beast was within a stride of the station wagon. On his last leap he chose to go under the vehicle instead of on top of it. Al was still cranking the Akeley when the six hundred pound brute hit the running board with the top of his neck just forward of his shoulders. He crumpled the steel like so much paper and the whole vehicle was knocked two feet sideways and almost went over.

Al went sailing through the air in a shower of camera lenses. It was a good thing we had tied the camera securely or it would have been wrecked. There was, of course, not nearly enough space between the chassis of the car and the ground to accommodate a bear of such size. I was sure Al would break an arm or a leg when he hit the ground, but some way he landed on his feet and ducked behind a tree.

By this time Frank had reversed his course. He literally dragged the bear away from the station wagon. The instant the up-ended Butch got to his feet he went after Frank and his horse. A bear is much faster on his feet than one might imagine. Butch was almost on top of Frank before the latter realized it. However, Frank had not spent half his life roping wild steers for nothing.

He then hooked his rowels into the ribs of his cow-horse, which responded with the speed of an uncoiling spring. The quarter-horse was running full tilt in four or five strides. He was going away so fast that when he hit the end of the rope, he snatched the bear off the ground. The beast landed on his back.

In the meantime, Red and Trigger had moved up behind the bear and as he rolled over on his back with feet up in the air Trigger dropped a loop around both hind legs and swung his horse to the right. Before the bear could get to his feet Trigger had taken the slack out of his rope and soon had the bear's back feet straight out behind him.

Frank moved his horse foward quickly and within a matter of seconds they had the bear stretched out flat on his back. I had come in a couple of times close enough to get pick-up shots with the Eyemo, and Al had made it back up on top of the station wagon and was rolling the Akeley.

It was a great sight to see how the two cow-horses worked. Each of them had turned facing the bear, but without allowing the ropes to become slack. The outlaw bear had managed to get over on his belly and he was trying to get the lariat off his neck, but the loop had pulled up tight and buried in the thick matted fur. Butch made a couple of vicious swipes at the lariat with his front foot and one of his sharp claws clipped one strand of Frank's rope. The resourceful Frank left his horse and ran back yelling, so that the bear would try to fight him instead of the rope. The plucky horse never slackened the rope one inch, although he had no rider.

Colcord yelled for Red to rope one of the bear's front feet, but the beast was moving so fast Red missed with his loop. Frank caught the lariat and was in the act of building a loop so he could drop it over the bear's foot, when the angry monster gave a vicious jerk with his back legs and Trigger's loop slipped off the hind feet.

Frank threw Red's rope down and made for his horse. He had a fair start but the bear was on his feet like a cat and right after him. When the rope slipped off the back feet and the bear started forward, it created slack in the rope between the bear and Frank's horse. As soon as the cow-horse felt the rope slacken he turned tail towards the bear.

Frank made a flying mount and as he came down in the saddle the bear was almost on top of him. The black beast pulled up short and reared up on his hind legs and took a terrific swipe at Frank's leg. In his frantic effort to get his foot in the stirrup Frank missed it, and the stirrup swung out towards the bear. The angry brute shortened his blow enough to catch the stirrup dead centre, missing Frank's leg by a couple of inches. He hit the stirrup with such force as to tear it loose and send it sailing through the air a distance of thirty feet.

Frank had had no time to get the split reins that dangled from the rings of the bits, and these horses had been trained to stand as long as the reins were down, but Frank drove his spurs into the horse and he leaped forward.

The bear had already started a second blow at Frank's leg, but the horse moved enough for the bear to miss the man. Instead he cut the horse on the back leg with his sharp claws. In some way Frank had managed to get hold of one rein by the time the blow of the bear connected. The cut on the mount had scared him badly, and he dropped his head and began bucking and running with the bear right behind him.

Frank was really on the spot. He was on a scared and hurt mustang with a bear tied to his saddle and he held only one

rein and only one foot was in the stirrup. The horse was snorting and bucking, while the bear was close on his heels, trying
to get at horse and rider.

I must say one thing: under such circumstances I have never
seen anyone who had as much control as Frank. He was sticking to that horse as though he had both feet in the stirrups and
both reins in his hands. Somewhere during the mad scramble
Frank finally got hold of the second rein, and he started raking
his horse with his sharp spurs from shoulder to flank.

The head of the horse came up and he stopped bucking and
started to run. In a few strides he had taken up the slack and
when the rope came taut it parted where the bear had cut a
strand with his claw. However, the rope jerked Old Butch off
his feet before it parted, and as he went down Trigger caught
one foot with a loop and made off on his horse, dragging the
killer by the one leg.

Frank had a second rope on his saddle and in a few seconds
he was back in the thick of the fracas. Trigger got tangled in
some small brush and the bear got up, but before he could make
a move Frank had another loop over his head, and the three men
soon had him stretched out again. This time Red caught a
front foot and he went in a third direction. Butch lay spread-
eagled now, flat on his back, his right hind leg stretched towards
the north, his neck towards the south-west and his right front
foot, east-south-east.

The outlaw had put up a terrific battle but the cowboys surely
had him in a bad way at last. All three ropes were so tight that
a person could have played a tune on them. I had run out of
film and was trying madly to load my camera. Al had shot four
hundred feet in the Akeley and was still rolling.

The boys kept the bear stretched out for a full minute and
he quit fighting and lay still. Frank was off his horse and on
top of him in a jiffy. With his jack-knife he cut the lariat from
the neck of Old Butch and with two tie ropes he quickly made
fast the fore feet and the hind feet together. Then he took
another tie rope and secured the mouth of the bear, tight shut.
All the time he was working, the bear was breathing very slowly.
When Frank had finished tying the outlaw hard and fast, he
stepped back and looked up at me.

"Anybody that saw the way Old Butch behaved would think
his mama was a wild bear!" was his comment.

That broke the tension. Everybody laughed in considerable relief, then we all started talking at once, each one trying to tell what struck him as being the funniest thing about the whole proceedings. The bear soon recovered from having been choked down, but he could only lie still. He was securely tied.

It really is a mystery why someone had not been badly hurt during all this mad scramble, but Frank Colcord was right when he said: "The Good Lord always takes care of fools and children."

CHAPTER ELEVEN

WILD BOAR

Foot by foot I moved forward with bow half-drawn and arrow in ready position. I kept my eyes focused steadily on a small opening in a low sprawling clump of sour oak. Inside the dense thicket I could hear the angry wild boar whetting his long curved tusks in cold fury. He was backed up against a huge pack rat's nest, composed of sticks, rocks and the leaves of pear cactus. His strong back legs were well underneath him and forward. He was ready to spring.

Just outside the brush and to either side of the tusker, Bill and Micky, my two boar dogs, were sparring for an opening. The wise old tusker was too smart to charge either of them. Should he charge one dog, instantly the other would rush in and slash him before he could turn to meet the attack of the first.

I was no more than thirty feet away when the angry beast suddenly shot out of the bush between the two dogs and bore down on me. He hurled himself through the air in an effort to strike me down. His mouth was wide open and the terrifying noise that escaped his throat was enough to curdle a hunter's blood.

I quickly drew and loosed an arrow. It struck him in the lower jaw, passed down his neck and embedded in the point of his shoulder. He kept right on coming.

As the arrow left the bow I leaped to the right. The left upper tusk of the charging beast cut two of my rear belt straps. The glancing blow spun me half-around, but I was still on my feet.

While shooting a wild boar picture on Catalina Island a few years ago I tangled with this tusker, which proved to be one of the most courageous and aggressive members of the porcine family I have ever encountered.

Al Wetzel, my cameraman, and I had taken one Akeley, one Sinclair and two Eyemo cameras and several thousand feet of

35 mm. Super Pan black and white negative film, my bows and arrows and my two boar dogs and boarded the boat, *Catalina*, headed for the port of Avalon, on Santa Catalina Island, off the southern coast of California.

Jack White, the head game warden for the island and super-intendent of the Wrigley cattle company, had met us at the dock in a Ford pick-up truck and we were soon settled in the bunk-house at Black Jack. This was the headquarters for all the cowboys and range riders who worked for the company and was the location of the comfortable and attractive ranch house where Jack lived. There we met Smokey White, Jack's son, Wally Opie, a lean red-headed, freckle-faced cow-hand, and 'Lonzo Lopez, a Mexican range rider.

Wally and 'Lonzo were assigned by Jack to assist Al and me in making the picture, and Jack agreed to be with us also in case he was needed. Of course, I did not know it at the time, but Jack and Wally were as fine ropers as they come, and Smokey, although only fifteen or sixteen years old, was well on the way towards being as good as either of the other two. 'Lonzo, having ridden the range for years, was thoroughly versed as to the best locations in which to find wild boar and was also a fair hand with the rope. It took us only a day or two to discover all these things.

The wild hogs on Catalina live for the most part in dense thickets of sour oak and huge patches of giant pear cactus. They seldom feed in the day-time except on dark, rainy days. There is, therefore, little chance to take motion pictures of them in their regular feeding grounds. They have to be found, roped, tied and transported to locations where the brush and cactus are not so dense as to exclude the sunlight.

There is usually such a section near the heavy brush, thus transportation does not offer much of a problem. But the roping and tying up of the tuskers can run into considerable danger. Once the boar were routed from heavy brush, Micky and Bill my two dogs, were well able to keep them cornered while we shot the pictures. If a hog was out in the open, the two experienced dogs would come in on either side of the boar and make him stand at bay.

If he tried to run they would soon overtake him and while Micky rushed alongside and got hold of the boar's ear, Bill would give the stern-end of the tusker a rough mauling. After a couple of breaks, the tusker would take cover in the first place he could find where he could protect his rear. These two dogs had worked together so long that they were more than a match for the toughest tusker, once they had him in fairly open country.

We spent the first day getting the camera equipment ready for action and selecting our horses. Al had not ridden a great deal and he had no desire to be in on the wild chases, but he had to ride a horse of some kind, in order to cover the necessary ground in search of hogs.

I was born on a farm in Alabama and had been riding horses since I was a small boy. Also, over a period of years, I had done considerable fox and wildcat hunting in Alabama, Florida, Wyoming and other sections of the country. I had a keen desire to see what the roping of wild boar would be like. I had seen cougar and bear roping in Arizona, but from what I could gather, boar roping was altogether different.

Jack gave Al a well-built bay gelding with a quiet, even disposition. My mount was a short-coupled, stocky roan with a blazed face, named Blondie. He was a well-trained, dependable roping horse, but bubbling over with nervous energy. Like a cat on his feet he never faltered when running full speed over treacherous footing. Normally, he was easy to handle and to keep under control, but when it was time for action, one had to be a fairly good rider to stay aboard.

By four o'clock on the morning of the second day we were up and out on the range. As the first rays of the sun broke over the landscape we came to a long wooded knoll, overlooking a narrow meadow of about the same length. We had no more than topped this rise when we spotted a long, rangy black tusker near the upper end of the meadow. He was headed towards some heavy brush near the lower end of the grass covered strip. Micky got scent of the boar at just about the time we spotted him and took off.

Wally was riding a lean black Roman-nosed mustang that could run like a racehorse, and Jack was on a strawberry roan that was just as fast. Smokey was mounted on a deep sorrel that was a match for the other two. Before I had time to think what was taking place, my head was snapped back and Blondie all but left me hanging in thin air. I clung to the reins and managed to get my balance in the saddle.

The other three, Wally, Smokey and Jack, had got the jump on me and Blondie by a full stride. The second I got set in the saddle, however, my mount pulled up abreast of the other horses. Each horse knew we were in for a chase and seemed determined not to be left behind. 'Lonzo and Al held their horses in. The former was leading a pack animal with all the camera equipment on him except one Eyemo, which Al carried in his hand.

As fast as the horses were, Micky was faster. His strain of greyhound blood gave him enough speed to pull well out in front of us, and he was almost on top of the tusker before that individual saw either the dog or us. Micky held his speed as he came in close. Finally the boar saw him and rushed to meet the attack.

Just before they met, Micky leaped high into the air and went a good ten feet beyond the boar. As he passed over the wild hog several feet off the ground, the boar reared and made a slash with his long curved tusk, but missed the plucky dog a good twelve inches. If he had connected, he would have cut Micky half in two.

As we raced towards the boar, the boys were busy getting their lariats untied and ready for action. Nobody was quite ready with a rope as we came into close range of the boar. He saw us just as he came back on to four feet after taking the cut at Micky and instantly forgetting the dog, headed for the brush, a good two hundred yards away.

The instant Micky hit the ground he turned and, before the boar knew it, was right alongside the tusker. He closed fast and caught the lower half of the boar's right ear, shut his powerful jaws on it and sat down. The wounded boar let out an angry squeal and gave his head a wicked side thrust that literally tore Micky's hold loose and sent the dog sprawling ten feet away.

Wally and Jack had been coming up fast on either side of the hog when Micky caught him and as the dog was thrown clear, two loops flicked out. The boar, having been almost stopped by Micky, changed ends and charged Wally's horse. The Roman-nosed black saw the boar coming and swerved to the left in time to miss the mad rush.

The sudden stop of the boar had caused the loops thrown by both men to overshoot the mark. It would take a little time for them to recoil their lariats. In the meantime, Smokey still had his rope swinging. The instant the boar saw he had missed Wally's horse he again headed for the bush. Smokey and I were right behind him.

I threw first but came nowhere near catching the hog. Smokey's loop, I was happy to see, settled right over the boar's head. Before he could flick the loop tight, however, the tusker had gone right through the noose without losing a stride. Micky had been busy keeping out of the way of the horses and had not been able to come to grips with the tusker a second time. He took another go at the boar after Smokey and I both missed.

The hog was going at top speed towards the brush, but no boar could stay long in front of Micky. While I hurriedly gathered in my lariat, I saw Micky come up behind the boar, and instead of going for his ear this time he caught the hog by the back leg and sat down. Bill, my other dog, bigger than Micky, but not nearly so fast, had not been near us when we first spotted the boar, but he had heard Micky barking and arrived just as the latter grabbed the hog by the leg. Bill was trying to head the boar off when Micky came to grips with him and when he saw that Micky had a good hold, he changed his course and came in from the side.

Bill weighed at least a hundred pounds and when he hit the boar with his shoulder it bowled the hog over. Micky held on as the tusker went down, but the rolling of the boar tore his hold loose. Instantly the hog was up and running, but Wally was ready with his second loop and he settled it over the boar's neck and pulled it up tight.

The boar hit the end of the lariat going full steam ahead. He up-ended and hit the ground with a heavy thud. Before he could get to his feet, Jack had snared one of his hind legs, and the two men soon had the angry tusker stretched out. The fighting boar made a swipe at Wally's rope and cut two strands of it, but before he could get into position to give it another slash, Micky nailed him by one ear and Bill quickly caught the other. Once they had the boar by the ears the big fellow was helpless. He would never be able to get loose until we had pried the dogs off.

I leaped off my horse and caught the boar by the back legs and kicked the front ones out from under him, so that he went down on his side. This was the first time I had seen a boar roped, but I had thrown many a wild hog after he had been

The African elephant is crafty and courageous, unpredictable and extremely determined when aroused

The author poses with a hard-won trophy

caught by Micky and Bill on other hunts. We soon had this ornery individual tied up and I pried the two dogs loose. They surely hated to let him go. He proved not to be badly hurt and we were glad. He would be a fine specimen to use in the pictures and I congratulated myself again, as I often did, on having such a fine dog as Micky; without him, the boar would almost certainly have escaped into the heavy brush.

We let the captive rest for an hour or so, then carried him on the pack horse a few hundred yards away from the heavy brush and turned him loose in thin cover. He dived into a small patch of cactus and turned to face the dogs. Evidently he had no intention of letting them get hold of his ears again.

In the meantime, Al and 'Lonzo had brought up the camera equipment, and almost at once we were set up and shooting pictures of the dogs working the boar. Two or three times he made a pass at one or the other of them, but every time he tried to catch one dog off watch, the other would get inside his guard and bite him before he could turn and meet the attack. The tusker soon learned that it was much wiser merely to stand the dogs, rather than try to fight them.

Al and his aid moved the Akeley camera in closer for a medium close shot, when suddenly the boar charged. At the time, the Mexican had his back to the beast and before he knew what was happening, the boar had hit and tossed him.

I was standing by with my bow and arrow ready, but before I could shoot, the boar was juggling the unfortunate range rider. Al, who had seen the beast coming, got clear, but the falling Mexican hit the tripod leg and sent the camera crashing to the ground. Again the boar tossed him before I could get in a shot. The hog had the poor fellow right on the end of his snout and was juggling the man much as a trained seal tosses a ball with the end of his nose. There was no way for me to shoot without taking a chance of hitting the Mexican.

Both dogs were trying to get hold of the boar, but so fast was the tusker slashing his victim, even they were unable to get an ear hold.

I ran to one side, hoping to get an opening for a shot. Out of the corner of his eye the boar saw me. He gave 'Lonzo one more vicious toss and came straight for me. I aimed for his brain and loosed the broadhead when he was almost on top of me.

H

The arrow flew high and struck the boar well up in the top of his head above the brain. It passed through his neck and into the fore part of his back, just behind the shoulder blade bones. I was moving to the right as the arrow struck and the angry tusker missed me by inches when he swept past.

As I leaped out of the path of the boar I drew another arrow from my quiver, and when the boar stopped and turned to face me I was ready. My second broadhead caught the tusker dead centre of the brain and he dropped in his tracks as though pole-axed.

The entire mêlée had lasted only a few seconds, but what a picture it would have made had some one been photographing it! Unfortunately for us, however, the boar had charged before Al and 'Lonzo had got the camera in place and ready. Besides, the beast had knocked the camera winding, along with the Mexican. This is one of the hazards of photographing wild animals; they just won't stick to the script or even to the wishes of the fellow trying to get the film shot.

As soon as the boar went down I ran to the wounded range rider, who, I felt sure, had been badly hurt. Fortunately, however, he was wearing a heavy pair of leather chaps covered with long thick woolly sheepskin. The tusker had cut these chaps to ribbons and had bruised the man's thighs and lower legs, but had cut only one gash, which was about three inches long and not more than a half-inch deep, in the calf of his left leg.

The stoical rider had taken the mauling without a whimper and was standing with his chaps cut to pieces and an embarrassed grin on his face. I probably would have been yelling loud enough to be heard for miles if I had got such a going-over from a boar. We were indeed relieved to find that 'Lonzo was not hurt worse, and felt sure that only the heavy chaps had saved his life.

For three weeks we stayed on the island and shot boar pictures with varying success. At least, there was never a dull moment. We roped a dozen or more boars, first and last, and each time there was a different problem. One boar chased Al over a cliff; another charged Jack on a steep side-hill and went clean over the back of his horse trying to get at Jack in the saddle; still another had been roped by Smokey, who when he got off his horse to tie the beast, was promptly chased up a tree. Wally lassoed one animal in heavy bush where he was not able to manœuvre his horse properly, and that gallant mount received an eight-inch gash in the shoulder from the tusker. Tough little Micky, who was mostly Airedale, had to be sewed up in three or four different places. Once he had a jugular vein cut so badly that I had to hold the wound on either side while Jack and Al sewed it up. On another day 'Lonzo had to climb a small sour oak to get out of reach of an angry boar, which promptly reached up and bit the high heel right off his boot. I had several close shaves while working the animals, but was lucky enough to escape unhurt.

There was one huge tusker we had seen several times but had been unable to get him into a spot where we could catch him. After we had the picture "in the bag" and had rested a few days and allowed the dogs to recover from their wounds, Smokey, Jack, Wally and I went out one morning, taking the dogs along, to see if we could find the prize tusker. He was the finest specimen I had ever seen and I wanted to bring him down with the arrow and have his head mounted for my den. Al had left with the film, so I had a little time I could spend before it would be processed and ready for cutting.

Any sensible person, I know, would have been satisfied after three weeks of thrills and spills, but a dyed-in-the-wool hunting archer is almost never really sensible; besides, this boar we were going after was a prize really worth having. This, of course, was going to be strictly a bow and arrow hunt, with no ropes used. Smokey, Wally and Jack just wanted to see the fun and went along merely as spectators.

A couple of times before this last hunt, Micky and Bill had already tangled with this tusker I was after, but in the heavy brush they had not been able to handle him. It was, in fact, this same boar which had partly severed Micky's jugular vein. The dogs had given the hog a fair going-over, but so far the tusker had won every round. The hazardous brush had been in the boar's favour and I was more than anxious to have a try at the prize to see if together, Micky, Bill and I could win the final round.

The sound of falling rain on the roof had wakened me at about twelve of the night before. I went to the door and found a cold wind blowing, accompanied by a gentle rain. "To-morrow," I said to myself, "will be a perfect day for boar hunting." It was good to remember that the picture was in the processing laboratory and to know that I had no further responsibility in that connection, just then.

Long before daylight we arose, had our horses saddled and were ready. The rain had ceased falling, but a light fog had drifted in from the Pacific across the island. There was little wind, and the air was cold and damp. The extra coolness seemed to act as a special tonic to the horses. Wally and Smokey were the first to climb into their saddles and their mounts were feeling so good that they both bucked across the coral just for the joy of living. Blondie had a slight hump in his back as I swung into the saddle and would have been glad to give me an exhibition, I knew, but I kept his head up and raked him in the ribs with a rowel, to remind him I was in no mood for foolishness. Jack's strawberry roan gelding, Peanuts, knew better than to try any playful tricks.

We had travelled no more than one hundred yards from the ranch when the dogs scented a bunch of hogs. They soon caught a medium-sized one and we had to pry them loose—as usual.

Within the next hour they caught three other wild boars and we had to free their quarries. There seemed to be boar everywhere that morning. Shortly after broad daylight we reached the vicinity where the big boy we were after usually ranged. The fog had thickened a little and even though the sun was well up, visibility was poor. We were working the north slope of a long rolling side-hill, partly covered with clumps of sour oak and small patches of giant pear cactus, when I heard Bill and Micky both barking in hot pursuit of a hog. They were coming directly towards us along the side of the hill.

As I urged my horse forward to meet them, I rounded a clump of cactus just in time to see Micky overtake and close with the big tusker we were after. The experienced dog came in on the up-hill side of the boar and caught him by the left ear. At the spot where he made contact, the ground was covered only by grass about two inches high and was clear of all obstructions.

As Micky closed with the boar the beast veered downhill. He was so big and strong he snatched Micky clear off the ground and threw him around in front of himself. The boar's feet got tangled with the dog and together they went, rolling over and over down the hillside. Micky had got a good hold and he refused to let go. The boar and the dog rolled a good thirty

feet, with first one on top, then the other. I was afraid the
tusker would kill my plucky Airedale, but when the hog
regained his feet Micky still had his hold on the ear.

At this point Bill went into action and caught the boar by
one ham, sinking his long fangs in deep. With one powerful
swing the boar swept Micky clear of the ground, but he had
braced himself and when the boar swung, the well-embedded
teeth of the dog ripped away a good portion of the boar's ear.

The instant he had torn clear of Micky, he headed for a low
clump of sprawling sour oak a few yards farther down the hillside. Bill could not begin to hold the tusker by the back leg,
and he let go as the hog made it into the brush.

Once inside the clump, the tusker backed up against a large
pack rat's nest and faced the small opening through which he
had entered. He had had all the fighting in open country he
wanted, and I knew that after such a going-over by the dogs,
he would not be coming out of the small clump of sour oak
unless he had to.

I could see no blood on Micky except around his mouth and
nose and that, I knew, had come from the boar. It seemed impossible that a relatively small dog like Micky could tangle with
a boar of this size without being killed, but the truth is, the Airedale never received a scratch. Together with Bill, he had won
the third round, and now it was my turn to put the porker
down for the full count.

The sprawling clump of sour oak was right at the foot of
the hill and my best approach was directly towards the opening
where he had entered the brush. If the tusker ran true to form,
he would not charge until I was quite near the brush. Yet, one
can never be sure just when an angry boar will charge, if he is
cornered by dogs. Only one thing is sure: he *will* charge, and
that with the speed of a wounded leopard.

As I eased forward, foot by foot, with bow half-drawn and
arrow in position for a shot, I kept my eye glued to the small
opening out of which I knew the hog would come at any second.
I could hear the threatening noise of the wild boar as he
sharpened his rapier-like tusks, upper against the lower. The
sound made by this action is a scraping click, not too loud, but
those who have heard it will agree it is not pleasing to hear.

While the seconds ticked past I thought of many other times
I had stalked cornered tuskers, no one of which had ever been

so formidable as this. Yet, more than once before now, I had barely managed to move in time to get out of the way. I wondered what would be the outcome this time, and I would gladly have backed away and left the wounded tusker. Some unexplainable urge deep down inside, which only a hunter can understand, kept me moving slowly forward.

Every muscle in my body was tingling, but was not taut. Tautness would be fatal, I knew: at such a time one wants to be alert, with each muscle ready for action but not tied up. Only the muscles pulling my bowstring partially drawn were under a strain.

Even though my brain recalled a thousand things, I never for a second forgot the danger before me, and beneath the seething turmoil of thoughts, I was able to act with a certain amount of cool deliberation. To say I was not afraid would be telling an untruth, but I did not have what hunters call "buck fever." Mine was a deep-rooted fear that tries the very soul of a man. Buck fever is something that envelops one with such restraint he is unable to think straight or to act with any given plan.

Just outside the dense brush in front and on either side of the boar Micky and Bill sparred for an opening, but the tusker was not thinking of them now. He had seen me and his cold, dark little eyes were carefully focused on me. The boar knew that man was his real enemy and was responsible for all his troubles.

I could not see the boar but I prayed for a chance to shoot before he should charge. I was no more than thirty feet away when the tusker shot out of the thicket between the dogs at top speed and bore down on me.

When yet ten feet from me he made a powerful leap, much like a lion makes, and came hurtling through the air, shoulder high. His mouth was wide open and the noise that escaped his throat was simply blood curdling.

I quickly drew and loosed an arrow. It struck him in the lower jaw, passed down his neck and embedded in the point of his shoulder. The arrow did not even slow him down.

As the missile left the bow I had leaped to the right. I felt the boar's tusk rip through the top of my trousers near the small of my back. His shoulder hit me a glancing blow that spun me half-around, but I was able to keep on my feet. Micky and Bill were right behind me. The boar had lost all fear of the dogs, and he whirled and charged for me again, but this time he was coming at me low and I shot a second arrow that caught him just forward of the shoulder blade bones. It cut through the tusker's body, partially severing the spinal cord, and passing through the lungs.

The boar seemed to stiffen and went down, then came to his front feet and faced me, but he could not advance. His hind quarters were paralysed. Instantly Bill and Micky had him by the ears. I dropped the third arrow back into my quiver, turned and walked away. I knew my opponent was down for the full count.

The dogs, too, realized that the battle was finished. They let go the ears of the boar and he slumped forward and lay still.

CHAPTER TWELVE

ALLIGATOR WRESTLING

ONE of the most interesting motion picture expeditions I have ever been on was made into the Everglades of Florida in 1941 in search of alligators.

Almost every living creature has a faulty characteristic somewhere in his make-up which man can use to his own advantage, provided he knows this peculiar weakness of whatever creature he may be hunting. The Florida alligator has an exceptionally bad fault that has proven his undoing on many occasions. By some freak of nature this reptile has a group of nerve centres under the throat and along the chest and belly. These centres are so sensitive that a man can by gentle rubbing with the tips of his fingers, put a fully grown bull alligator to sleep within a matter of seconds.

History does not tell us who was the first man that ever learned of this unusual trait in the scaly reptile, but it is safe to say that it was discovered by one of the tribes of southern Indians. Many years ago alligators were plentiful in Alabama, Georgia and Mississippi, as well as in Louisiana and Florida. The Creeks, Cherokees, Choctaws and Chickasaws were the predominating tribes of the southern States, while the Seminoles were of fairly late origin and are not a true tribe at all. There was no tribe of Seminole Indians until the eighteenth century when a portion of the Creeks first split away from that famous tribe, to form a nucleus for the new tribe to be known as Seminoles, meaning seceders. This small group became gradually a rallying point for renegades and outlaws from all the southern tribes already mentioned, and was also joined by an occasional runaway Negro slave.

In the early nineteenth century the Seminoles, led by a chief named Osceola, fought the troops of the United States to a standstill on more than one occasion. Besides being great warriors, the members of this late tribe developed into some of the best hunters found anywhere in the world.

Somewhere down through the years, the Seminoles had learned the trick of putting alligators to sleep by rubbing them on the chest and belly. Knowing this trick was one thing, but being able to accomplish it was a bird of a different feather. For some reason, bull alligators do not encourage such practices, seeming to think it's beneath their dignity or something. Anyway, they resent being man-handled for any reason at all.

The Seminole Indian, however, is for the most part a rugged individual that is hard to discourage, and if he decides he wants to rub an alligator on the belly and put him to sleep, he goes about the business of doing just that. Over a period of years this tribe found that the best and quickest way to accomplish this feat was to catch an alligator bare-handed and wrestle him until they could clamp on a combination hammer lock and leg scissors hold. Once they secured this combination they had little trouble in rubbing the alligator's belly.

While I was living in Miami, from 1925 to 1932, I met many Seminoles in the back country and hunted with several of them, but at that time I confined my hunting to the bow and arrow, and had not yet been bitten severely by the camera beetle. During that period I saw both Indians and white men wrestle alligators at water shows and at the Indian villages around Miami, but I had never seen anyone go into the Everglades or the Big Cypress and catch a really wild alligator, although I knew there were some of the Seminoles who had done this. I did see several that had tried it and had come out second best, having lost a hand, a foot, an arm or a leg. Some lives had been lost.

In 1941, however, while living in California, I decided that such a wrestling match would make a good, interesting short subject; so, with Al Wetzel, I returned to Florida to see if I could get such a picture. I wanted no tourist alligator or exhibition Indian. Nothing but a full grown wild alligator and an Everglades Indian would fill the bill.

The first week after we arrived in Miami we spent trying to find an Indian that would agree to perform this task, but found no one who was willing to do the job. Then one day I met Mike Osceola, a direct descendant of the noted war chief, Osceola. Although only nineteen-years old at the time, the youth was an inch over six feet tall and weighed a little over two hundred pounds.

He had just graduated from Miami High School as an honour

student and was one of the finest athletes in Southern Florida.
Despite the fact that Mike had had considerable schooling, he
was at heart a true Seminole. Although he realized that in
order to compete with white boys in the business world he would
need an education, his heart and soul still lived in the Everglades. During the three years it had taken him to complete
the white man's high school, he had spent every vacation back
in the Everglades with his people, leading the life he loved.

When I asked Mike if he knew how to wrestle an alligator,
he quietly admitted he had often done the feat, and readily
agreed to wrestle one for me so that I might get a picture.
Ordinarily, I might have been sceptical, but for some reason I
felt that, if there was an Indian in Florida who could manhandle an alligator, Mike was that Indian. He was so warm,
straightforward and friendly, that I liked him at once, and we
were soon in my hotel room pawing over a map of the
Everglades.

After some discussion he finally looked at me and said: "Mr
Hill, we don't need the map. I am a Seminole."

The way he said this made me realize how proud he was, yet
he respected me enough to believe that I knew what the capa-
bilities of a Seminole were. What he really meant was that he
knew the Florida Everglades like the palm of his hand and that
he had no need to use the white man's map to help him go
anywhere he wanted to go.

I folded the map, dropped it into my handbag and said:
"Yes, Mike, I know you are a Seminole; we won't be needing
the map."

We both laughed. Then we went into a discussion of the
picture, how long it would take to make it, what camp equipment and supplies would be needed and other details.

The next morning Al, Mike and I headed west across the
Tamiami Trail. Along the Trail near the Big Cypress we came
to a small Seminole village on the north bank of the canal that
paralleled the road in the manner as do so many canals in
South Florida. There we left the car with some friends of
Mike's. He borrowed a canoe into which we loaded our
cameras, camp equipment and groceries. Then following a
'Glades water course a mile or so north, we came to a small grove
of big cypress trees. There Mike's father had established a small
village that was being used as headquarters for a commercial

frog-catching business, which he owned. I gathered that he sold several hundred pounds of bull-frog legs each week at the market in Miami.

In this village we had lunch while Mike talked with his father about our intended excursion into the Big Cypress swamps farther north and west. It was easy to see how proud the old chief was of his son, Mike, but he was none too hospitable to Al and me. However, he did let us have a very large and well-made dug-out canoe, and we went on our way.

In the meantime, Mike had picked up a genuine Seminole costume, quite colourful as they always are, including a chieftain's hat. When he donned this regalia he lost all semblance of civilization and became a true Seminole. Standing in the centre of the graceful dug-out, he used a cypress pole about twelve feet long to shove the craft through the water. There was no paddle or oar: the push pole was all he needed to send the beautiful boat skimming through the water at a fast clip. We made much better time than would have been the case had we been using oars and paddles.

Mike never changed sides to turn the boat right or left, yet he handled it with the smooth grace of a flamingo swimming on a quiet lake. Around fallen trees that sometimes all but blocked the stream, through narrow openings between the huge cypress trees, he sent the canoe with smooth skill. Hour after hour we slid through the murky 'Glades water as though it had been warm thin air. No words were spoken after we left the frog camp.

The beauty of the country was breath-taking. We slipped beneath huge cypress trees whose heads were lifted more than a hundred and fifty feet into the blue skies. Spanish moss hung in sheets from every limb. Every now and then amidst the Florida oaks and the jungle vines there would be a slight opening in which grew the stately Royal palms with their smooth white trunks standing out in bold relief against the cobalt sky.

The variety of wild life about us, too, was astounding. Several times we saw the colourful wood duck glide gracefully between clumps of water hyacinth. White egrets, blue herons, ibis and bittern took wing, banked and circled above us. Snake-birds and kingfishers scolded as we moved through the dim shadows of the black mango. Occasionally a black bass leaped out of the water and snatched a moth or a flying beetle. Several times we saw the deadly cotton mouthed moccasin lying coiled on a partially submerged log or a floating patch of water grass.

Mike's keen eyes never failed to see every creature about us, despite the fact that he alone handled the boat. Once a white tail fawn slipped through a distant opening and, luckily, I had been watching the very spot when she appeared. I saw her for only a split second, and she was gone. Glancing at Mike, I knew he too had seen her.

A bald eagle screamed overhead and I realized for the first time that we were not beneath cypress trees any more. Only the blue skies and the bald eagle were above us. I saw, too, that the sun was no longer shining, but had sunk behind a forest of huge cypress trees in the far distance. So spellbound had I been by the majestic beauty of our surroundings that I could hardly believe it had been six hours since we left the village of Mike's father.

During that time Mike had not stopped poling the dug-out, nor had he sat down for a single moment, yet he seemed no more tired than when we started. His smooth muscles, the colour of polished copper, worked with machine-like precision.

Finally the Indian spoke: "We will make our camp as soon as we reach the cabbage palm hammock up ahead," nodding his head towards a forest of palms a half mile away.

While we moved towards the camp site I was thinking how lovely Florida must have been before the white man came. I could understand why the Seminoles loved it so much and why they fought so fiercely to keep it. A gentle spring breeze brought to our nostrils the smell of damp earth mixed with the scent of wild blossoms. There was in the air a balmy quality that was restful and soothing, and no sight of civilization obtruded on the scene. Only natural beauties, made by the hand of God that man cannot begin to match, stretched as far as the eye could see. No one but an Indian or perhaps another hunter who was a real child of nature, could understand the joy of living that filled my heart.

We made our camp amid the palm trees and as night closed about us the guttural grunts of the bull alligator could be heard in every direction. The love calls of the horned owl came from the depths of the swamps. Other night birds awoke and called to each other from many quarters. Deep-throated bull-frogs sang their songs of love. It was springtime and every living creature seemed to understand that the mating moon was fast approaching.

Next morning we found the den of a bull alligator underneath the high bank of a deep pool only a quarter of a mile from camp. There was a small white sandy beach at one end of the little pond, and the foot marks of the 'gator told us he was of considerable size. This small beach, we knew, was the spot where the bull alligator took his daily sun bath. Hurriedly we rigged two blinds out of brush nearby, one in which to set up our cameras and the other very close to the beach for Mike.

We spent a couple of days after that exploring the country and discovering other 'gator dens. We wanted to give the one we had selected as our first victim time to become accustomed to the blinds we had built near his sun parlour. In some ways the alligator is a stupid reptile, and few of the species are very observant. We learned by the fresh footprints and the smooth slides which the 'gator had made going in and out of the water daily since we had constructed the blinds that he either had not seen them or else was not disturbed by their presence. At any rate, he had continued to take his sun baths.

On the fourth morning, bright and early, we were waiting in the blinds with the cameras ready for action when up he came from the depths of his cave under the bank. It was a clear day and the sun rose warm and brilliant. In a short time it began to get hot and at about nine o'clock the old 'gator came out of his den and rose to the surface of the water in the middle of the pool, and swam in our direction to the sandy beach.

We never moved a muscle as he reached the sand-bar and crawled out several feet from the water, stretching his ten-foot length on the warm sand. Al was by the Akeley, ready to roll, and I had my hand on the switch of the high-speed DeBrie. We were to get our cue from Mike. The moment he came out of his blind and made for the alligator we were to begin shooting film.

The 'gator seemed not the least suspicious of our blinds: in fact, he had not even glanced towards them before stretching out to relax. We had left peepholes from which we could see both the reptile on the bar and Mike in his blind.

The Indian watched the bull alligator carefully for several minutes, but made no move. I wondered why he did not go after the 'gator, then I remembered he had told us the first day we reached camp that the best time to approach an alligator was when he was asleep. I realized now that he was waiting for the reptile to start napping before a move was made.

My heart was thumping like a trip hammer; it sounded loud enough to me to disturb the bull 'gator. Al was just as excited as I, but Mike showed no outward signs of anxiety as he rested on one knee in a partially squatting position, much like that taken by a track man on the mark for a hundred yards dash.

The big 'gator closed his eyes for a second, then slowly opened them again. Mike looked at us and grinned, as if to say: " See, the old boy is about to go to sleep, so be ready."

Again the 'gator shut his eyes, but failed to open them this time. For two, three, four, five minutes he lay without moving a muscle. I was about ready to explode with tension. Then there was a splash on the far side of the small pond as a black bass leaped out of the water to catch some flying insect that passed.

At the loud splash the sleeping 'gator only half opened his eyes and closed them again immediately. I was so tense that when the noise of the bass reached me I came very near turning on the camera switch. Again all was quiet except for the thump- ing of my heart.

How much longer, I thought, before Mike will make his move? Surely he knows the 'gator is asleep!

As though Mike had heard my thought he looked at us, nodded his head as a warning, and shot out of the blind with the speed of a frightened klipspringer.

As he dashed forward he let out a Seminole war-whoop that was enough to frighten a Sioux chief. I hit the switch of the high-speed camera and as it gathered speed it whined like the supercharger on an Offenhauser racing car. Al had the Akeley going.

The 'gator awoke with a start, but Mike's yelling seemed to hypnotize him for a split second. The youth was almost upon him as the reptile swapped ends and made for the pond. I thought surely he was going to make it into the water, but that Indian knew his alligator wrestling.

As the 'gator's nose touched the water and his eyes closed, Mike's strong left hand caught the upper and lower jaws of the reptile in a vice-like grip on the very end of the nose; at the same time his right hand went over the 'gator's back and caught the right foreleg of the monster on the far side from the Indian.

I saw Mike pull the 'gator's body tight in to his own right side, as he and the reptile together plunged head first into the deep pool of water. The two made a complete somersault as soon as they hit the water. The last I saw of Mike for almost a minute were the soles of his bare feet.

As the tail of the 'gator came out of the amber-coloured water and swung in a great arc, then disappeared, I stopped the high-speed camera and quickly removed the light brush we had been using for the blind. Al picked up the tripod for his Akeley and we hurried forward to set it up on the sandy beach.

While we were making the change of position and levelling off the camera, there was no sign of Mike and the big 'gator. All we could see to indicate their position was boiling muddy water. Al was ready, watching through the finder. I had left the high-speed behind, but stood by with a hand Eyemo ready to grab any action shot that presented itself.

Just as I was deciding the bull 'gator had dragged Mike into his den under the bank on the opposite side of the pond from us, the head of the boy popped above the surface of the boiling water, right in the centre of the pond. In a flash Mike grabbed a breath of air and went under again.

Immediately the 'gator's tail appeared with a swish. Two or three times Mike's head appeared, followed by his feet breaking the surface. The 'gator's tail would lash out, then his head would shoot above the surface and disappear again. I had never witnessed anything quite so exciting.

The first time the 'gator's head broke the surface, I saw that Mike's hand was still firmly gripped over the nose of the reptile, locking its jaws. The Indian not only had the death lock on the 'gator's mouth, but in addition the heel of his hand was covering the 'gator's nostrils so the reptile could not breathe.

Finally the desperate battle began to slow down. When Mike's head would appear he had more time to breathe. I noticed that the lashing of the 'gator's tail began to weaken, and I began to feel that Mike was going to win the struggle. At last he raised his head above water, breathed deeply a couple of times, then yelled: "Get ready! I'm bringing him to the beach!"

Immediately he disappeared under the water and for a full

three-quarters of a minute we could see nothing. What we could not see, and did not know until afterwards, was that Mike had sunk to the bottom and was walking on it, dragging the alligator with him.

When the courageous Indian next appeared he was on the edge of the sand bar. Almost unbelievably, he was still holding the 'gator's nose and right front leg. Mike lay on his back with just his head out of the water and the body of the 'gator was lying on top of him. However, Mike had a full scissors hold around the body of the reptile.

As the noble red man lay perfectly still, breathing rapidly, I could see that he had been badly weakened by the desperate struggle. I dropped my camera and ran down to where he lay. Kneeling down, I caught Mike by his right arm and shoulder and pulled with all my strength.

He looked up at me and grinned and nodded his head, meaning I was doing the proper thing. I was so excited that I had superhuman strength, for I literally dragged Mike and the two hundred pound alligator right out on to the beach. Ordinarily, I could not possibly have accomplished such a feat. Mike never let go either of his holds on the reptile.

Once on the bank, the bull 'gator rolled over and over, but Mike held on. Finally the reptile relaxed for a second and Mike let go with his right hand and began stroking the 'gator gently along the chest and belly with his free hand. At the first touch of the Indian's hand the big 'gator lashed out hard with his tail, but as Mike continued to rub him gently, the monster relaxed and in a matter of seconds lay as helpless as a sleeping baby.

Slowly Mike let go his scissors hold and pulled his leg from under the 'gator. The reptile moved once as Mike freed his legs, but a couple more gentle strokes and the powerful creature lay still. Mike stood up and moved around in front of the sleeping reptile, then for the first time he loosed his grip that had held the wicked jaws helpless for so long.

The 'gator lay belly up on the sand bar, sleeping, and as limber as a wet rag. Mike faced Al and said: "Well, that's the way to wrestle a bull alligator, or at least that's the way I wrestle one." We all three laughed.

Al and I exchanged glances. We knew we had just witnessed one of the most terrific feats of skill and courage it is possible for any man to perform. What made it more exciting was the

A ceremonial native
dance in the heart of
Africa

A native dance photo-
graphed for the film
Tembo

fact that we had a motion picture negative of the whole bout. What a picture and what an Indian!

Millions of people in various countries of the world have now seen that picture, and I can only say I hope they appreciate in some measure the strength, the courage and the skill displayed by Mike Osceola in subduing with his bare hands a reptile that is noted for feats of strength and savage fighting ability. At that, they could not have enjoyed seeing the picture so much as I enjoyed making it.

CHAPTER THIRTEEN

SHOOTING PICTURES UNDER WATER

Of all the exciting and downright fear-inspiring things I have ever done, I believe making an underwater motion picture some years ago off the southern coast of Florida was the most thrilling.

In the first place, I knew positively nothing about underwater gear and very little about the dangers involved when deep-sea diving. I became absorbed with the idea, however, that a good picture made beneath the surface of the ocean and showing the marine life to be found only in that setting would be most interesting, if one could secure such a picture. Having once decided to give it a try, there was nothing left but to go about the task of accomplishing it.

After considerable research I learned there was no water off the west coast of the United States that was suitable for underwater photography. The Caribbean Sea and the Atlantic waters around the islands off the southern coast of Florida were the best locations in which to shoot such below-water pictures, I became assured. I soon also realized that no suitable gear had been developed for use while making such pictures as I had in mind. A few types of diving bells and glass boxes had been used to take certain underwater shots, but they required cranes, winches and a regular salvage boat to handle them. I found, too, that all the equipment used by divers was extremely heavy and clumsy. To do what I wanted to do, the gear had to be light and easy to handle.

As soon as I accepted the fact that I would have to make my own gear to use in shooting the picture I had in mind, I procured some materials and built an underwater camera box in which I could use my 200-foot 35 mm. Sinclair camera. Experience as a toolmaker in earlier life stood me in good stead in accomplishing this task. Next, I built a diving rig. using a Japanese diving goggle and a small oxygen tank, which I carried fastened in a harness on my back.

It required some time to learn to breathe properly under water with this improvised gear. I had to inhale the oxygen through my nose and exhale it through my mouth, which made it very awkward. At first, I would sometimes get mixed up and try to inhale through my mouth, then I would strangle, but after spending several hours in practice, sitting on the bottom of a swimming pool in California, I learned to breathe fairly well without strangling. What bothered me most was, that the area inside the Japanese goggle was not big enough to hold a full breath of oxygen, and I could breathe neither fast nor deeply. By rigging a pressure valve and a small diaphragm, however, I was able to breathe well enough to stay under water a half-hour or more at a time.

After fashioning my camera box and diving device, I turned to the task of developing a bow and arrow that would shoot under water. It was my intention to hunt all manner of fish, including shark. Proper construction of a bow and arrow proved to be a much more difficult task than I had anticipated.

In the first place the limbs of the bow offered so much resistance going through the water that the weapon would not throw an arrow with enough speed to kill a minnow, not to mention a shark. Through experimentation, however, I learned that by using rubbers fastened on my bow immediately above and below the bow handle, and on to the string above and below the point where the arrow rests, I could get considerable speed. By utilizing a solid 11/32 dural shaft, six feet long, instead of a conventional arrow, I found I could shoot forty or fifty feet through the water.

For several weeks after I had all my gear in good order, I made various experiments under water to be sure they would work. I learned, for one thing, that it is much more difficult to shoot a bow with accuracy under water than in the air. There was a marked difference in judging distance, and furthermore, the arrow would not lose altitude when travelling through water nearly so rapidly as was the case when travelling through air. At the same time, the long clumsy arrow was much harder to aim than a short one of the usual length. In due time, however, I learned to shoot the bow fairly accurately up to thirty or forty feet. A few other flaws which I also ran into with my other gear gave me a little trouble, but finally I had them all eliminated and was ready for the real test.

Again I had Al Wetzel to work with me. Before we left California and headed for Florida, however, he had assured me that he wanted no part of underwater camera work. His purpose in going was to shoot some other material we were hopeful of getting and to assist me from topside in securing whatever underwater pictures I could get.

To be perfectly frank, I thought that once we were on the spot and ready to go, Al would weaken and probably would soon be right down on the bottom of the ocean with me, but as it turned out this was definitely only wishful thinking. Although Wetzel is a sportsman from the word go and has plenty of guts, he is not completely reckless.

On our arrival in Florida we secured the other picture material we had hoped to get in the Everglades. Then one morning we found ourselves several miles out in the Atlantic off the north end of Key Largo, just inside the reefs. Here the depth of the water varied from thirty-five to sixty-five feet; the bottom of the ocean was of white sand, and the water was as clear as the finest crystal. By using a glass-bottomed box to kill the ripple on the surface of the water, one could see the floor of the ocean just as clearly as the palm of his hand.

After considerable cruising around, we spotted an area of moosehead coral, sometimes called tree coral. This particular type of coral-rock accumulates or grows up from the bottom of the sea in the shape of a grotesque tree, though much larger than the average varieties of trees on land. The portions of the growth that represent the limbs of the tree are flat and more or less paddle-shaped, looking very much like the palms of the antlers on a moose. To carry the likeness further, these "palms" are rough and spiney, having sharp points along the edges and ends as do the antlers of the moose. Hence the name of moosehead coral.

Having failed to persuade Al to go under water to help me take pictures, I had brought along a young fellow named George Meggs, who in addition to having had considerable diving experience, had also done some underwater camera work. Besides George, Al and me, there were two boys who were to operate the pumps for George, as he would be using a regulation diving helmet rather than an oxygen device like the one I had. Also with us was the person who owned the forty-foot cabin cruiser we had rented to use while making the picture. Mike

Osceola completed the personnel of our small expedition.

Once we had located the moosehead coral, we dropped the hook and let a rope ladder over the side in preparation for our first dive. While we rigged up our gear preparatory to diving, Al constantly was looking over the side of the craft through a glass-bottomed box. When we were about ready to go over the side in order to make a light reading and to sort of size up the situation, I said as cheerfully as I knew how: "Well, Wetzel, what's the dope? What have you seen down there among the rocks?"

He took a good straight look at me and said without so much as a little grin: "I've seen plenty, at least enough to know that I'm not fixing to go down there, now or at any other time."

He hesitated just long enough to let his first words impress me, then he went on: "To be exact, there are three or four giant barracuda down there as big as my leg and as long as a shovel handle, one thrasher shark half as long as this boat, and several groupers that could swallow this box." He pointed to the glass-bottomed box through which he had been looking.

When Al mentioned the big grouper George pricked up his ears and said: "Maybe I'd better have a look around before we go below. I've never seen any giant grouper this far away from deep water." He took the glass-bottomed box and began looking down into the depths of the water.

I was getting more frightened every minute and I felt that if we did not make one descent pretty soon I would lose my nerve and not be able to go down at all. However, I managed to keep kidding Al as though there was nothing to be afraid of.

Finally George lifted the box frame over the side and said: "I didn't see any shark and the groupers are much smaller than they look."

"You see," he continued, "the refraction of the water makes the fish look more than twice their real size. It kind of enlarges them, you might say."

"But what about the barracuda?" I wanted to know. I had heard of two instances in years past, when I was living in Florida, in which a person had been hit by a giant barracuda, and in both cases the results were fatal.

"Well, there are two or three plenty big enough to knock a

fellow's arm or leg off if they should hit him, but you don't have to worry about barracuda unless you move quick," George said in a matter-of-fact tone.

"What do you mean, *move quick?*" I demanded, showing that my feet were getting cold. I had begun to wonder why I had ever thought I wanted to make an underwater picture, anyhow.

"A barracuda never attacks a man if he knows it's a man," George explained. "They strike at flashes like a fast moving fish or a quick moving hand or foot, never at anything that moves slow and easy. Oh, they may come in fairly close and have a good look, but they're nothing to worry about. Why, I've been diving many times in water where there were dozens of them and they never even paid any attention to me after the first minute or two."

I must admit that if George was in the least afraid, he was not talking like it, nor did he show any signs of uneasiness. By the time he had finished speaking he was over the side and into the water up to his shoulders.

"Okay, boys," George said, "start the pump and don't stop until we come back up." To me he said: "Mr Hill, you wait till I get down on the bottom before you start down. I haven't made a dive in some time and I may have trouble clearing my ears.

"And don't forget," he added as an afterthought, "to make sure your ears clear as you descend. The water here is close to sixty feet deep and if your ears don't adjust themselves you may burst your eardrums.

"I'll see you on the bottom, sir," and with this Al placed the diving helmet over George's head and on to his shoulders, and he disappeared down the rope ladder.

My heart was kicking up a storm inside my chest and my mind was racing a mile a second. "Wait until I get on the bottom before you start down," George's words were ringing in my ears. If he only knew what I was thinking! Waiting was the fondest thing I was of right about this time. In fact, I didn't care if it took him an hour or a week to clear his ears. Then the thought came to me that if I lost my nerve after getting into the water, I could always come back up and say my ears would not clear.

Al was again gazing through the glass-bottomed box and his

words snapped me back to the present. "He's on the bottom, Howard, and looking up for you."

As I climbed over the side, adjusted my goggles and was about ready to start down, Wetzel looked at me with a silly grin on his face and said: "Well, old fellow, I'll tell them that the last time I saw you, you looked plumb natural."

I don't know why, but his words burned me up. At that moment I could have choked him with pleasure. He could see that I was scared stiff, I guess, and just wanted to give me the works, as so often in times past I had shown him no mercy when he had been scared—like that time on Catalina Island when the wild boar got after him.

Well, anyway, I was so mad I was going down the rope ladder two rungs at a time and was more than halfway to the bottom before I realized my ears were hurting. I opened my mouth and immediately my ears popped and were relieved. I had no excuse to go back top-side. Besides, I was not half so scared now as I had been: I was too mad at Al for his ribbing me.

When I arrived at the bottom, George was waiting for me and he reached out and took me by the hand. The currents were so strong it was hard to stand on the floor of the ocean. That was the first time any man had held my hand since my dad used to lead me along the dark back porch after supper, and it felt almost as wonderful now to have George steady me as it had felt to have the protective hand of my father guide me in the dark so many years ago.

This was the very first time I had ever been any deeper in the ocean than one goes when he swims in the surf offshore, and as I looked about me I was amazed at such beauty as I had never seen before. It was as though we were in another world. The coral was of every hue and shade from a bright yellow to a deep purple. Some spots were as white as snow, while others were as black as the raven's wing. The fish which swam and drifted all about us, over our heads, and in and out between the masses of coral rock were of many varieties and colours. None of them showed the slightest fear.

The barracuda, three and a half or four feet long, first had a good look at us, then glided slowly out of sight into a forest of purple sea feathers that swayed back and forth with the under-currents. These currents ran in various directions and at times would lift us off our feet. It was a curious feeling to be carried in slow motion and it gave one the feeling of being in some dream world. I don't mind saying that when the barracuda all passed from sight, I felt much better and could then appreciate more fully the beauty of this undersea spot. The fiery bulging eyes of these creatures gazing straight at us and their long sharp teeth, which seemed to be grinning at us, were not a pleasing sight, and that's an understatement. I could almost feel them tearing through my flesh. I was more than careful not to make a quick movement of any kind while they were in sight.

The groupers which we had seen from above were not nearly so large as they had appeared to be from that point. We moved within ten feet of them before they eased around the opposite side of the coral rock to us. Not one of them would weigh more than a hundred pounds. We saw half a dozen Nassau groupers collected in a big hole in the coral. They were of a greenish cream, with big black spots the size of a silver dollar all over them, but in shape they were much like the ordinary grouper, a short thick fish.

After going completely around one huge clump of coral, we took a light reading and moved back to the rope ladder. I ascended first while George held the ladder to keep it from swaying too badly with the current. Al had inserted a Norwood light meter inside a large mayonnaise jar and I'd had little trouble getting a good reading.

As I told Al on emerging from the water, it was amazing how much light there was down there, sixty feet below the surface. When the meter was held towards the light tinted coral the reading was almost two hundred, while even the darker backgrounds were as much as one hundred twenty-five. The water was so clear that the coral trees formed shadows, just as distinctly as if they had been above water. Of course, we realized that the white sand bottom reflected some light.

Once back top-side without experiencing any trouble, I could hardly wait to get the camera ready to go below again. I had entirely forgiven Al and was amazed at myself for having been angry at him in the first place. What fools these mortals be, especially me, I thought to myself.

For several days we went out to the same locality and photographed many different kinds of fishes. George, Mike and I spent hours below the surface, taking motion pictures and simply gazing at the multitudes of different creatures that swam within a few inches of us. Angel fish (of which there were a dozen different kinds) would often put their mouths against the glass of our goggles and diving helmets and stare. They seemed to have as much curiosity about us as we had about them.

One day Mike and I decided to have a set-to with one of the big groupers. We had taken moving pictures of all the various fishes, and now we were going to try hunting them with the spear and the bow and arrow. Mike was not equipped with a regular spear such as underwater spearers of fish use to-day; he had only the usual Seminole variety, which his tribe throws at alligator, gar and other fish from a standing position on the ground above water.

Although he'd had no underwater practice, he succeeded after a few tries in getting it through a huge grouper. The big fellow took off with such speed that he snatched the seven-foot spear and pole out of Mike's hand and banged it against the coral so that it broke in half. We never did find the end which was stuck into the fish, nor did we ever see that grouper again.

I had better luck with the one I shot with the arrow. It was drilled through the head, just back of and above the eyes, killing him instantly.

At other places in much more shallow water, only eight to ten feet deep, we found crawfish, conches and other kinds of shell fish, which we caught and carried top-side to be cooked and eaten. The water and rocks at these latter places were not suitable for picture making, for the water was often roily, while the rocks were usually covered with moss, hence too dark. There was no white, clean sand in these places to reflect sufficient light for the making of good clear pictures.

After we had spent several days around the moosehead coral without seeing a shark of any kind, we were ready to believe that Al had been mistaken about seeing the monster of a thrasher shark, which he spoke of the first day, even though he insisted that he definitely had seen a big fellow.

George told me that he never worried about a shark of any kind unless the shark was following and feeding on a school of fish. He assured me that no shark would ever feed in water so clear and shallow as that in which we were working around the coral. He had proved to be right so many times that I felt he was probably correct in his reasoning about sharks, but just the same, although I had made the trip in the hope of shooting one with the bow, I could work up no enthusiasm about facing one in any spot. Privately, I felt that it would be just my luck to find one that was different from those which George had seen—one which might decide all of a sudden that he was hungry.

Neither did all the assurances I'd had from George comfort me any when one day I met my first shark face to face. George and I were sitting on a couple of rocks down on the bottom of the ocean, waiting for a big Nassau grouper to come out of a hole he had entered. Suddenly a huge thrasher shark came cruising by, just above my head. First, I saw a long shadow creeping over the white sand beyond me. Alarmed, I glanced up just as the monster passed over my head no more than six feet away.

He went past us for several yards, then turned and came back more or less towards me. He was approaching on my right at some twenty feet, but he had risen towards the surface by several feet. I realize now that he was probably just curious and was coming back for a second look, but at the time I could not be sure of his intentions. Furthermore, I figured that if he was trying to make up his mind about us, it would be a good idea to let him know that these creatures new to him on the bottom of the ocean had a sting that could hurt.

When George looked up I was already standing on my feet and had the bow in shooting position. He saw that I meant to try and get an arrow into the monster, so he started rolling the camera. Slowly and carefully I raised and drew my bow, took aim as best I could, at a spot about six inches in front of the shark's nose, and let go the string. The long dural shaft was on its way.

It caught the surprised shark dead centre of his circles, the gills through which he breathes water, and went completely through him.

The wounded giant lost all thought of us and started away in a hurry, then he slowed down and swam thirty or forty feet at about the same rate he had been making when the arrow struck. At that point he nosed towards the surface. Instead of continuing in that direction, suddenly he made a backward loop, much like an aeroplane makes, except that his loop was, of course, much slower and smaller.

As he headed downward he dived head first into the bottom,

bounded up a foot or two, levelled off and made one rush forward, then slowly glided to the bottom, belly up, and lay still.

The sea about us was so red with the blood of the shark that we had to wait several minutes until it cleared enough for me to go forward and claim my prize. The arrow was bent, but still had him transfixed, the broadhead sticking out on the far side. I could have made no more perfect shot had I thrown a hundred arrows, and I realized that I had made one of the luckiest hits of my bow and arrow career.

All of our party were so elated over our good fortune in having disposed of the shark and in securing moving pictures of the feat, that we decided not to push our luck further. We upped anchor, pulled in our ladder, loaded our prize aboard the boat and headed for the mainland.

As the sleek cabin cruiser cut through the blue waters of the Atlantic on our way homeward, Al said: "I told you I saw a big thrasher shark that first day, and this fellow looks just like him."

Whether this was the same one that Al had seen was highly problematical, we realized, but of one thing I was sure; this one was plenty big and had caused me some anxious moments before he sank to the bottom of the sea.

CHAPTER FOURTEEN

CRUISE ON THE SIROCCO

T H E sleek sailing ketch, *Sirocco*, cut through the water of the blue Pacific with the smooth grace of a swan. There was a gentle breeze, and the mainsails and foresails were set wing in wing. She was headed south-east by south, making for the port of San Lucas, Mexico.

Aboard her we were a group of happy fellows on a combination pleasure cruise and motion picture expedition. The party included Errol Flynn, owner of the *Sirocco*, Wally Heinz, his business manager, Al Wetzel and me, in charge of the picture expedition. In addition, the yacht carried a crew of four: the captain, two sailors, and a cook.

We had left Los Angeles harbour at Wilmington a few days before and were on our way to the Gulf of California. The first stop was to be Port San Lucas, a small fishing village on the extreme southern tip of the peninsula of Baja California. Those first few days we enjoyed smooth sailing and made Cedros Island on the third day out. We had skirted the island and were nearing Turtle Bay late in the afternoon of the fourth day, when suddenly the barometer took a drop.

In the western skies a backdrop of angry red formed a lurid canvas for an ugly storm cloud that rose to engulf us. In the heavens a graceful man-o'-war appeared near us. We watched the big bird as he banked, rolled and dived in a series of intricate manœuvres, riding the currents of the approaching storm. Singly and in pairs albatross flew by, skirting the surface of the gentle sea. A black merganza scolded loudly as he passed overhead. Seagulls, nighthawks, kites and swallows hurried landward to beat the storm.

Then of a sudden the tightly stretched canvas of the sails grew limp. The lazyjacks dangled straight down like sickened worms. The booms of the mainsail and foresail swung slowly aft as the last breath of air died away. The racing yacht staggered helplessly as she lost steerage way. The helm became useless as the stern slowly settled into the calm sea. There was no longer any time to watch the manœuvres of the birds we had been enjoying.

In the distance the frightening roar of the north-easter could be heard as it swept closer to us. The *Sirocco* lay dead in the water. We were experiencing the calm before the storm, and well we knew that the storm was about to strike. Hurriedly we dropped the mainsheet, and made it fast. While some of the fellows hauled down the foresail and jib, others were busy battening down the hatches.

A vermilion streak of forked lightning staggered crazily across the black face of the cloud. The stillness was shattered by a tumultuous clap of thunder. The long masts quivered to their very foundations. Then the north-easter struck with all its fury.

The impact of the first puff caught the *Sirocco* broadside and hauled her over to port. She pivoted on her keel and began to be driven helplessly before the nor'-easter.

Errol rushed to the steerage cockpit and started the auxiliary motor. When he slipped the clutch forward and opened the gas throttle, the propeller blades dug in and the drifting ship began to make headway. He swung the helm to port, and obediently the *Sirocco* turned her stern to the onrushing seas, which were building up rapidly.

The yacht, although well built and entirely seaworthy, was a nasty vessel to handle in a rough sea. Eighty feet long and twenty-two feet abeam, she carried only a four-foot freeboard. In really rough water she rolled like a porpoise at play. She was truly a "wet ship," as an old salt would say. Had we been given enough warning, we would have made a run for some protected cove, but the storm had caught us flat-footed and we had no choice but to ride it out. Heading into such a sea as was soon to be running, the *Sirocco* would not have stayed alive five minutes.

The waves rapidly grew higher and the troughs between became so narrow and deep that the ship did not have enough running room. She would glide down the steep side of a huge wave and plunge her bow into the one ahead. Tons of green water would come aboard and run the full length of the deck before she could free her head.

We soon found that by taking the oncoming waters on the

starboard quarter and cutting down our speed, the racer could negotiate the narrow troughs without shipping water. After a few minutes of experimentation, we learned the proper angle at which it was best to ride the mountainous sea. The wind was increasing with every passing moment and the waves continued to pile higher and higher. The *Sirocco* was shipping little water, but she rolled twenty to thirty degrees off centre as she slid off the back of one wave and climbed the face of the next.

The lines were strewn from stem to stern and it was impossible to stand above deck to straighten them out. The wind ripped the spreader light from the cross-arm of the foremast and carried it away. A freak wave caught the *Sirocco* head-on and a three-foot wall of green water raked her deck. I had seen the sea coming and grabbed on to the ratlines just in time. My feet were knocked out from under me, but I managed to hang on. One of the sailors was thrown against the mainmast with such force that his shoulder was all but broken, yet he was able to grab the guardrail and prevent himself from going overboard.

By now it was black dark and the north-easter was blowing a good sixty miles an hour. The captain sent Al, Wally and the two sailors below deck, then he himself remained to take the first watch, together with Errol and me.

All that night, the next day and most of the second night the wind drove us west-south-west, so that we were blown more than two hundred miles off course. We split up into two watches, Flynn, the captain and I working together, while Al, one sailor, and Wally comprised the other. The second sailor was suffer-ing too much from his injured shoulder to stand watch.

About four o'clock of the second night the wind began to slacken a little and by six o'clock the storm had blown herself out. Two hours later we had our first hot meal in more than thirty-six hours. It took two hours or more to clear the decks and by that time the wind had hauled around and was coming directly from the west.

We did not know our exact position, as we had no navigator, but we did know that land lay to the east of us. We hoisted all our working sail, rigged a huge spinnaker, and set our course due east. The sea had flattened, but was still choppy. The westerly breeze was made to order for the sleek racer: she took the bit in her teeth and leaped forward at terrific speed.

She had weathered the storm and come through it with few

scars, but those of us aboard her were dead on our feet. We had slept scarcely at all and had been wet and cold for the duration of the entire storm. The sun came out and the deck dried rapidly. The sailor who had been injured at the beginning of the storm had recovered enough by now to come on deck and take over the wheel. The rest of us, with a full meal inside us, sprawled out on the teak deck and were soon sound asleep. It was almost sundown before I awoke.

The next morning about eight o'clock we sighted land and by eleven we rounded Port San Lucas, sailed into the harbour. and dropped the hook. Errol Flynn had only ten days left to stay with us and he wanted to do some fishing. He had to get back to Hollywood to start another picture, so we decided to do no work with our films until he left. He had long yearned to fish in the Gulf of California, and we wanted him to spend all his time in having fun. Our work could wait.

Errol is a powerful swimmer and he enjoys skin diving and underwater spear fishing. We were able to spear several sharks, a couple of small manta rays, and many varieties of "pan fish," including several good-sized rock bass, which when fried we found to be delicious.

Off the end of the Cape, shark fishing was exceptional, and Al caught a huge hammerhead that weighed close to five hundred pounds. The blue marlin, however, seemed to have left the area. Almost every day we trolled for them, but had only one strike and failed to hook that one. However, we had little trouble in catching all the fish of other kinds we could possibly want, everything but the big blues. Yellow fin tuna, skipjack, yellowtail, dolphin and barracuda were there for the taking, and at the end of ten days Errol and the rest of us had enjoyed wonderful fishing.

When he finally left, aboard a small Beechcraft plane that flew over from Mexico City especially to pick him up, we cleared away and got down to work. Our objective was a short subject, featuring shark and another on marlin. The shark fishing film offered no real problem, as we succeeded in getting many shots of that species close to shore; the marlin subject, however, was something else again.

One day we followed the tuna boats to Goiter Banks, some twelve or fifteen miles north-west of the Cape and stood by while the fishermen spotted a school of tuna and began catching them. As they chummed the tuna to keep them near the boat, the blue shark moved in. After an hour or so they were so thick around the small boats that the men could not land a tuna, for as soon as a fish was hooked a shark cut him off before he could be landed.

The tuna boats pulled away from the spot and we sailed the *Sirocco* in where they had been, and started chumming with chunks of bait we had brought along for the purpose. Soon we had hundreds of the greedy devils all around the yacht, taking the bait the instant it hit the water.

Al and I got some good pictures of them as they surfaced, taking the refuse we threw overboard. I had a shark arrow rigged to a heavy line, rod and reel, and when one big fellow came to the surface to grab a large piece of chum, I drove the arrow right through his middle.

Before that wounded shark got fifty feet away, he was torn to pieces and eaten by the rest of the school. Within a half-hour I shot six sharks and not one lasted two minutes after being hit. One fellow was so greedy he swallowed my arrow and the toggle-type arrowhead, but the minute the rest of the sharks saw he was hooked, they went to work on him and he was soon eaten. Because they were cannibalistic, it was impossible for us to land any.

Finally, we decided to try to learn whether or not they would attack a man. We found a couple of two-by-four timbers, spiked them together, and slipped a pair of pants over them and tied them so that they looked much like a man's legs. On the ends of the two-by-fours, below the cuff of the trousers, we nailed two tennis shoes. Then we threw a couple of big pieces of chum into the water. As the hungry sharks came in to get the bait we hurled the dummy right into the middle of the school. Instantly, the monsters went after the dummy and tore it to pieces. I am sure that had a man gone overboard in those waters, he would have been entirely devoured in a matter of seconds.

One evening a live bait boat, which furnished the sardines for the tuna fleet that was working for the cannery in San Lucas, came in from Tiberone Island, which lies far up the Gulf. The crew reported they had run into a school of marlin swordfish off Sand Point, some sixty miles away, so early the next morning we pulled the hook and headed for the Point.

Native dance

Hippopotami live the greater part of the time in large
rivers and lakes

A bull hippo contemplating a charge

Our time was running short, and in order to reach the new location as fast as possible, we hoisted our sails and also employed the auxiliary motor. About noon we came in sight of Sand Point and dropped our sails.

While Al and I arranged an Akeley camera on the port deck and a DeBrie High Speed on the star board, the boys rigged a Zane Grey teaser and five lines, complete with baits, and got them into trolling position behind the yacht. Besides the five baits trolling back of the craft, I rigged a Japanese kite and, fastening a large cut bait on the end of a line without a hook, secured it to the kite line in such a way that it skipped along on top of the water.

Al had an Eyemo camera handy, so he could pick up any shots he could not get with the Akeley and the high-speed.

About the time we had everything ready, we came abeam of Sand Point. Just above the Point, in close to shore where a rocky cliff several hundred feet high formed the shoreline, the water was very deep. We slowed down the motor to trolling speed and headed the *Sirocco* towards shore.

As soon as we came into deep water things began to happen. First, a big marlin came after the Zane Grey teaser and gave it such a rap with his sword that he knocked it out of the water. Before we realized what was happening, five different marlin had every one of our baits and were off and running. The five reels running at high speed sounded like a swarm of bees. Even the cut bait I had fastened to the kite line with no hooks, was swallowed by a hungry marlin. It was not necessary to use the accepted method of getting the marlin take the bait, run a short way, then set the hook: these fellows were so hungry they grabbed and swallowed it on the move.

As the reels began to buzz, Al forgot all about pictures and made for a rod close by. He's a great outdoor cameraman, but he is also a most ardent deep-sea fisherman. I yelled to him to get to his camera.

He had no more than reached his Akeley when the first big blue took to the air lanes. He leaped several feet out of the water, shaking himself like a wet dog, made a graceful curve and dived back into the water.

The captain who was at the wheel when the fish struck, was hanging on to a rod with one hand and using the other on the wheel. Each of the two sailors had a rod and I had two. There

K

were marlin leaping in every direction. Several times there were three fish in the air at one time. We, of course, had never dreamed of getting more than one or two strikes at a time, and here we were with five fish hooked at once!

In a moment or two three of the marlin got themselves entangled and we lost all of them. I had only one rod now, but that was enough. The big blue on the end of the line had carried out a good two hundred yards of it and was still going. I began applying the brake and soon slowed him down.

In the meantime, the marlin which one of the sailors was plying turned back towards the yacht and started leaping near the stern of the ship. I turned my rod over to the free sailor and got the Eyemo camera and started making shots of the jumps.

The big blue near us had been hooked through one eye and he was really on the prod. He headed straight towards the port side of the *Sirocco* just under the surface of the water, and I was leaning over the guardrail, following him with the Eyemo. When within twenty yards of the boat he sounded, but I kept the camera rolling and my eye glued to the finder.

While I was leaning over the rail, waiting for him to come into view, he popped out of the water as though he had been shot from the bottom out of a cannon. He was within eight feet of the yacht and heading straight at me.

I leaped to one side as he came over the rail. His sharp sword missed my stomach by inches, and the fish landed more than half his length on deck. He gave a couple of flounces and was immediately back into the water and under the yacht. The line fouled around the propeller and was cut in two. The fish was free, but he came to the surface and made a series of six or eight long leaps into the air as he went away.

So close had I come to getting speared right through the middle that I forgot to follow as he went away. However, Al was on the job with the Akeley, and he made some wonderful pictures.

We soon got the last big marlin worked in close to the ship and had little trouble in bringing him to gaff. He weighed about 298 pounds and was the only one of the five fish we had hooked which we were able to land. However, we had suc-ceeded in getting the shots of jumping fish that were needed for the picture. In fact, we had got more than fifteen good jumps and some of them were close-ups.

Our script called for my shooting a marlin with the arrow. I rigged a lily-iron type of arrow point on a long shaft and fastened the head to a heavy eighty thread line, which was in turn attached to a 26 Von Hoff reel and a heavy shark rod. We got another cut bait fastened to the kite line and worked our way slowly back to the deep water near the shore where the other strikes occurred. Al stood by with the high-speed, and by using a 27 mm. wide angle lens, he was able to keep me and the bait in the same frame.

As we came in under the high bank a big blue rose to the surface a yard or two back of the skipping bait, then moved up to it. More than half his back was out of the water. Al saw him and rolled the high-speed camera. When the camera came up to speed, I quickly drew, aimed, and loosed the arrow. The head drove just under the dorsal fin about two inches and slightly forward of it. The arrow had hit the marlin where it would not wound him too severely, for there are no major blood vessels in that area. As the arrow drove into him the fish leaped up a foot or two, then turned towards the open sea, and was away like a scared pronghorn.

Dropping my bow, I snatched the reel and applied the brake very hard. I knew the arrow-head would not pull free and I felt that the heavy line was more than the fish could break. He had not gone more than a hundred yards when I was able to stop him.

The second I had him stopped he stuck his nose towards the skies and came out of the water, walking on his tail. I refused to give him one inch of line. Each time he leaped I rolled him, but he was hooked in such a way that he was almost twice as strong as if caught in the mouth. He made a dozen or more leaps through the air, and once or twice he made a very high jump and came over backward, performing a perfect arched back-dive.

We put a light skiff over the side and the two sailors got into it. I gave one of them the rod and they played him from the skiff. That marlin made more different kinds of jumps than I have ever seen made by any other fish. I am convinced this was due to the fact that the fish was not seriously hurt and was hooked in such a peculiar place. The boys soon had him within fifty feet of the skiff, and Al and I were grinding away with the cameras.

Finally the big blue quit jumping and started planing on top of the water. He would head first one way, then the other. He made one complete circle around the skiff, skidding along on his side. Then he straightened up and headed directly for the skiff.

The boys saw him coming and stood up on the seats of the little boat. The sailor who was rowing had an oar in his hand, and when he saw the fish was going to hit the skiff, he started to swing at him with the oar, but the marlin struck the side of the boat so hard that he knocked it three or feet sideways in the water. His sword hit dead centre of the skiff, just under the waterline and he went through both sides of the boat. Both boys were thrown out by the force of the blow.

Al and I each had been lucky enough to get a motion picture of the entire action. We had, of course, not expected to get such an unusual and spectacular shot, but it was a most thrilling sight to record on film, and has been seen by millions of people all over the world.

CHAPTER FIFTEEN

THE PSYCHOLOGY OF AFRICAN ANIMALS

Much more knowledge of the instincts, the habits and the psychology of wild animals is required by the man who hunts them with the camera, than is necessary for the hunter with the bow and arrow or with the various types of guns. Of the three essentials mentioned, I consider an understanding of the psychology of wild creatures the most important. If one is able to think after the same manner as the animal he is stalking, he has a great advantage over those persons who depend entirely on understanding the instincts and habits of the animals being sought. I am aware that many noted scientists claim that animals have little power to think and no power to reason, but the most successful stalkers have proved over and over again that this belief is erroneous.

In my experience over a good many years in hunting and studying animals, I have learned that some are stupid creatures and will react generally along a given pattern, while others are smart and alert and seldom fail to size up a situation from various angles before finally deciding what course to take. Rarely do these alert ones react in the same way under almost identical circumstances. I have often noted that a big herd of animals of the same breed or a mixed herd of several differing species are much more likely to do the same thing in the same way every time than is the case with a single individual.

It seems reasonable to conclude that a large herd cannot reason with as much clarity as a small group or an individual. It is a sort of mob psychology that actuates the large group. When a large mixed group is faced with a dangerous situation. there is little chance for the smarter animals to figure out what to do under the circumstances, for the simple reason that some weak-minded individual with no nerve will take some action at once, regardless of whether or not it is the wise course, and so startle the entire group into movement before the wiser heads have had time to figure just what is the safest course to take. It is the old story of some human being pulling a trigger or yelling "Fire!" and so starting a lynching or a stampede when wiser heads would have averted those catastrophes.

In the face of extreme danger, nervous fright can upset the wisest heads, even among human beings, and much more so those of wild creatures who so often must depend on quick action for survival. On the other hand, not all animals lose their heads when stricken with fear, and some seem even to be stimulated by it to clearer thinking. For this and other reasons, I have learned how unwise it is to make dogmatic statements concerning what any animal will or will not do under any given set of circumstances. It is safer to generalize without being too specific. The smart hunter continually studies the reaction of various species of game and remembers what he observes. Experience is still a great teacher, though even that is not an infallible guide.

When we first arrived in Africa in 1950 to begin shooting the feature picture, *Tembo,* we knew nothing, comparatively speaking, about the various animals of that continent except what we had read. Any good hunter, however, knows enough to be afraid of all animals and to trust none of them. The word *afraid* here is not meant to imply being panic stricken, but only a fear great enough to assure caution and respect in the presence of any wild creature. The easiest way to get killed by a dangerous animal is to be so afraid that one acts without thinking. Action prompted only by fear is seldom wise or accurate.

Each new species of animal we encountered, we approached with the greatest caution. As to the big five which are considered the most formidable, the lion, the leopard, the rhino, the elephant and the buffalo, we never at any time in the presence of one of them allowed ourselves to become careless. On the other hand, it is almost as dangerous to become over-confident as it is to be frantic with fear. A certain amount of confidence is a great asset. so long as it is tempered with good common horsesense, but when confidence becomes cocksureness in a hunter, he is fast coming to the end of the trail.

It never pays to underestimate the potentialities of any wild creature, especially in the jungle. In the first place, that is his home and he has the advantage. I have never seen a camera hunter who was a real woodsman become guilty of over-confidence, but I have seen a number of mere camera enthusiasts who had little fear of any animal. These were cases where ignorance was bliss. Such a fellow in Africa needs the aid of two good white hunters when he goes out for pictures; otherwise, he will not be coming back.

In America, one of the most successful types of hunting when seeking the bovine animals such as the moose, deer, antelope, elk and mountain sheep, is pass shooting, sometimes referred to as drive shooting. Usually a number of hunters will spread out and make a drive through a certain area, while others take up a position on a pass or trail leading from one locality to another where the animals are most likely to pass. Many times the creatures being driven will all but run over the hunters who have taken up such stands.

In Africa, this type of hunting just described is of no earthly good when used in hunting the multifarious types of antelope and gazelle that abound there. In fact, the only time I saw this type of hunting used successfully was in conjunction with elephants.

At one of our camps in Tanganyika, not far from Musoma, there were tens of thousands of animals grazing on the open plains and the low rolling knolls covered by thorn brush. We located a few spots which were natural passes through which these beasts travelled daily. Using the natural cover that occurred near these passes, we fashioned blinds and left them for several days so the animals would become accustomed to them. These blinds were not elaborate and gave no cause for suspicion. The animals paid little attention to them. In fact, they fed and walked by them every day as though they did not exist. We even had boxes fastened on legs inside these blinds to simulate cameras, so that when we did place the real instruments near the small openings through which to shoot scenes, they would cause no suspicion.

Then one morning, long before daylight, we stationed cameras and cameramen inside the blinds, but not an animal came near them. They did not see the cameramen, I am sure, but the creatures were so thick in the vicinity that long before there was enough light to secure pictures, the beasts that were downwind of the blind smelled the human scent and soon had the source of it spotted. Their alert attitude naturally caused other animals nearby to become suspicious and they would not approach the blinds closer than a hundred yards or so. The moment one group of animals smelled the human scent and were successful in locating the position of the cameramen, they would begin snorting and stamping their feet. This peculiar behaviour would be seen by other groups and the alarm was relayed. Within a short time every creature within five hundred yards knew that man had been spotted and furthermore, knew his location.

It was useless to stay inside the blinds because no animal would come near. After a few fruitless attempts, we decided to try other methods. We rounded up a couple of hundred native beaters and sent them far below the area of our best natural blinds and started a drive towards our position. Soon a large number of animals were gathered in front of the beaters, but they somehow knew or feared that they were being driven into some kind of trap. Confusion ensued for a short time, but finally the herd started running parallel with the line of beaters. Eventually reaching the end of that line, they cut back behind the natives.

The next day we added more beaters and made a line in a half circle. Again we soon had a large herd in front of the beaters, but no sooner did the wild creatures realize they were being driven in a given direction than they stampeded. Finding they could not go around the end of the line, they cut back and went right through the line, almost running down several of the native boys who were reluctant to give way.

For a couple of weeks we tried every method we could think of to drive the beasts, but they consistently refused to go in the direction we wanted them to take. Whenever they broke through our line, they went as fast as they could in the opposite direction. Although we used jeeps and trucks to help the beaters, the animals simply would not be driven.

One day a big herd of gazelles of various kinds had broken our line and Wayne Stotler and I had tried to get around them in two jeeps. We chased them for two miles across the plains before we were able to head them off, and after we finally got in front of them, they swerved to the right and left of us and kept right on going.

From a local British chap I learned that the reason these animals would not be driven was because the method had already been in use for so long by the native tribes: all the animals feared to be driven lest they should run into an ambush of native bowmen or spearmen. I was nearing my wit's end as to just how we were going to get close-up pictures of the various animals when it was impossible to get within a hundred yards or little less of them. Even at that distance they would not stand quietly for more than a minute or two before taking off. I was about ready to give up in desperation when an idea hit me and, as nutty as it seemed, I decided to give it a trial.

A few days later I gathered another company of native beaters and we went down to a spot where we had two blinds fairly close together. After the cameramen were inside the blinds and all ready for action, I strung out my line of boys to the right and left of the two blinds and started a drive *away* from the blinds. Within a quarter of a mile we had gathered a couple of thousand animals before us, and they made a break to cut back. Playing up, we yelled and did our utmost to keep them from going through our line, but they could not be stopped.

As soon as they got beyond our line they kept right on going and many of them passed within a few yards of the blinds, so that the fellows got some excellent pictures. Every day for a week we tried to drive the beasts away from the blinds and almost without exception they would break through our line and run by our blinds. Only a time or two after getting through our line, did they fail to go close enough for the boys to secure good shots. It was as simple as falling off a log, once we had it figured out.

The natives were amazed at how nicely the animals co-operated. When we go back to Africa again, the herds, I feel sure, will be wise to this trick, because by then the tribesmen will have used it often enough to have proved to the wild creatures that it does not pay to do the exact opposite to what man is trying to make them do. They have that much sagacity, I am sure.

Another bit of psychology we used to advantage in forests where the cover was fairly thick was this. By careful stalking and with the aid of a good native tracker or two, a herd of animals, usually water buck, elephants or buffalo, was spotted. As soon as we were sure of their exact position, we would send a group of natives far to the windward of the animals and have them set up a lot of noise, while a few picked fellows with the cameras would sneak behind the beasts and downwind of them. Invariably the creatures would become so interested in the distant noises and faint odours of the decoys that we would be able to get near enough to secure good close-ups.

Using this method is very dangerous, however, if the subjects are either Cape buffalo or elephants. Both these creatures have a way of getting angry when they are unable to figure out just what is going on, and if they are watching in one direction from which they hear and smell human beings, then suddenly happen to discover some man close by, they are liable to make it very rough on the intruder.

One day while we were employing this method on a small herd of elephants in tall grass and scattered timber, some of the fellows were almost killed. I had climbed a large tree from which I could watch the boys sneak up on the herd. They in turn were to watch me, and from my position I was to signal them when the elephants were all facing in the direction where we had sent the decoys.

At this particular spot the ground was fairly level but there was an occasional deep *donga*, or ditch. The beasts were, however, in such high elephant grass that it was hard to locate them. At any rate, I had been watching the herd from my position in the tree top for an hour or more and I felt sure that there were thirty-three head of them. (It pays to watch every member of a herd in a situation like this.)

As soon as the native boys who were acting as decoys had reached their position and started to make a lot of unusual noises, the leader of the herd started rounding up the rest of the band. It was a group of cows and yearlings, but we had not seen either a bull or a calf. Cows with young calves usually stayed where there was more cover than in this particular spot. Realizing that cows with young calves are much more alert and short tempered than a group of this kind, we figured we had no cause to worry on that score.

The boys with the camera began making a sneak up-wind towards the herd at the same time when the boss cow had begun to round them up. Even though the grass was tall, from my position in the tree I could look down and see my men most of the time at this juncture; Casumway, my head tracker, took the lead, Wayne Stotler and Ed. Hill came next, then Arthur Phelps, my cameraman, was bringing up the rear.

When I left California on this African expedition it had been only nine months since I had suffered a crushed left knee in an accident, followed by three operations, so all the time I was on this trip I not only could not run, but in tall grass I could not even walk fast. For this reason I seldom went very close to a herd of dangerous beasts, unless the object was to kill one of them with the bow and arrow. As it turned out, it was a good thing I did not go with the camera crew on this particular day.

The fellows worked in fairly close to the herd and were watching me for the signal to tell them when all the animals were together. I counted the beasts a dozen times and every time I was sure there were thirty-two of them in sight. Besides, the leader was standing calmly in the centre of the bunch, testing the air with her trunk, and every once in awhile she would call softly. Finally, I felt satisfied that there were no stragglers, so I gave the signal for the fellows to move in closer.

The boys were in single file about five yards apart, following a well-worn elephant trail. I saw Casumway go out of sight down into a deep *donga*. Then Wayne, following back of him, started down and was out of sight all but his head, when a very large bull elephant, that not one of us had seen, came out of the tall grass in the bottom of the *donga* and into the trail.

All at once I saw Wayne back up quickly and raise his rifle to his shoulder. I knew something had gone amiss, but from my position in the tree I could not see what had caused this unexpected action on Wayne's part. After a couple of seconds he ducked down out of sight and he, Ed. and Arthur started back towards me on the trot.

About that time I saw Casumway come up on the other side of the ditch, running like the Devil was after him. It turned out to be the big bull elephant that was pursuing, and he promptly emerged from the *donga* only twenty yards behind my tracker. This boy, Casumway, knew that beast better than anybody else I met while in Africa. Right then he proved how well he understood the creature.

Casumway knew he had no chance to outrun the bull, but before the beast had a chance to get into stride, the hunter had a good twenty-five yard start. Before the bull was even out of the *donga*, Casumway had quit the elephant trail and was headed

at right angles to it through the heavy grass. He ran only a
few yards, then made another tack and came back towards the
ditch paralleling the course of the trail. The eyesight of the
elephant is notoriously poor and the bull ran several yards past
the spot where Casumway had left the trail before he realized
which way the black boy had gone. He turned off the trail
with trunk lifted high, screaming as only a mad bull elephant
can. Of all the sounds I have ever heard it is the most blood-
curdling.

The instant Casumway heard the bull enter the grass he ran
back into the elephant trail and headed towards us. He was
running very low, using his hands part of the time to keep his
balance, but he was going like the wind. By now all the cows
and yearlings knew that man was near and they started to fan
out and try to locate the intruder.

Casumway had given the big bull the slip as slick as a whistle.
The angry monster ran in circles, trying to locate him, but was
never able to figure which way the boy had gone. Wayne and
Ed. had seen that Arthur got safely back to the tree and he lost
no time in climbing up to safety beside me. The other two
then started back to see where Casumway had gone, but he met
them only a short way from where Arthur and I were in the big
wild-fig tree. We were happy, indeed, to be joined very soon
by Wayne, Ed. and Casumway.

They could have killed the bull, all right, but since the herd
had been aroused and there was no chance to get pictures, there
was no point in shooting unless that was necessary to save a life.
It was wonderful to sit high up out of danger and watch the
herd scream and run in circles, looking for Casumway.

This native hunter seemed not the least alarmed: he said he
had got away from many herds of mad elephants, and I believe
him. For a good half-hour they searched the tall grass, but we
were downwind of them and they could not get our scent.
Besides, the noise being made by our decoys a quarter of a mile
upwind of them kept them somewhat confused.

Finally they decided they could not locate their enemy, so they
headed across country towards a dense forest a mile or more
east from where we had found them. Many continued to trumpet shrilly in their uneasiness and high displeasure. The bull
and the boss cow brought up the rear.

Had Wayne failed to hear the bull and to back away quickly

from the *donga* he would have met him face to face in a few more steps. Wayne, however, an alert and experienced hunter, was back out of the ditch and out of sight when the bull stepped into the trail. At that point the beast had seen Casumway and had started after him. The boy had already been underway when the bull saw him or I might have lost at that spot the best native hunter I found in Africa.

CHAPTER SIXTEEN

ENCOUNTER WITH
HIPPOPOTAMUS

THE Hippopotamus *(H. amphibius)* found in and around the
large rivers of Africa, is a type of the family *Hippopotomidæ,*
whose closest relatives are the pigs. Hippos are the largest of all
non-ruminating even-toed mammals living in the world to-day.
As far back as the pleistocene epoch there was a variety of this
beast and naturalists are unable to find any characteristics of
the fossil remains which would distinguish them from the
hippopotamus that still occurs in Africa. This prehistoric beast
was found over almost all of Europe, while dwarf species were
living in Crete, Malta, Sicily, India, Burma and northern Africa.
To-day a tiny variety, the pygmy hippo, no bigger than a pig,
lives in the rain forest of West Africa. This little fellow is less
aquatic in habit than its larger relative.

All hippos are clumsy looking beasts with soft greasy hides
more than two inches thick in some spots, but they can move
with surprising speed and agility when perturbed, considering
the fact that some individuals have been known to measure as
much as fourteen feet in length and to weigh more than three
tons. It is easy to imagine the dangers a hunter is in when confronted by such a monster at close quarters.

Despite the fact that hippopotami live the greater part of the
time in the large rivers and lakes, they often come out of the
water and feed for a considerable distance inland. I have seen
them as far as ten miles away from any considerable body of
water. They eat aquatic plants, grass and leaves and have sometimes been known to devour the entire vegetable and cane crops
of the natives.

While at most times the hippo is a lazy, easy-going fellow that
enjoys minding his own business, he is not averse to taking up
the cudgels if the need arises. A wounded or cornered hippopotamus is a strong, agile and dangerous adversary. Old bulls
often become outlaws and will charge on sight, without provo-

cation. Mothers with young are extremely jealous, alert and aggressive.

When travelling through the water, this animal prefers to walk on the bottom, rather than to swim. If frightened and anxious to get away he may even trot along the bottom of a lake or stream. Naturally, the extremely heavy bulk of such a creature becomes more manœuvreable in the dense medium of water than when on land.

During the mating season the bulls fight considerably to win the admiration of some fickle female, who although she seems to enjoy watching the battle never condescends to take part in one. We learned from the natives that the old bulls often fight to the death. However, we never actually saw one so killed, but we did see several that had huge chunks bitten right out of their sides, shoulders, necks or legs. Incidentally, both the canine and incisor teeth of the hippo are well developed, and he does not hesitate to use them when necessary. When one remembers that the lower canine teeth or tusks of the bull may often weigh from four to seven pounds each, it is easy to imagine the harm they may inflict. One big fellow I saw, who had evidently been in a battle, had a hole bitten out of one side, big enough to hold an inflated football, yet it seemed not to cause him too much inconvenience.

Near Rutshuru I met a tea planter who told as an example of the strength with which the hippo can bite, the story of an angered bull that bit one of the planter's huskiest native workmen completely in two with one vicious snap of the jaws. I also heard of several occasions on which hippos had attacked small boats and had bitten out the side planking as if the hard wood had been so much soft putty.

The meat of the hippo, more like beef than pork and much less greasy than the latter, is delightful to the palate and is more desired by the natives than that of any other animal in Africa. The loin is exceptionally tender and juicy. Though most of our party preferred the flesh of the eland (largest of all antelope), the Tommy gazelle, the impalla and the dikdik, yet we greatly enjoyed the loin of hippo.

During our stay in Africa we photographed many hippopotami, but fortunately we succeeded in staying out of reach of these ponderous subjects At that, we had several close brushes with the ungainly monsters. Once while travelling up a small river, the Tarini, in a boat which we had improvised from some soft, half-rotten boards, we rounded a sharp bend in the stream and met a bull hippo almost head-on. We had carried a five-horse outboard motor along with us and had it fastened on to the back end of the flimsy little bateau, so we were cruising along at a fair rate of speed.

When we confronted the hippo he opened his cavernous mouth and started for us. I was in the front end of the craft and the instant the angry bull spread his jaws and headed for us, I rammed a paddle clear down his throat to his tonsils. Evidently, he was not expecting this bit of aggressiveness, and it stopped him cold. However, he clamped his jaws shut like a giant pair of spring scissors, snapping off the two-inch handle of the hardwood paddle as though it had been a piece of macaroni. He coughed out the blade of the paddle and was again anxious for combat, but by now Ed. Hill, who was running the motor, had given it the gun and we were out of reach.

We would not have thought of entering a stream of that size with the makeshift craft had we known there were hippopotami in it. For several weeks we had been camped at a spot nearby, and not having seen nor heard any hippos, we did not even suspect that there were any of the species in the vicinity. After seeing this one too close to enjoy the view, we realized there were evidently some facts about the stream which we had not learned during our stay nearby. When I told the local headman (chief) of one of the tribes who lived near the river what had happened, he laughed as though it were a big joke. Then he said that often during the rainy season the hippos came up the stream from Lake Victoria, the margin of which lay only about thirty miles west of where we were and into which the Tarini flowed.

One thing I could never understand about the natives of Africa was the peculiar sense of humour they possess. Many times I noticed that the most tragic happenings were to them a huge joke. I suppose the grimness of nature and the struggle for survival had not only inured them to tragedy, but had even made some aspects of stark tragedy amusing. I was born and reared in Shelby County, Alabama, where the coloured population outnumbered the whites, and I was brought up among Negroes. In fact, they were my regular playmates and constant companions on my father's farm until I went away to school, and one of the outstanding characteristics of all the

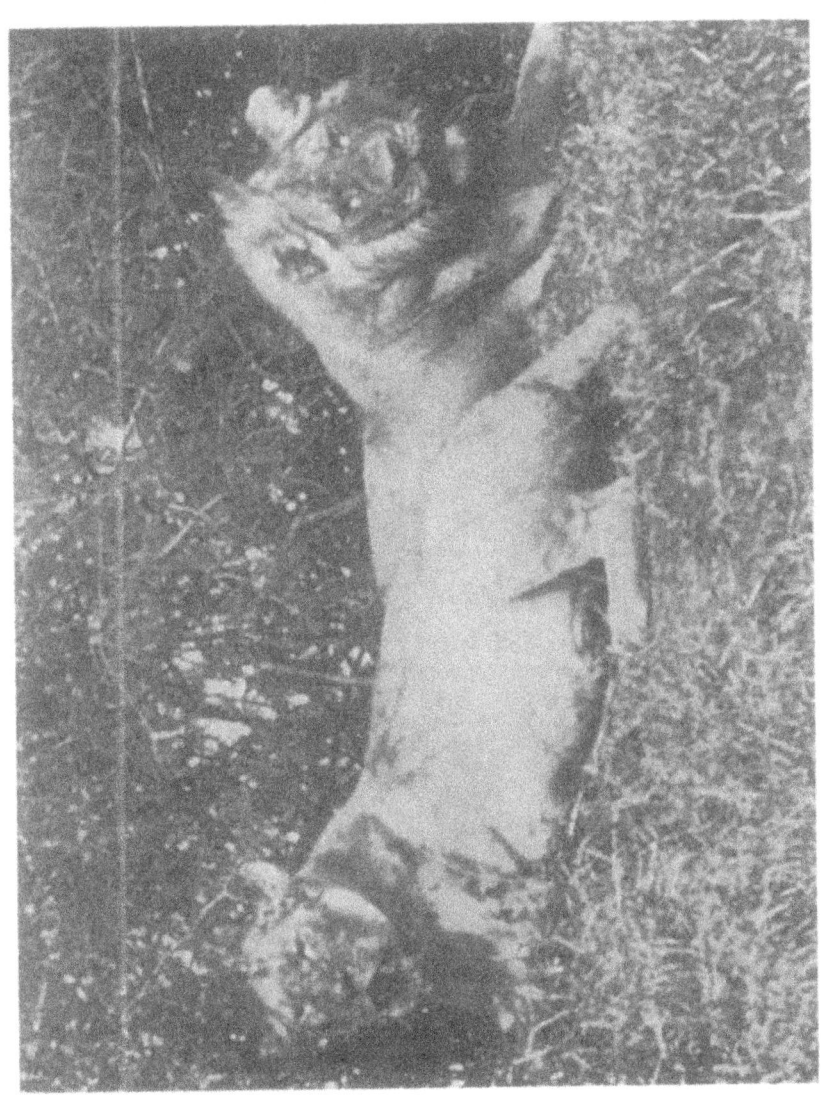

Lion and lioness
at home

A study in black and
white

coloured folk in the south was their sympathy. Never once did I know one of them to consider anything sad or tragic as a laughing matter. Yet it remains true that all the native Africans I ran into on my expedition over there had this most unusual trait. Anyway, this native chief really got a bang out of our surprise encounter on the Tarini and our narrow escape from the bull hippo.

Another time while we were preparing to photograph a large number of the beasts at a spot along the Rutshuru River in the Belgian Congo, something happened that was really funny, even to us white men. On that particular occasion little danger was present, but the way the thing happened and the reaction of those involved was amusing. We had discovered a deep pool in the river just below an abrupt bend, and in this pool lived more than a hundred hippos. At this point the stream was a good hundred yards wide and the pool some two hundred yards long. Right in the centre of the river was a small island or sand bar. In one respect the hippo is much like the crocodile: he enjoys lying on the warm sand and taking a sunbath, especially in vicinities where he is seldom molested.

The bank on which we had decided to make pictures was considerably higher than other spots surrounding the pool, and we had carefully selected it, so that should any of the hippos become angry and decide to attack, they would have to come up a considerable incline to reach us. At the same time, there were three or four spots along the bank by which a hippo *could* approach us if he were sufficiently determined.

A local native had shown me the place several days before, and I had scouted out a way by which we could come near it in a jeep. The last hundred yards or so, however, would have to be travelled on foot. This particular spot was closed to hippopotamus shooting and, unless the life of a man were seriously endangered, no one had a right to shoot one of the beasts. I felt sure that it was this protection which accounted for the large number of hippos in the pool. One should remember, however, that they were in no sense of the word tame hippos.

At any rate, one morning Mike, Ed., Wayne, Casumway, the local headman called Big Nothing and I arrived near the river in two jeeps with all our camera equipment. Knowing how prone the fellows in the party were to take chances when we had rifles along and realizing that there would be considerable explanation to be made if we should be forced to kill one of the beasts, I had decided not to take any rifles with us. In most instances such a practice is not safe, but I felt fairly certain that by using a little common horsesense we could avoid having any trouble with the creatures. All of us knew the temperament of the beast and about how much interference he would stand for before starting a fight, as well as approximately the speed at which he could run.

When we had reached the spot beyond which we could not use the jeeps, we turned them around and headed them in the direction from which we had come, figuring that if we were forced to retreat, the vehicles would be in a strategic position for a fast exit. We left the motors running, too, because we knew that without rifles we were taking a chance.

While the boys were unloading the equipment, Casumway and I worked our way down near the edge of the water on top of the high bank to make sure there were no stragglers hidden in the few clumps of low rhinoceros brush that grew about in scattered patches. We saw no such animals and went back to the vehicles and told the boys they need have no fear, as there were no hippos nearer than the river.

Carl Mikule, whom we all called Mike, was a fast and indus-trious worker. No sooner had I said the road was clear than he shouldered an Akeley camera attached to a heavy tripod, picked up a heavy dry cell camera battery that weighed not less than fifty pounds, and headed for the river bank. His complete load must have been close to a hundred pounds. The rest of the outfit collected their loads and also started for the bank. I was the last one to leave the jeeps, because I wanted to make sure that nothing we might need immediately was left behind.

I had gone only a short way from the jeeps when I heard a yell near the river. Convinced that we had overlooked a hippo in some of the brush thickets and that it was after Mike, I knew instantly it was he who had given the war-whoop. Though there were some intervening clumps of brush, I could see almost to the water's edge. Before I had time to think twice I saw Mike coming back up the hill in overdrive. Right behind him was a big bull hippopotamus blowing saliva in the Texan's hip pockets, but losing ground at every stride. All the members of our party saw and heard Mike coming, and they too reversed their field and headed back for the jeeps.

I stood in my tracks without moving, to be sure Mike was out of danger. I saw there was no cause to worry in the least, because that tall Texan was covering the ground with the speed of a spooked mustang, while the fat, stubby-legged hippo made slow time. At the speed the beast was making uphill, I could almost have outrun him with my stiff knee, broken a few months before in a hunting accident.

Of course, it was not funny that the hippo had charged Mike, but the laughable part was that he had forgotten to drop either the clumsy camera or the heavy battery. I must say that they were in no way retarding his speed. Never in my life have I seen a man, even without a heavy load, make better time than he was making. Mike is about six feet two, with long powerful legs. We were all in the jeeps when he arrived and he just stepped aboard the one I was driving, camera, tripod, battery and all.

His foot landed right in the middle of the little pick-up box or bed in back of the seats and as he came aboard he yelled: "Let her go, Bud!"

Everyone was choking with laughter, but I never cracked a smile. We started the jeeps moving forward, but when we reached a spot where we could see the hippo, the bull had turned back and was again close to the water. He had got no farther than forty yards from the stream at any time.

Mike still held the camera on his shoulder, though he had set the battery down automatically as he squatted in the box of the jeep when it began to move forward. The instant I saw that all the danger was over I could hold in no longer. I screamed with laughter and so did everybody else, including Casumway and Big Nothing. At our rude outburst Mike realized for the first time that he still held the camera. Then it dawned on him that he had also forgotten to put the battery down until he had reached and boarded the jeep. Having a terrific sense of humour and being a regular fellow in every sense of the word, he instantly realized how funny he must have looked with a camera, tripod and a heavy battery outrunning a hippo uphill. He joined in the merriment and I think he enjoyed the incident more than we did. It may not sound funny as I have told it, but the way it actually happened was a riot.

When I got so I could talk without laughing, I said: "Mike, why didn't you drop the camera and battery?"

"Man," he replied, "when I came face to face with that fiery eyed hippo and he opened up that cavity of his, and I got a peek at those molars, I didn't know I had a camera or battery. All I know is, my feet got scared and started going places, and the first thing I knew was, they'd brought me to this jeep. What more could a fellow ask than that?"

We laughed again and Mike continued: "I could hear that baby snorting right behind me and I had no desire to become entangled with his bicuspids. I knew he didn't mean *maybe*, and I think I proved to everybody that my head was working: I didn't stand for any rough stuff, did I?"

We had to admit he had not stood upon the order of his going, but had gone at once. What a really wonderful sport he was, I thought, to take such a ribbing and get as much fun out of it as the rest of us did.

Finally when we had all settled down to the job of getting some pictures, Mike told us just what had happened. The hippo must have been lying close up under the high bank in shallow water where we could not see him when Casumway and I had gone down on our first reconnaissance trip. He probably had not known we were there or he would not have stayed near the bank: either he would have come for us or else have retreated into deep water. He evidently had intended to come up on the bank and feed or lie down, and had been on his way over the steep bank when Mike arrived on the scene.

Anyway, Mike had reached the steep river bank and was in the act of setting down the battery when the head of the monster appeared over the bank within about ten feet of him. The nearness of the man must have startled the beast so that he felt he was cornered. Either through fear or anger he opened his jaws and started for Mike. It was at that point that Mike had yelled and that his feet, as he said: "started going places."

Several times during the day we had to take to the hill as other bulls advanced towards us. We kept a close watch, however, and were able in each case to spot them long before they came to the bank. It was necessary for them to come through several yards of shallow water to reach us, and we could see the tops of their backs the minute they entered the shallow stretch.

The hippopotamus pictures used to illustrate this volume were taken on the Rutshuru River, in the Belgian Congo.

CHAPTER SEVENTEEN

WE MEET THE PYGMIES

Our tired foot-safari of five white men and more than a hundred native blacks rounded a sharp curve in the jungle trail through the great Ituri forest in the Belgian Congo of Central Africa which we had followed since early morning. From my position at the head of the long column, I caught a glimpse of a naked Pygmy warrior dart across the trail and disappear into the dense undergrowth.

He moved with such speed and agility that I had to think twice to be sure that what I had seen was really a human being and not a dog baboon or some other wild animal. I was almost sure I had seen the gleaming side of a hunting spear. It had to be a Pygmy warrior I decided. However, in order to check, I stopped dead in my tracks, turned and faced my head boy, directly behind me and pointing to where I had seen the figure, I said: "*Mutu kidogo hapa!*" meaning literally: "Small man here!" I had spoken in Swahili, which is understood by practically all natives of Central Africa. My head boy replied in the same dialect: "*Indio, bwana. Indio.*" ("Yes, master. Yes.")

Now I was sure that what I had glimpsed was a fleeting Pygmy warrior. The African natives have much better eyesight in the dark forest than do white men. I had no desire to burst unexpectedly upon a frightened Pygmy village. The tiny villagers might shoot poisoned arrows first and ask questions later.

If the information given me by Pat Putnam, an American who had spent almost forty years among the little people, was correct, we should be drawing near a small village of wild Bambuti Pygmies. Pat had told me that he was sure the little folk would become friendly and would co-operate with us in getting motion pictures of a real animal net-hunt, but he warned me not to surprise the camp.

He said we should keep all guns out of sight and that I should remove my arrow from the bow and put it into my quiver as soon as I was in sight of camp. Also that I would be wise to unstring my bow. He assured me that the little people were excellent archers and would know when I unstrung the bow and placed the arrow in my quiver that my intentions were not hostile. He also told us that if any of our party carried guns the Bambutis might stampede and leave the vicinity, or then again, he said, they might conceal themselves in the dense bush and take a few shots at us with poisoned arrows.

Howard Bigelow, my interpreter, Arthur Phelps, cameraman, and Wayne Stotler, Ed. Hill and Carl Mikule, who made up the rest of our small motion picture company, were soon gathered at the head of the line. My wife, secretary of the outfit, was in Nairobi during this part of the expedition.

I was sure that the Pygmy warrior we had just seen would reach the camp and give warning of our approach long before we could possibly get there. All the rifles in our safari had been concealed in various packs, so we knew that the little man had not seen any guns, even if he had been watching us for some time before he took flight.

Howard Bigelow had been a missionary in Africa for several years, some time previous to this trip, and although he had had little experience with Pygmies, he did have a fair knowledge of several wild tribes of African natives, and he was of the opinion that we should continue our line of march as though we had seen no one.

I led off and we moved quietly forward. We had gone only a short way around a couple of more bends when I smelled wood-smoke. I must say, that detecting this odour as we moved through the dark jungle with its towering trees and the deep, mysterious shadows beneath and beyond them, made for a spooky feeling. I could imagine I saw Pygmy eyes looking at me from all sides.

The fact of the matter was that those eyes were actually watching us, but we did not know it. Less than a half-mile from where we had glimpsed the frightened warrior, we came on to a Pygmy village. A dozen or more leaf-covered huts were nestled in a small clearing, yet there was no sign of life.

I realized that the little people had taken to cover and I knew, too, that they had taken their bows, arrows, spears and hunting nets with them. There was nothing in sight except the bare huts, the cook fires and a few cooking utensils.

Feeling more than a little nervous, I walked cautiously forward, but I tried not to show it. All the native bearers in my column were bleary-eyed from apprehension and if some one had made a false move, they would have dropped their packs and have been off like a herd of frightened antelope. With a show of confidence, which I did not feel, I walked to the centre of the little group of huts and slowly removed the arrow from my bowstring, dropped it into the quiver on my right shoulder and then unstrung my bow.

I raised my right hand and looking into the dense shadows of the forest, spoke in Ki Swahili. "*Yambo!*" I called, which means "Hello!"

Giving the forest my best smile, I repeated: "*Yambo!*" this time a little louder.

By now all the other fellows had joined me, unarmed in any way. We chatted among ourselves a few seconds, and I again raised my hand. This time I yelled: "*Yambo!*" and I had to laugh out loud as my voice carried through the quiet jungle.

Then, from behind the trunk of a huge mahogany tree about forty yards away, two elderly Pygmy warriors, armed with bows loaded with keen broadheads, came forth. They advanced a couple of feet towards us, then stopped and looked back into the dense forest. We knew that this was a signal for all the concealed Pygmies to keep us covered, so that if we made a false move they would give us a shower of arrows. It was a tense moment.

Slowly the two little warriors came towards me, their strung bows held at *ready* position. They were brave, I had to admit, but were taking no chances. I made a couple of steps towards them and they pulled up sharply. Their beady little black eyes were watching me like those of a cornered leopard. I stopped, naturally.

It seemed they did not like my advance, and at that moment if there was anything I wanted to do it was to please the couple of little fellows. As yet they had made no sound of any kind.

After I stopped, they soon began moving cautiously towards me again. Finally they got within six or eight feet of me and again they stopped. I could see that the two little guys were even more scared than I was, and that was plenty. Slowly I extended my hand, grinned, and said in a tone just above a whisper: "*Yambo.*"

This time the older of the two (who later turned out to be the second chief of the group) whispered in reply: "*Yambo.*"

Man, was that ever sweet music to my ear! I stood with my right hand still extended. The second chief slowly advanced and, lowering his bow, started to shake, but when his little hand was within inches of my big mitt his nerve simply failed him. He withdrew his hand and stepped back one step, then looked over his shoulder at the other warrior who still stood with bow half-drawn, watching me like a hawk eyeing a chicken. The second chief was making sure that his companion was ready to give me the works if I tried to harm him, the leader.

He must have had lots of confidence in his assistant because after one reassuring look he stepped forward once more and touched my hand, then quickly withdrew his. I still had not moved a muscle, but was grinning like a cat eating mucilage. I was doing my very best to be ingratiating.

Finally he actually shook hands briefly with me, but as I clasped his little hand lightly he watched it carefully, as though afraid I were going to break it off or perhaps squeeze it to a pulp. All this time the rest of my party had not moved a muscle nor said a word.

As soon as the leader had shaken hands with me, he backed up to his partner, took up his stance and held me under his bow while the second little fellow came forward and shook hands with me. As soon as he had done so I took my eyes off him, glanced down at his bow and said: "*Mashalie uta. Mzuri. Iko Mzuri.*" ("Bow and arrow. Good. Very good".) I held out my hand to show that I wanted to see his arrow.

He removed it from the little bow, stepped over and stuck the broadhead down into the earth two or three times, then handed it to me. He had stuck the arrow in the ground to remove the poison on its point before he let me have it, which showed he did not want to hurt me. I looked the arrow over carefully and gave it back to him, saying: "*Uta iko misouri.*" ("Arrow very good.")

He replied politely: "*Santi, Sana.*" ("Thank you, Sir.") Not all Pygmies can speak Ki Swahili, but the little folk in this particular camp could all speak it, we later found.

I then withdrew one of my own big broadheads and wiped the keen steel blade over my hand to show that it was not poisoned, then holding it by the blade, I extended the feathered end to him. Eagerly he dropped his own weapons beside him and took the arrow.

The second chief of the village, who had been standing with bow ready to shoot all this time, could stand it no longer. He lowered his bow, came forward briskly and began looking at my arrow. I took another broadhead from my quiver and handed it to him.

The two Pygmies began chatting like a couple of magpies and pointing out to each other different parts of the missile. The leader looked back towards the forest and said two or three words in his own tribal language, which few if any white men can understand, and made a motion with his hand.

In a few seconds several quarters of the bush became alive with Pygmies. There were fifty or more, men, women, children and tiny babies. They came forward slowly, eyeing us cautiously. All of them, especially the men and boys, were most interested in my arrows. While they chattered back and forth among themselves, the rest of our group eased forward and asked to see the bows and arrows of the Pygmies. Within five minutes all fear had been dissipated and the little folk were laughing and asking questions.

When Bigelow told them we had come from Pat Putnam's camp and wanted to make a motion picture of a Pygmy net-hunt, they agreed to put on a big one for us. All of them knew Pat Putnam and seemed to love him. If we were friends of his, they would help us in any way they could.

We moved the bearers into the clearing and soon had opened a sack of salt. The little people ate it as if it had been sugar. They began building houses for us to sleep in, but they forgot one small item: they were making the houses for us just the same size as those they were accustomed to building for themselves. Of course, we could not begin to get into the little huts, which they were covering with big *magongo* leaves. We hated not to use the quarters which they were so hospitably providing for us. Even the babies hardly big enough to walk were dragging a leaf at a time to be used. However, the little people saw the joke of the size question when it was pointed out to them, and we stretched a tent fly and rolled out our sleeping bags.

The Bambutis were wonderful hosts and I am sure were actuated by a genuine desire to have us happy, comfortable and well-fed. They gave us fresh meat (which they hunt and kill more successfully than any of the tribes of bigger natives), along with mushrooms newly gathered, and some kind of greens that made a crisp and wonderful salad. We later discovered that even the young children knew which mushrooms were safe for eating, viands that I would certainly never trust myself to pick out among all the violently poisonous growths in that overwhelming Ituri forest. Night soon settled down and after our long trek that day it was wonderful to rest in the cheerful glow of several large camp-fires.

The Pygmies were like a bunch of happy children, more amicable and optimistic and friendly than any other natives we had met in Africa. They seemed genuinely happy to have us as guests and they agreed to put on a really authentic net-hunt for us and demonstrate how they catch a great deal of their animal food. This had never been photographed, and I was eager to get moving pictures of the clever use they make of nets and the way the whole village participates in a hunt.

Soon our cook boy had our supper prepared and we ate it with pleasure. The fresh meat our hosts had given us turned out to be the flesh of young duiker, which had been caught only that day. The mushrooms were tasty and tenderer than any I ever ate before. while the salad was excellent. It was long after midnight before we turned in. In the meantime, we had shown the little people many gadgets of civilization which they had never seen before.

During the evening I shot a bow and arrow contest with a couple of their best archers. Their little bows were fairly accurate at close range, but beyond twenty yards the Pygmies did not shoot them well. They were astonished at the way my bow would shoot at fifty and sixty yards. The great penetration and speed of my arrows sent them into a hysteria of approval. Instead of being sorry that I could outshoot them, they would yell with glee when I made a good shot. Before I went to bed I had fallen in love with the whole tribe. They were so friendly and straightforward and smart that all of us agreed we liked them better and had more respect for them than for any other tribe we had seen in Africa.

We understood that these little folk were the greatest hunters in the whole continent and were sure these particular villagers would help us to get a good picture. We got into our bedrolls, knowing that we had no cause to worry. There was a warm feeling around our hearts. We were among friends.

We spent several days with the little people and they put on a most successful net-hunt for us. We were able to photograph authentically all the preliminaries necessary for the hunt, and were quite lucky in getting several shots of blue and red duiker (small antelope) actually hitting the net. It was necessary, however, before taking any pictures, to search diligently through the forests for breaks where the sunlight was allowed to shine through openings between the huge trees that towered in the Ituri Forest. We had carried along a roll of silver paper, from which we improvised reflectors to help concentrate the meagre light that filtered through breaks in the heavy timber. For the most part, we used the Eyemo hand cameras to secure the action shots, but Akeley and Sinclair were used to good advantage in making shots of the Pygmy camp and the preparations that preceded the actual hunt.

The Bambutis were so co-operative and worked so untiringly that we were sorry when we had to leave. All our party had fallen in love with them by then, and we were unanimous in the opinion that nowhere else in Africa had we found a people so wonderful as these little folk.

CHAPTER EIGHTEEN

MAJI MOTO

SLOWLY the half-ton pick-up truck eased down the steep side of the Riff Wall. The V-8 motor whined at high speed in low gear, the brake pedal was pushed well down. As each tyre bounced off a boulder, it slid several inches before the knobbly tread could take hold again. The narrow, rough treacherous tracks, that could scarcely be called a road, winding through the lush dense jungle growth, was reminiscent of an animal trail. One wrong move or the slightest mistake in the judging of distance would send our truck catapulting down the boulder-strewn mountain side. We held our breath and prayed that we could make the last half-mile to the valley below without a mishap. These tracks winding through the jungle were used much more by the beasts of the forest than by motor vehicles. Casumway. in the truck with me, sat forward on the front edge of the seat, his arm well braced against the instrument panel, his keen black eyes watching carefully the road ahead.

For more than half a mile we had travelled at this snail's pace coming down the side of the Riff Wall from the high plateau country above, in South Central Tanganyika, heading towards the plains below. We were on our way to Lake Manyara and Maji Moto. We had left Ngorongoro Crater early that morning, leading a small motor safari of two trucks and two jeeps. Somewhere, an hour or so back of us, came a one and a half ton truck and the two jeeps. Over the rough narrow tracks we could make much faster time in the half-ton pick-up than in the heavy truck. On leaving Ngorongoro that morning, I had told the rest of our party that we would wait for them at the native village in the valley below the Riff Wall, where we would have to leave the main tracks and go north to Maji Moto. Our maps did not show any road from the village to Maji Moto, but we had been told by the caretaker at Ngorongoro Crater that we could get the necessary information from the natives at the village. In order to save time, we had decided that I should go ahead as fast as I could from Ngorongoro to the village and try to obtain the necessary information by the time the rest of the safari arrived.

I was beginning to believe we were going to make it safely down the steep side of the Riff Wall when we rounded a sharp curve and came on to a straight stretch of road. Through a small opening in the jungle growth we could clearly see the plains below. ' However, as we half-skidded and rolled through the next sharp curve in the road, Casumway's excited warning grabbed me with the snap of a bear trap!

"*Simama, simama, Bwana! Mkubwa tembo, mingi, mingi hapa! Simama, simama!*"

When translated from Ki Swahili, native dialect, this meant: "Stop, stop, Master! Big elephants, many, many here! Stop, stop!"

Casumway was not jesting. No more than fifty yards down the road in front of us was a great herd of elephants. In a few seconds a hundred questions raced through my brain which only augmented the fear that already gripped me. Would I be able to stop the truck? Would these elephants charge? Why had I taken the chance to travel down this treacherous road without first sending Casumway ahead on foot to make sure there were no elephants in the road? How dumb could a fellow get? These and many other such thoughts came to me before I could reach forward and cut the ignition switch. I realized, however, that this was no time for panic. A quick application of the brakes would lock the wheels and cause them to skid out of the ruts. Once out of those deep ruts, we would go over the side and fall a thousand feet below. I applied the brakes a little harder. I could feel them take hold and the truck slowed down a bit. One rear wheel hit a boulder and almost bounced out of the tracks. All four wheels skidded a foot or so, but managed to stay in the ruts. We were less than forty yards away from the beasts now and the rear end of a big bull elephant almost covered the road. There were mamas, papas and babies, the most dangerous of elephant herds, I well knew. Yet the truck still went forward.

The bull in the middle of the tracks had a limb of an acacia tree in his trunk the size of a man's leg and was switching it back and forth over his rump as though swatting flies. Luckily for us, the elephants had not got our scent, for the wind was in our favour. Nor apparently had they seen us. Fortunately they were all headed down the road, facing away from us. Even though they had not got our scent, nor yet seen us, they must have heard us coming. Nevertheless, they did not seem in the least perturbed, nor did they show any signs of sensing our approach.

We were less than thirty yards away from them now and it seemed I could not stop the truck. At this point the big bull gave the limb a mighty heave and threw it over his back into the road, where it landed with a terrific thud. I was sure he had seen us and was making ready to charge.

I was so frightened that I shoved down with all my might on the brake pedal and locked all four wheels. The truck started to skid. I grabbed the door catch and made ready to bail out if the truck started over the side, but miraculously the vehicle stayed in the deep ruts and finally amidst a crushing of rocks and gravel it came to a stop.

The rear end of the big bull, still blocking the middle of the road, was not more than seventy-five feet in front of us, much, much too close for comfort. We waited breathlessly for a couple of minutes, minutes that seemed like hours. The bull never moved except to wave his huge trunk around and switch his paddle-like tail. Finally the whole herd started to move down the tracks. A few yards, and they were out of sight around a sharp bend.

Casumway started to open the door of the pick-up. I stopped him abruptly. The rear end of the big bull had no more than disappeared around the bend when his head re-appeared, his great trunk raised high into the air, testing the breeze. He was looking straight at the pick-up. As he gazed at us his tremendously big ears waved back and forth.

Casumway realized now why I had not let him open the door of the truck. I am thoroughly convinced that, had he been in sight, the bull would have charged. He evidently had known that the truck was there all the time, but for some unknown reason had not definitely connected it with man. He was suspicious, but he was not sure. I could see that he was nervous and a bit perturbed, but as long as he did not see a human being he would not become angered. He came towards the truck, still watching very closely and testing the air with his trunk.

We never moved a muscle. I was positive he had not distinguished us inside the cab of the pick-up.

There was a giant rubber tree near the tracks where the old bull stopped in his advance towards us. One of its huge limbs came out over the road. When the bull came to it he reached up and encircled it with his trunk, then with one mighty heave tore it from the trunk of the tree and dashed it to the ground. The strength of the beast was appalling.

At last he turned his stern and shuffled down the tracks, letting out a bellow that could be heard for miles. When he was gone from sight, I realized I had not breathed normally for some time. I heaved a great sigh of relief and waited. Casumway and I exchanged glances. We grinned but never spoke. I felt as a man must feel when he has been pardoned from the death chamber. How close we had come to death we will never know. Had the elephant either seen or smelled us, I am convinced, that would have been our finish.

We waited a good fifteen minutes before we moved, spoke or got out of the cab of the truck. Before we finally ventured forward, we lowered the windows and listened. We could hear the great herd a considerable distance below us, tearing the limbs from trees and pulling the vines out of them. Finally we silently opened the doors, got out of the truck carefully, and quietly went down the road. Fifty yards below where we had last seen the elephants, they had turned off the tracks and headed down the steep Riff Wall at right angles to the road. At the spot where they had left the trail, we stopped and could hear them plainly a good 300 yards down the mountain side. From the number of tracks and the amount of devastation left in their wake, we estimated there were at least 150 in the herd.

After clearing the road of all the broken limbs and small trees left by the herd, we made our way down the side of the Riff Wall to the plains below. Here the road straightened out. It paralleled the course of the Wall at a distance of a few hundred yards.

A mile or so farther along the trail we came to a clear, cool brook that emerged from the Wall. It continued beside the road for a hundred yards or more. On either side of the stream there was a wide strip of forest, mahoganies, acacias, wild rubbers and other varieties of jungle growth spiralling high into the sky.

At one spot between the road and the brook there was a clearing. In it was parked a light panel truck, and beside it a white man was eating his lunch as he sat in a camp chair.

Not having seen a white person other than those of our own company for six weeks and more than 800 miles of travel, I stopped and spoke to him. It was most unusual to run across one lone white man so far out in the bush. He proved to be an Englishman and was so cordial that I pulled the pick-up off the road and had a chat with him.

I learned that he was connected with the Tanganyika Game Commission in an official capacity and was on his way to Arusha for a meeting. He told me that in his younger days he had been quite a sportsman and hunter. He had lived in Tanganyika for over forty years and was well acquainted with all the best hunting country in South and Central Africa. I told him that we were in the territory making a motion picture, and that the rest of my safari would be along shortly.

Being a Game Commissioner, and having been a successful sportsman hunter he, I felt sure, could give me information regarding Lake Manyara and Maji Moto.

"By the way," I said: "Are you familiar with the hunting conditions around Maji Moto?"

At the mere mention of the name, his expression changed and his keen blue eyes fairly sparkled. He looked me over carefully before he spoke and what he said was a direct question rather than an answer.

"I say, my boy, you're not thinking of taking a safari into Maji Moto and making camp, are you?"

"That's the reason for my being here," I said.

"I have hunted that area several times in my younger days," he went on, "and even though I have shot game in most all of Africa, I want you to know that the game around Maji Moto and Lake Manyara is the most dangerous I have ever encountered. For what reason no one has been able to learn, but these animals are simply mad. A great number of them will charge on sight, without provocation." Apparently warming to the subject, he continued: "There have been several hunters killed there in recent years, and it seems each season the beasts become more treacherous. I myself while walking through the forest with a companion was tossed there by a cow buffalo. Returning from an elephant hunt, I was charged without warning and she

This crocodile, shot with bow and arrow,
had killed a native guide

Crocodile killed by an arrow on the
Semliki River, Belgian Congo

The author and a friend proudly hold a gigantic python killed with bow and arrow

Howard Hill sails along in a jungle-made blind, unaware of the deadly python ahead

tossed me before I could get in a shot. My life was saved by my companion who felled her with two shots in the head from a double elephant rifle."

What the Britisher was telling me, only corroborated what I had already heard from the natives. Yet, knowing how prone the natives are to exaggerate the dangers of all animals, I had not been too much impressed. But hearing it from this experienced hunter, I was sure there was considerable truth in what he told me.

The Englishman evidently knew I was more than a little impressed with this information. He looked at my pick-up truck and when he saw the California licence plates, he smiled and said: "To my knowledge, no one has ever camped in the area of Maji Moto except two Americans." At this point he laughed. "We refer to them as the crazy American chaps." He hesitated.

"What happened to them?" I asked.

"Oh, not much. The second day they were there and while they were out hunting, a rhino found their camp and destroyed it completely. When they returned, even the two crazy Americans decided to clear out. I tell you, my young fellow, Maji Moto is a most dangerous vicinity and I would advise you to forget it. It is no place to make camp or to shoot pictures."

During the next few minutes I learned from him just how to get to Maji Moto. I would first have to persuade the natives to build a bridge across a swift, narrow river. According to his information, this river washed the bridge away during the rainy season every year and another had to be built by the first party that wanted to go to Maji Moto. At the moment the bridge was out.

Finally we heard the big truck and the rest of the safari coming. The commissioner looked at his watch and got up, folded his camp chair and climbed into his truck.

"I say, old chap, I must be running along. It's getting late and I have a long way to go. It has been grand seeing you and I wish you the best of luck."

Without further words he drove away. As I stood watching him leave, I was sure he had already put me in the class with the other "crazy Americans."

When my men came up with the rest of the safari they pulled off the road into the clearing. While we had our lunch, I gave them all the information I had obtained from the commissioner.

M

They, of course, were interested and impressed, and agreed that it would be most dangerous to camp near Maji Moto. However, we had spent many weeks and travelled hundreds of long weary miles to get there, and none of us was prone to give up now that we were only twenty-five miles or so away.

We kicked the idea around for quite a while and finally decided we would at least have a look at the place. It was possible to camp where we now were and go to Maji Moto every day, but the fifty mile drive over the terrain necessary to get there was too difficult and would consume too much time. We decided, if we were to work the country at all, we would have to camp somewhere close to Maji Moto.

Now that we had learned that this place was out of bounds for other safaris, our desire to see it had a greater fascination than ever. We found the native village nearby and learned it would take a week or ten days for the native workmen to build a bridge. Despite this delay, we decided to have it done.

While Wayne and Mike took the pick-up and went into Arusha 150 miles away to get some needed supplies, the rest of us established camp and helped the natives construct the bridge. In five days it was completed. However, it was not strong enough for either of the trucks. On the morning of the sixth day, leaving the trucks behind, we headed towards Maji Moto with the two jeeps well loaded with camera equipment and a light camping outfit.

Because we had heard so many exciting stories about the viciousness of the animals of Maji Moto, we entered the dense forest beyond the first river with a great deal of caution and some anxiety. The old tracks over which no one had travelled for many months were partially blocked by new growth in several places. Our native boys, with the aid of machetes, cleared each of these obstacles in turn and we finally arrived at the last river which formed the south boundary of Maji Moto.

This stream, even though narrow and shallow, was extremely swift. After considerable inspection as to the best route to use in crossing it, we drove one jeep through. The bottom of the river consisted of soft, shifting sand, and once or twice the heavy jeep all but stalled. but we finally made it safely across. Then we rigged a chain from the back bumper of the first jeep across the river to the front bumper of the remaining one and had no difficulty in getting the second jeep across.

A few hundred yards beyond the river we came out of the thick forest on to a wide flat plain. The dim tracks wound through high buffalo grass. I was driving the lead jeep and Wayne Stotler, some thirty yards behind me, was at the wheel of the other one. I was cruising through the high grass in second gear, and was rounding a sharp bend in the trail when I all but ran into a big rhinoceros. He was standing with his hind quarters in the road.

I made a quick lurch to the left in order to miss him and at the same time trampled down on the accelerator. The big rhino swapped ends with the agility of a polo pony, and made a mad lunge at the side of the jeep. I was sure he had us, but as the accelerator went down, the jeep leaped forward. He missed us by inches and ploughed into the high grass on the opposite side of the tracks. In a flash he was out of the grass and back into the road, this time behind us. He came after us with all the speed he could muster, snorting at every jump. The jeep was rolling at a fair clip by this time and I felt sure he was going to have a rough time to catch us. However, we never started to pull away from him until we had attained a speed of over thirty miles an hour.

A hundred yards or so from where we first came on to the beast, the road led out of the tall buffalo grass and across a long wide smooth meadow of short bunch grass. The ground was firm here and the road straight. I was sure then that the angry rhino could never catch up with us unless the motor failed. I could easily have pulled away from him, but I was aware that Wayne was not far behind me. I knew that should we pull away from the beast he might stop, turn back and catch Wayne head-on as the latter came out of the tall grass.

I drove just fast enough to keep about twenty yards distance between the jeep and the oncoming rhino, until I had lured him a good 200 yards out into the open meadow. In the meantime Wayne had his jeep out of the high grass and was coming in back of the rhino. Seeing this, I immediately shifted into high gear and pulled away. He soon gave up the chase and stopped; then he heard Wayne's jeep coming in behind him and immediately turned to face Wayne. At once he charged head-on at the oncoming jeep.

We had stopped to watch the show. This was not the first time a charging rhino had been after our jeeps, and I felt comfortably sure that Wayne would be capable of outmanœuvring the angry beast. It looked for a few seconds as though the jeep and rhino were going to meet head-on, but at the last instant Wayne made a sharp turn to the left and the rhino shot by on the right side of the vehicle, missing him by a foot or two. Before he could stop, turn and charge again, Wayne was well ahead of him and going fast. The disappointed and tantalised rhino stopped, pawed the ground with his front feet and snorted a few times, all the while shaking his head.

At that moment, I thoroughly believe, that particular rhino would have charged a locomotive had one been close at hand. As there was nothing else in sight to charge, he finally calmed down a little, turned and started trotting back towards the high buffalo grass. We were too far away from him for his liking. He was one mad and disappointed rhino as he left us on the open plains.

We soon came within sight of Lake Manyara. It stretches north and south and is about thirty miles long by six or eight wide at its greatest width. The Riff Wall that also runs almost due north and south at this point is parallel for the most part to the east side of the lake. Incidentally, this is the same Riff Wall that starts in Egypt and runs from there down into North Rhodesia, a distance of over 3,000 miles. The Riff Valley in Egypt is bounded on one side by this freak of nature, and perhaps it is from this valley that it takes its name.

In some places along its course, the wall rises to more than 2,000 feet above the surrounding country. In flying from Alexandria, Egypt, to Nairobi, Kenya, a great portion of this outcropping of rock can be seen from the plane.

The distance from the shore of the lake to the steep rock cliff that forms the wall at this point varies greatly. At a couple of places it is but a few hundred feet, while at others it is two or three miles. There are places where the wall runs straight and fairly close to the lake for more than a mile, then cuts sharply back away from it. The ground near the shore of the lake is usually sandy, but in a few spots there is a black mud or gumbo-like soil.

A strip of meadow runs along the edge of the lake and varies in width from a few feet to a mile or more. Where this meadow stops, the forest begins and runs back to the wall and in some places also along its sides and up to the top. Giant acacias, wild rubbers, mahoganies and a variety of thorn bush constitute the forest. The thorn bush are found mostly near the edge of the meadow and near the top of the wall. The dense forest and an abundance of grass and water make the semi-isolated area an ideal feeding ground for many varieties of big game animals.

From the top of the wall eastward, the country is almost void of forest. There is considerable cultivation by both natives and whites and this fact offers little encouragement for wild life. However, nowhere in Africa did we see a more natural and ideal spot for big game animals than here at Maji Moto and Lake Manyara, and nowhere else in Africa did we find such an abundance of the large animals.

There were two main herds of elephants that lived in this area. One numbered about 125 head, while the other had well over 200 animals. Once when we were tracking the smaller herd through the forest, they led us to the second and larger herd. Seldom in this modern time is one fortunate enough to see so many elephants at once. There were well over 300 around us.

The name Maji Moto means in the Ki Swahili language "water hot." About half way along the eastern shore of the lake where the Riff Wall comes within 200 yards of it, a high rocky cliff goes straight up for more than a thousand feet. Out from under this cliff a series of large sulphur hot springs rise at boiling temperature. Several small brooks are formed by these gigantic springs. As they run towards the lake, over the yellow sands, they fan out and form half a dozen shallow, swift running streams. To these hot streams the elephants come at night and stand in the steaming sulphur water for hours. Oftentimes they drink huge quantities of this sulphur water and it acts as a purgative to the beasts.

The native chiefs claim that this water has great healing powers. They told me that the elephants had learned that if they drank this water, it cleaned out their system and they had no disease. They said the reason the elephants stood in the water for long periods of time was to allow the healing powers of the water to take the soreness out of their bruised and lacerated feet and legs. They told me that for many hundreds of years the natives from far and near had come to Maji Moto to bathe and drink the water for health purposes. I cannot verify the accuracy of these statements, but I can truthfully say that I have watched on a moonlight night many elephants come to this spring and stand in the water for hours. I have also seen them drink it in great quantities. Nowhere else in Africa, I can attest, did I see elephants whose skins were so smooth as those at Maji Moto; whether it resulted from the sulphur water or not, I do not know.

However, there were no natives living nearer than thirty miles of Maji Moto, except on the west side of the lake. All those who came to bathe and drink, crossed the lake by boat. The chiefs assured me that the wild beasts in this district were so vicious that no natives dared grow crops or build a village anywhere nearby. Some of the native boys in our safari who had old sores on their feet and legs, which we had been unable to cure with medication, soaked themselves in this water only a few times, and the sores were healed.

Most all of the bovine animals came to the hot springs to drink, but we saw only the elephants stand in it for any great length of time. Late one evening there were three Cape buffaloes wallowing in a pool of hot water and black mud near the shore of the lake. However, most Cape buffalo wallow several times a day during the hot dry season in any convenient mudhole. The same habit is followed by the rhinos. The reason for this is to discourage flies, ticks and other insects that attack these creatures in swarms. Even though the rhinoceros hide looks like armour plate, it is fairly soft and the heavy creases in the skin are very tender. The ticks fasten themselves to the hide at the flanks, ears and other vulnerable spots where the skin is pliable.

There are several types of tick birds that follow the rhinoceros and buffalo. It is not unusual to see a dozen or more of these birds on top of the back of a single rhino. Often-times one is able to locate these beasts by first seeing a flock of tick birds flying above them. Once we saw an old bull rhino lying stretched out in the open meadow and there were more than fifty tick birds giving him a thorough going over. He seemed to be enjoying the cleaning, because he lay perfectly still and let the birds walk all over and around him, pecking off the ticks.

Several miles below Maji Moto spring we located a spot where we decided to set up camp. There was a low narrow backbone of ground that came out across the meadow from the Riff Wall to the edge of the lake. Along the narrow ridge there were several giant thorn trees. Where it ran out near the lake, there were six or eight of these trees in one clump, forming a semi-circle. The closed side of the semi-circle was towards the Riff Wall while the opening faced the lake. We set up camp under these trees, inside the half circle.

Between the trees on the side facing the Riff Wall we lashed heavy timbers to form a strong fence that would withstand the best efforts of any of the heavy animals except an elephant. It was not likely that elephants would come so far away from the forest to make an attack, a good quarter of a mile. The trees at our camp could be easily climbed if rhino or buffalo disturbed us.

In front of the opening towards the lake we parked the two jeeps in such a way as to block anything coming from that direction. However, we were entirely vulnerable to lions and leopards, but that was a chance we had to take.

Before sunset we had our camp well established. There were herds of wilde-beeste (gnu), zebra, impala and a small number of reed buck and wart hogs visible from our camp as the sun went down. The place was literally alive with animals and as it began to get dark, more herds came out of the forest on to the plains.

Just before total darkness, we spotted with the aid of our field-glasses a herd of about 200 Cape buffalo feeding out on the meadow a mile or so north of camp. We heard lions roaring in the distance in several directions. Three lordly giraffes ambled by, stopped and had a good look at us. These docile, lovely creatures are to me the most fascinating of all living animals. Every time I see one of them I am reminded of what the backwoods farmer said when he first saw one at a circus. He looked at the giraffe a long time most carefully without saying a word. Finally, he turned to his wife beside him and said: "Honey, there just ain't no such animal."

We stayed up late that night, even though we were worn out from travel and extremely tired from the strenuous day's work. The distant roaring of lions, the grunts of hippos in the lake and the weird maddening laugh of the hyena made us nervous. We could not help remembering the warnings given us by the English commissioner and the many tales that had been told us by the natives. The plain truth was, we were scared. We did a lot of kidding to ease the tension. Finally, we went to bed and were soon asleep.

At about four the next morning I was awakened by the low growl of a lion close at hand. I was out of bed and from under my mosquito netting in a couple of seconds, flashlight in one hand and rifle in the other. Listening carefully for the next growl, Ed. Hill was beside me with his rifle cocked and ready. It was at this tense moment that the deep-throated rumble of a male lion very close to us broke the stillness. As the strong beams from my nine-cell flashlight enveloped him, he cut the growl short and quickly faced us. He was no more than sixty feet away, a huge old male with a ragged unkempt mane. I could see the scars about his face and nose that told of his many fierce battles. He was staring straight into the strong rays of the light. The black tip of his tail whipped from side to side; he was ready for the kill! Back of him I could see five other full-grown lions, two male and three female. They were also looking in our direction, but fortunately seemed not to be angry at the moment.

Ed. started to raise his rifle slowly. I knew that this was no time to start trouble. One shot and the whole pride of six lions might be upon us.

I whispered: "No, no! Ed.!" and cut off the light.

The next ten seconds were the most tense I have ever experienced—six lions only a few yards away, with an angry leader ready to charge, was enough to scare the daylights out of anyone.

Again the stillness was broken by the growl of the old male. It seemed no closer than before. We waited another few seconds. When he growled a third time I thought it sounded a little farther away from us.

It was at this point I became aware of my knees trembling like a quaking aspen leaf in a gentle breeze. I waited a full half-minute and turned on the light. I could see six lions moving away with the tough old male bringing up the rear. As the light struck him he again turned to face us. I lost no time in cutting the beam; it seemed to infuriate him and I had no inclination to displease him at that hour of the morning.

Ed. and I waited a full minute in the still darkness. Not another person in our camp had been awakened except my head tracker, Casumway. He was directly back of me, only a couple of feet away. He whispered: "*Simba ku-ondoka*" ("Lions going away.")

Casumway was right. The lions had gone a hundred yards

or so towards the forest. There they set up a chorus of roaring that brought all the rest of the camp out of bed on the double. As flashlights were turned on, I yelled at the top of my voice. "Turn off those flashlights."

The other fellows had not seen Ed., Casumway and me standing in the darkness.

After a few less tense moments I told Casumway to start a fire. But now we could hear the lions roaring inside the forest towards the Riff Wall. The fellows would hardly believe us when we told them how close the cats had been to our camp and how near we had come to being charged by them.

We sat up the rest of the night, and believe me, there was no one sleepy! So went the first night at Maji Moto, and the weeks that followed offered us many another thrill we shall never forget. But that is another story.

CHAPTER NINETEEN

ONE MEMORABLE DAY
AT MAJI MOTO

A F T E R we had been camped at Maji Moto a couple of weeks our supply of staple foods began to run low. One morning when we arose about daylight there was considerable fog hanging over the area, and as there was no chance of shooting pictures under such conditions, it seemed to be a good time to replenish the larder. Wayne, Ed. and Mike got in one of the jeeps and headed back to our base camp to get more food.

Arthur Phelps, our native boys and I planned to stay in camp and get everything ship-shape while the other fellows were away. However, they had been gone less than an hour when the sun burst through the thick blanket of fog, and within a matter of moments the latter was completely dissipated. A clear blue sky above us, with only a few fluffy thunderheads near the horizon, made it an ideal day for picture taking after all.

Cleaning camp was quickly forgotten and soon Arthur, Casumway and I were headed north along the lakeshore in our second jeep, looking for animals to photograph. We knew how dangerous it was to play hide-and-seek with the big game around Maji Moto with only one jeep at our disposal, but by now we had seen so many animal charges that we were getting used to it. If anything did go wrong with the motor or the steering apparatus while ducking elephants, rhinos or buffalo, we would be gone goslings without the other boys and the jeep they were in. If a fellow, however, spent too much time thinking about *all* the things that might go wrong in a place like Maji Moto, he would soon wind up in the madhouse. Besides, the little motor was purring like a kitten with a saucer of cream and the steering gears were working perfectly.

We passed up a big bull rhino caked with fresh black mud and two giraffes that we saw feeding on the thorn brush near the edge of the forest. I told Arthur I had a feeling we were going to have some wonderful luck. Just then Casumway, sitting in the back of the jeep, touched me on the shoulder and pointing off towards the lakeshore, said:

"*Kifaru! Maba, toto, haka!*" This meant: "Rhinos! Mother, baby, there!"

"*Indio, iko mousiri!*" ("Yes, very good!") I replied.

I could see the big mother rhino with a half grown calf, standing in the deep mud at the edge of the lake. I stopped the jeep and Arthur hurriedly climbed back in the rear of it and got his camera ready for work.

We had already fastened the tripod securely in place and had the camera mounted, but Arthur had to get a light reading and set his lens. I told him to set his focus on the four-inch lens at infinity, as we would stop a considerable distance away from the two beasts to secure our first shot. I planned to move the jeep into position directly between the rhinos and the forest. They would have to come within close range of us to reach the cover of the timber if they chose to run, I reasoned, while if they made a charge it would be our turn to take cover. At any rate, we could take our first shot with the four-inch lens, then switch to the two-inch.

Arthur soon had things set and I started the jeep. I kept several hundred yards to the right of the animals until I got between them and the forest. Then I headed straight towards them and we were within a hundred yards of them before the mother saw us and turned to face in our direction.

Sixty yards or so from them I came to a deep buffalo wallow about three feet deep and several yards long. I swung the jeep sharply to the left and stopped broadside to the wallow. The reason I stopped behind it was that I knew if they charged us they would have to slow down to come through the mudhole, thus making it easy for us to elude them.

As soon as we stopped I cut the ignition switch and the motor stopped. One can hardly get steady pictures with a four-inch lens if he is shooting from a jeep with the motor going. Besides, I figured I had plenty of time to start it again if the beasts should charge. Art took a 20-foot shot as the two rhinos looked us over. Then they came walking towards us and he ground away as they came.

At thirty yards they stopped and had another good look. Arthur switched to a 27-mm. wide angle lens. The mother advanced about ten yards towards us, then stopped again and gave three or four loud snorts, and as the *toto* (baby) came up in back of her she lowered her head and up went her tail. This time she came with full determination to toss us.

Arthur yelled: "Here she comes, Howard!" as if I were asleep.

I yelled back: "Stay with her, boy. Stay with her!" I could hear the camera humming.

When she was about five yards short of the buffalo wallow I stepped on the starter, but nothing happened. The mama rhino came very near going head-first into the mudhole, but she slid to a partial stop, then ploughed through the heavy mud and came on. I was frantically tramping on the starter.

It finally took hold and the motor started. The rhino threw mud on Arthur as she made a swipe at the back end of the jeep with her long sharp horn. The little car had literally jumped out from in front of the angry beast.

She chased us for at least 100 yards, but the ground was pretty bumpy and Art had so much trouble keeping himself and the camera in the jeep that he had no chance, whatever, of getting any more pictures. As soon as the big rhino saw she could not catch us, she went back and got her baby, and they lost no time in disappearing into the forest.

As it later turned out, these were some of the best rhino pictures we secured on the entire trip.

A mile or so farther along the lakeshore we spotted six big buffalo bulls lying on the beach beside the lake. They had neither seen nor heard us and were enjoying the warm sunshine. I manœuvred the jeep into position between them and the forest, just as I had done in the case of the rhinos. This time, however, I did not cut the switch. Knowing that an idling jeep motor does not affect the short lenses too much, I told Art to use the wide angle lens entirely this time.

As we came in and stopped, the buffaloes got up and milled around nervously for a moment, then started on the run for the forest. They were going behind us, so we stayed where we were and Art got a good shot of them as they passed some forty yards from us.

I was just about to comment to Arthur that these buffaloes must not be natives of Maji Moto, since they had showed no fight, when suddenly they stopped to face us. They had come close to the edge of the forest but had not entered it. I was almost sure they had stopped for only a brief moment to have a last look before continuing their flight, but I had another thought coming.

They gazed at us for only a few seconds, then came trotting towards us. All six of them were spread out, forming a front about twenty yards wide. We held our ground and waited. At about fifty yards they slowed down to a walk, but kept right on coming towards us. Arthur was making pictures as they came. At about twenty-five yards they stopped. He got two or three individual close-ups as they looked down their noses at us.

In the meantime, they closed ranks and stood almost side by side, facing us. A huge brute near the centre of the group gave the ground a rake or two with his right foot, throwing dirt and grass into the air. Then he gave his massive head a vicious shake, sending saliva in all directions. This was the signal for something to happen, and it did. Six angry buffaloes lowered their heads and started straight towards us.

By that time I was anticipating such a move and I came out on the clutch and down on the accelerator. We were away and across the flat like a scared jack rabbit. Buffaloes are about the slowest of all big animals on the run although they can get away exceptionally fast from a standing start. We already had some wonderful buffalo pictures, so we did not crowd our luck further, by trying to work this bunch any more. Some experienced African hunters claim that buffaloes never charge in groups but I can only say that this is what I saw these six do.

We soon came to a point of timber that jutted out on to the plains within a couple of hundred yards of the lake. We stopped the jeep near the forest at this point to have a good look at the plains beyond, in order to see if there were any interesting animals feeding there. Arthur was using the field glasses and Casumway was watching a huge gaggle of Egyptian geese that were about to settle in the lake.

I happened to be observing a couple of zebras that were feeding a few hundred yards away. They had not yet seen us as we were partially hidden by the tall grass and thorn bush that grew near the edge of the forest. All of a sudden both zebras raised their heads and looked towards the forest to our right. Thinking that perhaps more zebras or other animals were approaching from that direction, I followed their gaze. To my amazement, I saw a flock of ostriches coming towards the lake at a fantastic speed.

An ostrich, once he gets moving, can trot away from any animal in Africa. The cheetah or lion can catch him by stalking and then charging, but once an ostrich really gets going he can trot past a herd of antelope in full flight.

These birds were running for all they were worth across the open meadow towards the margin of the lake. They were a good quarter of a mile away, but if they held their course they would pass within one hundred yards or so from where we were. I told Arthur to have a look with the glasses and see if he could tell what had alarmed the stupid birds.

He took one look, then told me that something was after them, and that it appeared to be several hyenas. I put the glasses on them and saw that a pack of wild dogs was giving chase.

Although normally a wild dog has no chance to outrun an ostrich over any given distance, yet once a pack of these dogs sets after any prey, they maintain a fast pace and keep running until their victim, no matter what it is, gives out. African natives claim that a wild dog can run all day at a good rate of speed, without rest. I cannot verify this statement, but after having chased wild dogs for miles at a fast rate in a jeep, I do not doubt the truth of it.

Our first thought was to wait until the dogs got right in the middle of the plain, then intercept and kill them before they could get back into the cover of the forest, but we decided to wait and see what the ostriches were going to do. We did not have long to wait, because the birds were really travelling. Although the dogs were losing ground at every stride, they kept right on following.

As the birds approached us, we could see that most of them were only half grown, but these could run just as fast as the older ones. We could hardly believe our eyes when they swept across our bow and right out into the lake. They never lost a stride when they hit the water.

Lake Manyara is extremely shallow in most places, seldom more than three feet deep. For the first hundred yards or so the water was no more than a foot deep. The birds travelled in the water at the same speed as they had on land, the only difference being that they merely picked up their feet a little higher as the water became deeper. They were several hundred yards out in the lake before they finally stopped and turned around to look back.

The dogs must have known they were beaten: when they came to the lake they stopped and gazed at the fowl a moment or two; then they waded out into the water and had a drink. This trick of the ostrich was one of the cleverest I have ever seen a wild creature employ to get away from an enemy. There was no way in the world for the dogs to catch the birds in the shallow lake. As soon as the dogs got into water more than two feet deep they would have had to swim, while the ostriches could trot about in water that deep almost as well as if on solid ground.

When we realized that the chase was over, Arthur got his rifle and I my bow and arrow. We made a sneak on the pack of dogs. I managed to kill two of the seven with my bow and Arthur got the other five with his ·30-06 before they could make it to the forest.

There are two creatures in Africa that are despised and hated by everyone; hyenas first, and wild dogs second. After once seeing these ruthless, slinking, filthy killers at work, a man never forgets his disgust at the sight. They breed so fast, however, and become so cunning that both seem to hold their own, despite there being no law to protect either. Several Game Commissioners and wardens with whom I talked told me that thousands of antelopes and gazelles are killed by these despised canines every year.

After we finished with the pack of dogs, we made some pictures of the ostriches standing out in the lake. I later spoke to several white hunters about this unusual incident, and not one of them had ever seen an instance like it, but they said they had been told by the natives that it did sometimes happen. It thrills me even now to think of having seen this trick of the ostrich, and I would say that he is not too dumb a bird after all.

We worked several miles farther up the lakeshore and ran into a big family of baboons, but they were so wild we failed to get any good pictures. However, we found a herd of eight or ten giraffes and were lucky enough to get good shots of them.

We always enjoyed photographing these lovely creatures. They are such magnificent and yet lovable animals that I cannot understand how anyone could bear to harm them. Many times we saw them stand behind thick clumps of thorn trees with only their heads protruding above the tops. There they would remain and quietly watch us until we came within a few yards of them. Not one ever offered to harm us in any way. In parts of the really wild country we visited, where few white people had ever been, some of the giraffes were so tame they would hardly run at all. They would stand and gaze with their big innocent eyes, fringed with extravagant eyelashes, while we shot all the pictures we wanted.

All of our crew loved animals and we killed very few of them and then only for food, except of course, the predators, including wild dogs, hyenas, jackals and in some sections lions and warthogs. Of all the wild creatures in Africa the stately inoffensive giraffe is my favourite. I have spent many hours just watching them, and even though they seldom play or do anything out of the ordinary, they are still fascinating.

We had had a wonderful day, filled with thrills and unusual incidents and we made some great pictures, but no longer was the light bright enough to take any more shots, even though the sun was still far above the horizon. We took the motion picture camera off the tripod in the back of the jeep, packed it away and headed back for camp.

Arthur remarked as we turned towards home that he had had enough excitement for one day. Little did we suspect that the greatest thrill of all was yet to come.

At one place where the Riff Wall runs parallel to the lake for half a mile or so and very close to it, we came on to a big herd of some two hundred elephants. They were heading south along the fringe of trees that grew just under the Wall, which at this point rose straight up for 1,000 feet or more. Immediately under the Wall was a narrow scope of forest about seventy yards wide, then a flat grass-covered meadow of about the same width between the trees and the lake. We were right out in the middle of this strip of meadow when we came abreast of the herd of elephants in the fringe of forest.

They were strung out for one hundred yards or more and were hurrying right along. The calves and yearlings were in a swinging trot, while the cows were moving along just under a

Young cheetahs—
harmless at this age
but potential killers

The author with two young cheetahs

A lion cub stands his ground

trot. I steered the jeep fairly close to the lakeshore where we could see a little better, then moved abreast of the leaders and stopped to watch them as they hurried past.

There were at least a hundred cows in the herd, but we saw not a single mature bull. There were, however, several cows as large as most bulls grow and their tusks were even longer than those of ordinary bulls, though I noticed that they were much smaller in diameter. One tremendously big cow was bringing up the rear, and I realized at once that she was the boss of the herd. She kept trumpeting every few yards, and when she came up to a straggler she would give him a prod with her tusk. Most of the time her trunk was straight up, testing the air.

She could hear the motor of the jeep but the sun was directly in her eyes when she looked our way, and the reflection of the light off the surface of the lake must have troubled her vision no little. However, she knew that mankind was about and she definitely did not like that fact. By the time she was opposite us, she had succeeded in speeding up the herd to a fast trot.

I moved the jeep forward again until I was a little ahead of the front of the herd. Fortunately, there was an opening through which we could get a good view, and I stopped the car again. By now there must have been fifty or more of the cows and yearlings trumpeting shrilly. It's a sound that makes the hairs at the back of one's neck tingle. The beasts were talking back and forth and getting up more speed all the time. We could hear the angry scream of the matriarch above the rest of the din as she brought up the rear. Finally she gave a mighty trumpet that was different from all the others, then was quiet. She was crossing the opening just opposite us at the moment and she was making good time.

Once more I pulled up even with the leaders and waited. We were getting a terrific kick out of watching the huge beasts drive through the forest. Although they were not stampeding they certainly were losing no time. When they were considerably more than halfway between the point where we had discovered them, and the big forest to the south into which they were heading, they topped a little hill. Beyond it was a wide shallow gulch or *donga* and as the elephants entered it they were lost from view.

As they disappeared from sight I noticed they were not trum·

N

peting any more. I had kept watch very carefully, but had not seen Big Mama, the boss cow, come over the hill. After a wait of a few minutes we had seen not a single elephant come out of the gulch and not one sound had we heard from them. I felt sure that something was afoot, and I kept my eye on the open space, convinced that the boss of the herd had never come across it and gone into the gulch with the others. I mentioned this observation to Arthur and he said: "Let's get out of here while the getting is good."

My curiosity was working on me, however, and I wanted to see what was up, so I just kept the motor going and waited. What I saw a few seconds later satisfied all the curiosity I ever expect to have concerning elephants.

About thirty yards away, exactly opposite us and taking cover behind a dense acacia tree was Big Mama sneaking up on us and making no more sound than a ghost. She had her big ears straight out and her trunk high in the air. She had spotted us and was coming in for the kill.

The instant I discovered her she came around the side of the tree in high gear. Her great ears were flapping like a couple of wagon sheets in a wind storm and she was screaming blue murder. This maddened challenge sent a chill of fright through me that still wakes me up at night, more than two years later. For a second I was frozen, but just for a second.

She was within twenty yards of us before I could get the jeep under way and, believe me, I poured on all the power I had. The back wheels were throwing grass, gravels and dust in the old girl's face, but it only made her madder. She came on still faster if that were possible. She was no more than ten yards from us before we picked up enough speed to hold our own.

As soon as I saw we were losing no ground in second gear I jump-shifted into high and we pulled away from her, but not until we had gone a good 400 yards.

In all my years of hunting and photographing all manner of beasts I have never been so scared for so long a time. It seemed as though it took a week to get away from that she-elephant. All the time Arthur had been yelling that she was gaining on us, but I just kept quiet and prayed that we would make it. Never again, I promised myself, would I mess around in a jeep with a herd of elephants, if I could just get out of this scrape.

Even after we got out of danger I never slowed down until we reached camp, some six or eight miles from the scene of the race. When we did pull into camp we stopped without a word having been spoken since we had left the mad elephant far behind. Cheerfully Casumway came out with the only word of English he knew.

"Okay," he said, grinning as he climbed out of the jeep.

He was right. After that day it was okay just to be alive.

CHAPTER TWENTY

CROCODILES ON THE SEMLIKI

T HE crocodile is not only the largest of all reptiles, but it is also the most vicious and the most dangerous. He is capable of and often does perform feats of strength that would seem im-possible, if not known to be true. For the most part he lives on a diet of fish, but if large animals come into or close to the water in which he lives and so afford him the chance, he does not hesitate to attack them. Natives of different tribes in Africa have been killed and devoured by this unwholesome creature.

Though he lives much of his time below the surface of the water, he breathes air, notwithstanding which fact he has been known to stay submerged for unbelievable periods of time. According to some scientists, the crocodile, like the alligator, has the type of skin that is capable of obtaining a certain amount of oxygen from the water surrounding him. The amount of air thus absorbed, however, is not sufficient to keep either of these reptiles alive indefinitely, especially if the individual is active while submerged. In some areas where these creatures hiber-nate during the colder part of the year, they lie for days with-out moving.

In Florida I once saw an alligator lie so long in shallow water during his hibernation period that moss grew on his head and back and covered those portions of his body to a depth of two inches. When warm weather arrived, however, the old fellow came to life and cleansed himself of this parasitic vegetation by rolling over and over in the mud. According to some natives I met in Africa, the crocodile often follows the same procedure of hibernation as does the alligator.

It is in localities where crocodiles abound and have not been hunted with rifles that they often become man-eaters. There lives in British East Africa an English trader who calls himself Rufiji, who has spent some forty years catching crocs and selling their hides. He told me that while camping on the shore of Lake Victoria in quest of the dread reptile, he had known large crocodiles catch and drown a full-grown zebra, as well as water buck, impala and half-grown Cape Buffalo. These statements sound incredible, I know, but it has often been proved that a twenty-foot croc is capable of prodigious feats of strength in the water.

While my party and I were camped near the mouth of the Mara River in Tanganyika, a native chief called Long Foot told me that his tribe lost many cattle every year to this deadly reptile. On the east shore of Lake Victoria where crocodiles and hippos live in the same vicinity I learned, first hand, that the croc, despite his courage and strength, will give ground when a hippo approaches. One day, while photographing crocodiles along a beach of Lake Victoria, I saw a large male hippopotamus wade ashore right in the middle of a dozen or more huge crocs that were sunning themselves. As the hippo came into view, all the reptiles made for the water and left him in sole possession of the beach. It would seem that the crocodile should have considerable advantage over the hippo in the medium of water by reason of its speed; however, from all I could learn from the natives and from what I have observed, the hippopotamus is king of the lakes. This beast has one of the biggest and strongest mouths of any living animal and once a hippo gets hold of a croc he can easily break him in half, while a crocodile has no chance of killing a full-grown hippo, or river-horse as he is sometimes called. I saw one of these ungainly creatures that had been badly wounded on a back leg and the teeth marks were definitely those of a crocodile, which to me proved that occasionally, at least, the two do engage in combat.

There have been so many conflicting stories told as to man-eating crocodiles that one hardly knows what to believe, yet I am convinced that almost any crocodile more than twelve feet in length would not hesitate to catch a man if found in deep water. One native boy about twenty years old was knocked from the bank into the Mara River and eaten by crocodiles while we were camped nearby. I shot a couple of the biggest reptiles in the vicinity with a lily-iron type arrowhead that had a flex areoplane cable attached, and we dragged them ashore and cut them open, but failed to find either the boy or any part of his clothing. There were many large reptiles in the river at the point where the boy was caught, however, and evidently I failed to get the culprit.

At one time many of these cold blooded reptiles could be found along the small streams, as well as in or near the large rivers and lakes, but of late years the creatures abound only in the big streams and lakes. Especially is this true in vicinities near civilization. Specimens up to ten feet long can still be found in small streams and ponds in the back country. Practically all of the native tribesmen are deathly afraid of the reptiles and when taking a bath or going for water the blacks select a shallow riffle where the crocodiles have no chance to get a victim without exposing their own hides.

Some of the largest crocodiles we saw in Africa, eighteen to twenty feet long, lived in the Congo River. Of all the crocodile infested streams on the Dark Continent, however, the Semliki, in the Belgian Congo, is the most noted. This river flows from Lake Edward into Lake Albert. Although not a large river, as streams go in Africa, yet it is deep and fairly swift. We had secured a considerable amount of motion picture footage of crocodiles in various places, but no matter where we went, whenever those reptiles were mentioned, someone would speak up and tell of the great numbers to be found along the Semliki.

After we had shot most of our picture, *Tembo,* and were headed back towards Stanleyville, we stopped by Lake Albert for some elephant hunting and had a go at the Semliki, which runs into Lake Albert at the south-west end of that body. It is necessary to go some twenty miles by boat to reach the Semliki. The closest village of any size near the river is Kisenyi and most hunters hire a boat there and make the run across the lake to the mouth of the stream. There is a sand bar, however, which blocks the mouth of the river, making it impossible for a sizeable boat to go out of the lake and up the river.

The natives at a small village near the mouth of the Semliki own a few skiffs and dug-outs, but no sane white man would risk travelling up that stream in one of these contraptions. Most people, however, who make outdoor adventure pictures, have a few bats in the belfry, anyway, so when we arrived at the mouth of the river in a Greek fishing boat that could get no closer than 200 yards to the mouth, I made arrangements with the headman of the village to take us up the stream in one of their canoes.

He assured me that he had a great war canoe. I had seen war canoes on the Congo that were fine, seaworthy craft, so I did not hesitate to strike the bargain with him. Shortly thereafter I saw three villagers coming out of the mouth of the river in the war canoe. Two of the men were paddling and the third was continually bailing water with a half-gourd that held about three gallons of water at each dip. I felt a twinge of concern, and when the canoe drew up beside our launch my heart sank.

Of all the beat-up, rotten, water-logged contraptions I had ever seen, this one was the worst. It was made of six rough, hand-hewn boards about eighteen feet long and sewn together with sisal cord. To keep the boards from collapsing the black boys had cut or bored holes through the side planking and had inserted sections of small tree trunks about the size of a man's leg. Then with pitch and moss they had chinked the gaping holes where the boards failed to fit close together. No wonder it required continual bailing! Had no one bailed it out, it would have sunk in ten minutes. There had not been one nail or piece of wire or any other kind of metal used in the entire construction of this monstrosity.

We got out a big box of rags and oakum and went to work, chinking the thing, but after a short time, we found that it was impossible to stop the leaking. In fact, when we forced the packing in tight enough to stop the entry of the water at one place, it spread the boards at some other spot, so that soon the packing we put in gave way and water poured in. Finally we gave up trying to prevent the leaks and three of us got in and rigged a tripod and set up a camera. With the added weight it required two natives to keep the canoe bailed out sufficiently to keep it afloat.

One of the native boys assured me that this war craft was perfectly safe in the roughest water, adding that he had made many trips across the lake in it; there was no need to worry. Knowing, however, that most African natives could teach Paul Bunyan much about lying, I still did not feel completely sold. We finally got it loaded, and with plenty of misgiving Ed., Wayne, Arthur and I, together with the crew of three natives, headed up-river. The seven of us and the camera equipment did not seem to overload the canoe, but only to make it leak faster. Even before we reached the village, a couple of hundred yards up the river away from the lake, Ed. had to take another half-gourd to assist the bailers in preventing the vessel from sinking.

We stopped at the village where the natives indulged in a little conversation and had a swig of *pombe* (their own brand of beer). They picked up two more bucks, each armed with his own half-gourd and we were about to push off when one of the native women came running towards the craft with a two gallon gourd of beer. The bucks were already feeling high. That native brew which serves them for beer has the kick of a Missouri mule. I was at the front end of the canoe and when I realized what the gourd held, I refused to let it be taken aboard.

One of the bucks who had just joined our party protested, but I told him if they had even one more drink I would neither pay them for the work already done nor proceed any further. I waved away the woman with the beer, shoved the boat off the bank, and pointing up stream, yelled: "*Sasahevi indoka hapa! Pasi, pasi!*" ("Go this way immediately! Quick, quick!")

Three of the bucks began to paddle and two to bale. We had gone less than fifty yards when my eyes bulged at the sight of a big croc swimming across the Semliki with only his eyes and the tip of his nose above water. I got a shot at him with the Eyemo camera while Arthur was grinding away with the Akeley. The reptile came within twenty feet of the canoe before he sank beneath the surface of the murky water. As long as we could see him, he was looking straight at me and seemed not the least afraid. In fact, it seemed to me as though he probably had breakfast on his mind. I said to the other fellows:

"Thank Heaven. that crocodile doesn't know how loosely this canoe is put together!" Wayne and Ed. laughed a bit shakily.

"One slap of his tail could sure put the skiff out of commission and dump us all right in the river!" Ed. agreed.

The more I thought about the situation the more frightened I became. I handed the Eyemo to Ed. and got my bow and arrow ready for action. We wanted to get a picture of my shooting a croc with the bow, and although I hadn't anticipated such prompt action I figured I might as well be ready.

The native crew was really hopped up on the *pombe*, and they were laughing and paddling like mad. The crazy looking canoe made good time. We rounded a curve in the river and for a good quarter of a mile on both banks we could barely see the ground for the huge crocs that lay sunning themselves.

There must have been 500 in sight, if there was one. I could hardly believe my eyes.

As we hove into view they slithered into the river. We knew by the great swirls in the water, made by the powerful tails of swimming crocs that these creatures were all around and under the boat. Arthur was shooting pictures and I just stood there in the bow of the boat with bow and arrow ready. I don't mind saying I was scared stiff.

One of the native boatmen struck a big fellow with his paddle and the monster up-ended. His great tail came several feet out of the water and made a sweeping curve as he lashed at the paddle. The boatman hoisted the paddle out of reach of the reptile and ducked low inside the canoe just as the tail swished over his head and struck the water with a terrific force. All the native boys roared with laughter. Even the one who had ducked just in time to save his head thought it was very funny.

" What a sense of humour these fellows have! " I thought, but perhaps it was the influence of the *pombe* that made it so keen.

The loud laughter sent every crocodile in sight scampering for the water. I yelled: " *Sasahevi simama!* " (" Stop immediately! ") They cut their raucous laughter short.

Most African natives are just like children, very hard to handle at times unless one keeps them under control with a firm hand. They are quick to sense any weakness and to take advantage of it, and once allowed to get out of hand they lose all respect for those in authority and often become dangerous.

On the other hand, they well understand right from wrong, and will hold in high respect anyone who demands obedience. Every now and then some buck who has drunk a little too much beer will try to run a bluff and if permitted to get by with it, trouble is sure to develop.

Our policy was to be more than fair with the natives of all tribes we encountered, but at the same time to be very firm. Following this rule, we had no real trouble at any time. I had never seen these particular boys before they came rowing the canoe out to our fishing boat. Had I allowed them to take the gourd of beer aboard I am sure we should have had trouble in keeping them under control, but the moment they saw I would not allow them the *pombe*, their respect for me increased.

At any rate, after they had scared all the crocodiles away, I ordered them to beach the boat. We then got out and took cover in the grass and waited for the reptiles to come back to the bank. While we waited, I told them that I had made a bargain with the headman for the use of the boat and for the necessary men to paddle it, that if they were not willing to do what their chief had promised, I would be forced to tell him of their conduct and that I would not keep my end of the bargain.

They agreed that I was right and said they had not meant to spoil the trip, but had just forgotten that we were making pictures. I said no more and for the rest of the trip they were very quiet and stuck strictly to their job. They were really expert boatmen, I found, and could paddle hour after hour without tiring.

After we had rested for about half an hour, some of the crocs had come back on to the banks and we continued upstream. A mile or so farther up the river we came to another bend. Beyond it was a low flat sand bar about twenty-five yards wide and fifty or sixty yards long. On this bit of sand the crocodiles were literally stacked on top of each other. By now the paddlers had learned that we wanted to get as close as possible to the creatures.

There was not a whisper as we came closer and closer to the bar. The crew made not the slightest splash nor did they touch the sides of the canoe with the paddles. The way in which they were co-operating was wonderful.

I got set for a shot at a monster on the very end of the bar nearest us, and at about twenty-five yards I drove a broadhead arrow right through his chest. The big fellow had been asleep and when the arrow struck him he leaped straight up a couple of feet and swapped ends. His great tail caught another croc amidships and knocked him right off the bar.

The wounded monster made a run at another brute nearby, but the intended victim saw him charging and scurried into the water. Evidently the injured reptile thought the other crocodiles had been responsible for his wound and he meant to retaliate.

The natives had seen the arrow go right through the tough reptile and they were amazed at the penetrating power of the broadhead. About the time I had a second arrow on the bow the wounded croc saw us for the first time and started for the river. In the meantime the canoe had glided to within ten or twelve yards of the bar.

As the reptile scurried towards the water he offered another broadside, but this time I drove an arrow directly under and just back of his right eye. It hit the brain. The impact sounded as though the missile had hit a block of hardwood.

The big croc plunged into the river and began up-ending; first his tail would come out of the water, then his head would appear. There was no use shooting again. I knew the second arrow had done the trick.

The paddlers handled the canoe most skilfully, keeping it clear of the threshing croc. At the sound of the second bowshot every croc on the bar had plunged into the river. The noise made by the reptiles churning the water sounded like thunder. The river all about our craft was boiling as the monsters made for deep water. The one I had shot soon stopped moving and turned belly up, but before we could get to him, he slowly sank to the bottom.

The moment a crocodile dies he will sink and will not rise again for several days. In this case I knew the victim would never rise, because crocodiles are cannibals, and where that many were gathered together and as hungry as they must be, I was sure the rest of the clan would devour him before the day was over. The water was a dark amber colour and one could see no more than a few inches down into it. We wasted no time trying to find him.

Beaching the canoe on the sand bar, we ate our lunch. The natives never carry anything to eat on such a trip, but we had plenty of food for them as well as ourselves.

They had done a swell job of paddling and of keeping the water bailed out of the leaky canoe. When I complimented them they were as pleased as children. My stock had taken a considerable jump in their estimation after they had seen me kill the huge croc with the bow and arrow. They said they used bows to shoot fish, but were not able to kill crocodiles with them.

I showed them some of my arrows and let each one shoot a few times. They used the pinch draw, or savage loose, as it is sometimes called and were able to draw my bow only a few inches. They told me they had never seen a white man shoot a bow before, and that they had never dreamed any bow could shoot so hard. Each of them wanted to buy my bow, but when I told them it was worth a hundred and fifty dollars they looked at each other, giggled like a bunch of adolescent girls, and said: " *Yeye wishka*," which meant literally: " She is finished," or about the same as the French "*C'est fini.*" In other words. there was no use to discuss the subject further.

We started the return trip down the river about one o'clock, but it had become overcast and there was not enough light to shoot pictures. We saw literally hundreds of crocodiles. At one spot right on the river bank, we came abreast of a small herd of six or eight elephants feeding near the water. I bounced a few blunt pointed arrows off their ribs and they stampeded through the marsh grass and were soon lost from sight.

Naturally, we made much better time returning with the current than we had made in travelling against it, so our arrival at the native village was long before nightfall.

I paid the headman what had been agreed and he divided half the amount among the five bucks who had gone with us and put the other half in his pocket. He explained to me that it was his boat and that he had made the bargain, so he felt he was entitled to half. To me it seemed he was getting much the better part of the bargain as he had done no work, but the paddlers seemed to think it was a fair split, so I said nothing. When the boys paddled us out to the launch, however, where we could not be seen by the headman, I gave each of the five a generous tip and they were more than pleased.

Under the influence of the bonus, they told us that if we would come back some other time, they would fix the boat so it would not leak and they assured me solemnly that they would never again laugh and frighten the crocodiles.

I promised them I would return the first chance I had, and I still mean to keep that promise. However, the next time I am going to take my own canoe, and it will not be laced together with sisal string, believe me.

CHAPTER TWENTY-ONE

THE KING OF BEASTS

No other animal in the world is quite so well known as *Panthera leo, the lion.* Although he is generally accepted as the king of beasts, many persons who have had an opportunity to observe and study him closely, realize that this impression is erroneous. The fact is that no single lion nor even a pride of them would dare attack a mature bull elephant or rhinoceros.

While in Africa, making the motion picture, *Tembo,* I took advantage of the opportunity to discuss the subject of the relative qualities of the lion and other big game with many well qualified authorities, and not one of them accepted the lion as king. Several white hunters, who had spent many years in the African bush, agreed without exception that the bull elephant is in reality master of the wild animal kingdom. In addition to the opinions of experts, my own observations bore out what they told me. On several occasions I personally observed instances in which full-grown maned lions gave way to both the elephant and the rhinoceros.

Once I was waiting on a high bluff of rock near an elephant trail with my camera ready as a group of my men went through the forest below my position to drive out a herd of elephants. A lone bull that had strayed from the herd chanced to come along the trail, leading in a northerly direction. At the same time there happened to be three lions going south along the same trail as that being used by the elephant. From my elevated position I could see them approaching each other. Long before they met, the lions scented the elephant and they stopped in their tracks, calmly gazed for a few seconds in the direction of the approaching elephant, then they left the trail and took cover in a clump of heavy thorn bush some thirty yards from it. The big bull, apparently not having either seen nor scented the lions, stayed in the trail, and when he reached the spot where they had turned aside, he raised his trunk and sniffed the air. Definitely, he got the scent of the cats, but he seemed not in the least disturbed. At any rate, he went right on up the trail just as though he had not smelled the lions.

On another day, while waiting in a camera blind near the edge of a forest close by a strip of meadow in Tanganyika, I was amazed to see an unusually big maned lion walk out of the forest and head across the meadow towards a lake that lay immediately beyond it. It was early evening and there was not enough light for making pictures, so when I saw the lion I picked up my field-glasses to gain a closer look at him.

He was an impressive creature, looking every inch a king of beasts. It had been a very hot day and out on the edge of the lake beyond the meadow there was an ornery old bull rhino lying in a mud wallow. The reason I knew he was ornery was because we had already had several brushes with this particular bull when we were crossing the meadow in jeeps. In working the country north of this meadow, it was necessary for us to cross it often, as our camp lay a mile or so south of it. Without exception, every time we had to pass through the meadow, this ill-tempered old individual would come for us. It is a fairly easy matter to out-manœuvre a rhino with a jeep if the ground is not too rough, and this meadow offered good footing, so we always managed to get by the battle-scarred old beast without too much excitement.

These experiences we had had with the bull rhino made me more anxious to see what would happen when the lion got near the old fellow, who evidently considered this meadow his own preserve. As luck would have it, the lion could not see the rhino, lying as he was half submerged in the black mud, and the wind was in the old bull's favour, preventing the lion from scenting him.

I felt sure the lordly-looking beast had started for a drink of water before setting out on his night's hunt. Anyway, he was heading straight towards the spot where the rhino lay in the mud, apparently asleep. I was deeply interested in watching the affair.

The rhinoceros has a wonderful sense of smell but his eye-sight is notoriously poor. The lion was still fully one hundred yards away when I saw the bull rhino slowly raise his head. Evidently he had scented the approaching lion. With unbeliev-able speed the ungainly looking rhino bounded to his feet and faced with his nose into the breeze. He trotted anxiously forward a few steps, stopped, sniffed the air, and gave a loud snort. He was on the prod and ready for action, but as yet he had not actually spotted the lion.

The big cat, hearing the snort, looked up and saw the ugly champion of the meadow. Immediately, the lion crouched low and growled. I could barely hear the growl, but feeling sure there was going to be a fight, I was highly excited. The muddy old rhino gave another snort and kicked dirt high into the air with his back feet, then came up-wind towards the lion on the double. The cat lay crouched very low to the ground and eyed the oncoming bull. When within about thirty yards of the lion, the rhino stopped. He had still not spotted his adversary, but he was looking in first one direction, then another, trying his best to locate him. Then suddenly he saw the crouching cat and shot forward.

He drove to within twenty feet of the cat at top speed, then lowering his massive head and without slowing his pace, he made a pass at the lion. The latter remained crouched low in the grass until the head of the rhino went down, then leaped high into the air, and the rhino shot under him. You simply would not believe how suddenly a rhino can stop and change ends, faster than any polo pony I ever saw. The cat had barely hit the ground before his enraged adversary was driving towards him again, head down.

At that point the lion let out an angry roar and headed for the forest as fast as his legs could carry him, with the rhino in hot pursuit, snorting at every jump. Few animals can run so fast as the lion and it could easily be seen that the big beast had no chance to overtake the fleeing cat, but I will say, he did his best.

The lion hit the forest no more than thirty yards from where I stood concealed in my flimsy brush blind. All the way across the meadow the lion had roared as he ran, while the rhino let out a snort every time he hit the ground. It was one of the most thrilling and exciting events I have ever witnessed. The angry rhino ploughed right through the underbrush after the yellow cat, but soon lost sight of him. So anxious was he to come to grips with the feline, however, that he literally tore holes through the underbrush looking for him.

After five or ten minutes the muddy monster trotted back to the meadow, where he shook his head vigorously, snorted several more times, then kicked sod and soil skyward with his back feet. I don't think I ever saw any other animal quite so perturbed. It is doubtful that any living creature can get more angry than does the rhinoceros, and this one seemed fairly to cultivate a mean disposition.

I only wish those who contend that the lion is king of beasts could have seen that one high tailing it across the meadow with the only thought in his mind, escape. I never did see that lion again, but the beat-up old rhino could be found any day, somewhere near the meadow if not in it. He seemed to hate every creature except the Tommy gazelles, the impala and the zebra. These he allowed to feed on the meadow he had appropriated as his own at any time, but wildebeeste, giraffes, wart-hogs and all other animals in that region were charged on sight. The only time we saw him give ground was when the elephants came down to the lake to drink. As soon as he saw or smelled one of them he took out for the forest, without putting up any kind of argument, but I'll bet it made him mighty mad. Evidently, some elephant had made a believer out of him; at any rate, he wanted no part of the tusker.

While camping in this same spot in East Central Tanganyika, we discovered a rolling plains country some little distance below our main headquarters. On the plains were vast herds of antelope, as well as zebra, wildebeeste and Cape buffalo. Usually where great numbers of such game abound there are also many lions as well, because as a rule lions follow the herds of other animals, so that getting food will be easy. It is my opinion that the big cats prefer zebra meat to any other fare. The reason for my thinking so is that we found five or six zebras killed by lions to one of any other animal species. Needless to say, we discovered plenty of lion spoor in this plains country, where these vast herds fed.

We decided to hang a few lion baits and see if we could get some pictures of the big cats. One morning Ed. Hill and I took a jeep, some heavy Manila rope, a rifle and two local Mohammedan native blacks and made a run down to the rolling plains.

Near the edge of a small forest that lay along the bank of a rivulet running through the plains country, we came on to much fresh lion spoor. After constructing as rapidly as we could a couple of blinds from thorn bush just inside the forest near the

The result of a deadly argument between a python and the
bow

No man can tell what any animal will do

spot, we rode out on the plains to get a couple of zebras to hang for bait.

It is the custom in that section to hang lion bait in a tree, in order to prevent its being eaten by the buzzards, hyenas, jackals and other vermin as soon as it is placed. Any lion that may find this can easily jump up and pull it down, or he may even climb the tree and help himself. At any rate, we spotted a herd of several hundred zebra a mile or so north, so we went after them. A quarter of a mile beyond the point where we came within rifle range of them, was a high rocky bluff, covered with scrub acacia trees and thorn brush. From this high spot could be seen all the surrounding plains country. The zebras saw us coming and began milling around as is their custom at such a time, but they never took to heel.

Ed. and I had agreed to allow the native boys to take a hind-quarter of the first zebra we should kill. The Mohammedan religion requires that any meat which is to be eaten has to come from an animal whose throat has been cut with a knife before the creature is dead. For that reason a Mohammedan native boy will hurry to any game that has been brought down, in order to cut its throat before life is spent.

When we drove within about two hundred yards of the herd, we stopped the jeep and I got out with the rifle. Followed by the two boys, I moved forward, away from the jeep the distance required by the African game laws, and selecting a fine fat zebra near the end of the herd, I took aim at the top of his shoulder and fired. There was a loud smack as the bullet struck, and the zebra went down. He had no more than fallen, however, when he bounded back on to his feet and took off away from the herd and in the direction of the high bluff already mentioned.

The rest of the herd, frightened by the report of the rifle, headed south in the opposite direction from that taken by the wounded beast. I took careful aim and again fired. This time the zebra up-ended and went down to stay. The two Moham-medans, knives in hand, were off like scared jack rabbits, making all speed for the downed animal.

In the meantime, Ed. came up in the jeep to where I stood and said: "Howard, you killed a zebra with that first shot." He pointed off to our left in the direction taken by the main herd.

I looked where he was pointing, and sure enough, about three hundred yards away there lay a dead zebra. What had actually happened, we learned later, was that the first bullet had missed its mark on the animal I was shooting at, and instead of going through the shoulders, had passed through the top of the neck, then after passing through kept right on its high speed way and struck a second animal in the chest cavity, just above the heart. The second zebra had stampeded with the rest of the herd and had gone a good two hundred yards before the bullet did its work.

Meanwhile, because we had been looking in the direction of the animal I had killed with my first shot, we had momentarily forgotten the second victim and the native boys. Just then, two of the most blood-curdling screams I have ever heard came to us across the grasslands from the direction of the Moslem boys. As we looked towards them we could see two dark spots moving towards us and followed by two big yellow cats. Never have I seen boys run so fast, but despite their best efforts, the lions were about to overtake them. I had no chance to hit the lions without endangering the boys, for they were between me and the beasts.

I laid a ·375 bullet to the right and behind the two fellows. It struck the ground no more than a foot in front of the cats and sent up a big puff of dust. Both lions swerved sharply to the left and I fired a second shot that hit the ground right under the belly of the foremost cat. The animal leaped high into the air and when he came down, he pulled up short and stopped.

The second one stopped too, but the boys kept right on coming. I held my gun ready, but did not fire again. I had no desire to kill the lions unless it was necessary in order to save the lives of the boys, and by that time they were a considerable distance in front of the beasts. The lions, surprised and no doubt somewhat bewildered by the concussion of the rifle bullets hitting so close to them, soon turned and trotted back towards the dead zebra.

As quickly as the boys had recovered from their fright enough to think and talk, they told us what had happened. They had reached the struggling zebra, they said, and had cut its throat when they heard a growl, and looking back, saw the two tawny cats bearing down on them. At that point they had screamed and taken to heel in our direction.

Actually, the lions had been lying on the high bluff, watching the herd of zebra, and when I had felled the one that was heading in their direction, they had immediately left their hiding place and started for the dying animal. We learned later that lions have been known to behave in this manner quite often, and we had no doubt that they regularly used the high bluff as a lookout. Anyway, when they had approached the zebra, they found that the native boys had beaten them to the kill, and they simply meant to get rid of the boys so they, themselves, could devour the zebra in peace.

When the boys had sufficiently recovered from their narrow brush with the lions, we secured the zebra that had fallen on the plain. Having hoisted him in a tree near one of our blinds, we then went for the one upon which the two lions were feeding.

Foolishly enough, we had not taken a camera, as we had had no idea of seeing lions before we even set the bait. It would have taken too long to return to camp and get a camera, so we decided to secure the second zebra and hang it near our second blind, as originally planned. Then, we thought, if the lions cared to, they could go there and finish their meal.

There was, of course, the possibility that the two lions would not relinquish the kill without a fight although they had not made it. Ed. and I decided to give it a try, anyway, and see just how much nerve was possessed by these particular cats. We knew we could always outrun them in the jeep. We had no desire to kill them. Dead lions make poor motion pictures and our sole purpose was to secure good pictures.

The native boys wanted no further truck with the cats, so we left them by the little river and headed the jeep towards the carcass of the second zebra. The lions saw us coming long before we got anywhere near them and, switching their long tails from side to side, they stopped eating and faced us. Ed. had his rifle ready just in case we should have to protect ourselves. We merely wanted to move their dinner and lure them to a spot where we might later have a chance to photograph them.

I was driving, so I kept right on going straight towards them until we were within fifty or sixty yards. A lion can move very fast, once he charges, and that was about as close as I felt it safe to go.

We were cruising at about thirty-five or forty miles an hour and I felt sure I could pick up speed fast enough to out-distance them should they suddenly decide to charge. However, when the cats still held their ground at that distance, I turned the jeep to the left and started in a wide circle around them.

I think the beasts would have charged if we had kept heading straight for them, but this new tack was upsetting. They kept turning to face us but they quit thrashing their tails, a pretty good sign that they were not going to come for us immediately.

While they eyed us and tried to decide just what to do, I started blowing the horn of the jeep and I pushed in on the clutch and gunned the motor, then let out on the clutch and accelerator so that the motor backfired two or three times, sending out a black puff of smoke at each blast. Evidently those cats had never seen nor heard such carryings-on, for they turned towards the safety of the high bluff at a long lope. I repeated the performance with the jeep, blowing the horn and causing a motor backfire. The lions, now thoroughly frightened, never stopped to look back until they were more than halfway to the rocky bluff.

Ed. and I cut in to the carcass and quickly fastened it to the back bumper of the jeep, then headed for the river. When we reached the two Moslem boys they could not understand how we had been able to take the kill away from the lions, but they were very happy for the reason that they would have plenty of meat to eat. One hind leg was removed and we hung the rest of the carcass in another tree, near our second blind, then made our way back to camp.

During the next few days we spent many hours in the blinds, but failed to get any pictures of lions. They never touched our bait, even at night. Finally we decided that the game all around was so plentiful that the cats must prefer to make fresh kills instead of eating the spoiled meat of baits. We never again saw the two lions that had given the native boys such a bad time.

CHAPTER TWENTY-TWO

AFRICAN ELEPHANTS

T H E African elephant, not to be confused with the smaller and more docile Indian branch of the family, is crafty and courageous, a most unpredictable creature and an extremely determined one when aroused. His craftiness is shown by the fact that although he may be perfectly aware of the presence of man, yet he often will show no outward sign of that awareness. Seldom does he give any evidence of anger until he suddenly charges. Particularly is this true if he knows the exact whereabouts of man. Many times when an elephant has scented a human, but owing largely to his own poor eyesight has not been able to decide on his exact position, he will become uneasy and in some cases display considerable anger. His displeasure is increased, no doubt, by the fact that he does not know in what direction to attack the intruder.

By far the greater number of elephants will stampede the instant they get the scent of man; there are, however, so many exceptions to this rule that the experienced elephant hunter anticipates the possibility of a charge. No dangerous animal should ever be taken for granted, and especially is this the case with the elephant. Those members of this species that have had little or no contact with white hunters may display much less caution than others that have been hunted by riflemen. By the same token, such beasts which inhabit unsettled and out-of-the-way sections, may be much more likely to charge than more experienced ones. However, an elephant that has been hunted and perhaps wounded will fight with more courage and sagacity when cornered or brought to bay than one that has had no previous encounter with man.

In Africa, the natives for the most part seldom attack the elephant, for the simple fact that they have no suitable weapons, and his lack of aggressiveness on the part of the natives may be largely the answer to the boldness of those beasts found in the back country. The fact is, that where elephants have not seen nor had any experience with men armed with the deadly high-powered rifle, they have no reason for being afraid. On the other hand, if they have been hunted by riflemen, have seen their own kind killed, and have perhaps felt the pain caused by the hot slugs from a heavy gun, they develop a fear and a hatred of man that often borders on insanity.

Facts have shown that some elephants after a few encounters with riflemen have become so cunning that they are all but impossible to track down and kill, yet they themselves may plan crafty methods by which to seek out and kill the white man. Many individual beasts after having been wounded, have become deadly and insatiable killers.

A wise and experienced elephant may know that man is tracking him, but instead of fleeing to safety, the beast is liable to lead the hunter into a trap where he can be ambushed. The more I learn about the sagacity of the elephant, the more I respect him as an adversary in the wilds. One must even feel an admiration for him, grudging though it may be.

Some scientists with little or no experience in stalking big game have often made the statement that no wild creature has a sense of reasoning, as I said earlier in this book, but that all wild animals act purely by instinct. On the contrary, all professional hunters, guides and experienced sportsmen know that such thinking will eventually lead one to sudden destruction. It is not a good policy to match wits with a cagey elephant or buffalo, a grizzly bear, a lion or a leopard too often if one has a desire to live out his allotted span.

Some of the true experiences related by such noted hunters as Selous, James Hunter, George Wood, Sir Albert Peace, the Hill boys (Harold and Clifford), Petrus Jacobs, Piet Schwarz, William Finaughty, Hartley, Gifford Teask, H. Biles, and Jan Vilgoen should be adequate proof that many animals become so smart the hunter must use all of his wits as well as his trusty rifle in order to save his own scalp. Ned Frost, Roy Glasgow, Frank Colcord, Wally Gravett, Col. Theodore Roosevelt, and many other well-known and widely experienced American hunters have told of encounters with grizzly bear which prove beyond any doubt that that beast possesses the power to reason. It seems to be another evidence of the egoism of mankind that he would believe himself to be the only living creature with a corner on brains and reasoning power.

As an illustration of the facilities for thinking possessed by the elephant, he has been known to run a man up a tree and upon discovering that he could not push the tree down or pull it up, has then placed his head against the trunk of the tree and shaken it with all his might in an effort to dislodge the person who was seeking safety. Often in a situation like this, the elephant, after making every effort to get at his foe and failing, has been known to leave the vicinity, later to sneak back quietly and under cover to wait until the intended victim, thinking the beast had gone, left the tree, only to be charged and killed. Who could deny that this is reasoning power?

In Tanganyika I met a white hunter named Thurston who had been attacked by a wounded elephant. He told me that the bull hit him with his trunk and knocked him several feet. The blow knocked the gun out of his hands and momentarily stunned him. When he regained consciousness he was lying face down and the elephant was standing directly over him. Not knowing where the elephant was as he came to his senses, the hunter turned his head to one side to have a look around. The elephant, seeing the man was not yet dead, seized him by his ankles, raised the man above his own head, gave him a couple of swings and threw him against a tree several yards away.

The poor fellow hit the tree a glancing blow and fell with both legs broken and his pelvis cracked, but still conscious. This time he landed flat on his back. Hearing the elephant coming towards him, he closed his eyes and played dead. For more than half an hour the beast stood over him. Finally the bull decided the hunter was killed, so he buried the man under a pile of leaves, limbs, trash and dirt, and went away. Thurston, however, had managed to get his arms over his mouth and nose without the elephant noticing the movement. This action had protected his mouth and nose enough that he could continue to breathe beneath the rubbish.

When the elephant had gone, some native boys who had been with the white hunter when the elephant had charged and had been able to escape, came back and found him. They uncovered the fellow and carried him several miles to a mission station, where after a day or two a doctor arrived and set his broken bones.

Seldom does one find an elephant quite so gentle as this one was. Usually when a wounded elephant succeeds in getting his adversary within reach he tries to obliterate him, and is more liable either to mash the victim flat, stick a tusk through the man's body, or to tear his limbs off, one at a time, than merely to bury him.

When we went to Africa to make the picture, *Tembo*, in 1950, I took along from California as my interpreter the Rev. Howard Bigelow, a Baptist minister, who had spent nine years some time before as a missionary in Africa. During those years he had bagged some forty-odd elephants, most of them rogues that were killing the native villagers and destroying their gardens. He often told me that elephants would not face the fire of a heavy rifle. His theory that all elephants would turn aside when shot head-on at close range, even though not hit in a vital spot, was corroborated by other missionaries we met and talked with in Africa. However, I was never able to banish from my mind the fact that I had read many stories by other more experienced elephant hunters that in no way agreed with this assumption.

A few months after our party had returned to the States we were shocked to receive word that Howard Bigelow, who had remained in the Belgian Congo, had been killed by a wounded elephant. I learned from a friend, at whose mission station Howard was working at the time of his death, that he had been killed because he did not believe an elephant would face fire. Bob Bothwell, the missionary, wrote me the story, substantially as follows:

Howard Bigelow had wounded a bull elephant (with only one tusk, it happened) and the beast had gone into some high grass. Bigelow immediately followed and when he came up fairly close to the bull it charged him. He began shooting it in the head, but despite the fact that he hit the beast three times at close range as it came for him and the fact that each bullet hit the bull in the fore part of the head, the shots did not stop him. Neither did he turn aside. Once the beast had Bigelow down, he gored him with his one tusk, which killed him quickly.

Altogether, the preacher had shot the elephant five times through the head with a ·375 Magnum rifle and each bullet had gone completely through the head of the bull, but not one of them had hit the brain. The enraged creature still had enough strength and determination left to carry out his deadly intent. Howard was a fearless and experienced hunter, but he had underestimated the courage and the reaction of some elephants. All the charging individuals he had shot previously had turned aside when hit in the head, but this one reacted differently and kept right on coming.

The four native boys who had been with Bigelow on the hunt had run for safety when the beast started his charge. Later, they went back and found not only the body of the white man, but also that of the bull which had died a short distance away. It was they who carried the report of the tragic incident to some plantation owners twelve or fifteen miles away and who in turn gave the account to Bob Bothwell.

There was once a very famous British hunter named William Finaughty, who said of the African buffalo: "On no account should one ever follow a wounded buffalo unless in open country. Many good men have lost their lives through neglect of this precaution."

Other men almost as famous as Finaughty have said substantially the same thing concerning the danger of following wounded elephants, lions, rhinos and leopards. It matters not how well one may be able to shoot a rifle nor how powerful that weapon, sooner or later every hunter who fails to exercise every precaution will be overcome by some beast, especially if hunting alone. The danger in hunting African big game is great enough without taking needless chances.

Sometimes sudden excitement will cause even the most experienced and cautious hunter to commit an act that is unwise and extremely dangerous. I shall never forget an encounter which Ed. Hill, Wayne Stotler and I had with a very large and angry bull elephant in the Belgian Congo. We were walking in a hippopotamus trail through high grass near the Rutshuru River, following the spoor of several elephants, and the signs had led us into the dense forest that bordered the river. As late afternoon arrived without our having sighted the quarry, we decided not to pursue them any farther and turned back towards camp. We had with us our head native tracker, Casumway, and were moving along another hippo trail when we came to a narrow neck of dense thorn brush that joined two large patches of the same kind of cover. Suddenly we came abreast of a very large bull elephant no more than forty feet off the trail.

We could see about half the animal. His chest and fore

shoulder were in plain view, while his neck, head, trunk, rear legs and most of his belly were hidden behind the brush. The bull was feeding on some vines and had no idea that mankind was near. By sheer luck the wind was directly in our favour.

I was carrying my elephant bow and arrow, while Wayne and Ed. each carried a ·375 Magnum rifle, as did Casumway. On seeing the elephant so near at hand and realizing that he did not know we were near, I thought that at such close range the open chest shot would be a perfect one for the arrow. Had I taken time to think twice I would have known better and would not have taken such a chance at so close quarters and under such poor shooting conditions. We did not take time, however, to consider the best possible approach to the problem, but immediately went into action.

I motioned for Casumway who carried my rifle to come near me so that I could take my gun should the beast charge after I had driven an arrow into him, as I confidently expected to do.

Ed. and Wayne faced the beast and I drew and raised my bow and let drive, aiming for the region of the heart just back of the foreleg and low down in his chest cavity. In my haste to get the arrow into the bull before he discovered our position, I had failed to notice a thin vine that hung down in front of me about ten feet away. It was not in the direct line of the point of the arrow, but an arrow seldom leaves the bow in a perfectly straight flight. The back end usually makes a couple of fast swerves right and left before the friction on the feathers has time to straighten it up and hold it steady on its course. As the long, extra heavy arrow left the bow, the back end buckled to the left and the front part of the shaft struck the dangling vine, so that the arrow ricocheted sharply to the right. As a result, it missed the entire chest cavity and shoulder.

We did not know it at the time, but the arrow had struck the surprised elephant in the jaw. The sharp broadhead cut through the skin and muscles, struck a lower jaw tooth and folded back on itself. The darting missile had hardly passed from sight when there was a metallic crack as the tempered blue steel blade struck the flat hard tooth of the beast.

There was an ear-splitting scream and a sound of breaking trees as the wounded bull ran through the thorn scrub as though it were so much broom sedge. He headed up-wind directly away from us. Had he come our way with the same explosive speed, I am sure I would never have had time to drop my bow and take my rifle before he was on top of us. I also doubt seriously that Wayne or Ed. would have had time to take aim.

As it happened, we got only a fleeting glimpse of the bull's rear end as he tore through the bush like a runaway locomotive. When he made the end of the patch of thorn trees some two hundred yards away, he cut to the right and headed for the river swamp. Then of a sudden he stopped, reared on his hind legs, and made a complete turn, at the same time trumpeting an angry challenge calculated to turn to white the black hair of a hunter. Above the tops of the grass we could see the arrow shaft protruding from his right jaw.

Three or four times the big bull reared on his hind feet and turned in a circle, before he succeeded in getting his trunk around the metal shaft of the broadhead. Finally, he pulled it free and tossed it high into the air.

After getting rid of the arrow he ran back towards us a good hundred yards, reared up above the grass and turned completely around again. Definitely he was looking for us now, but we were crouching low in the hippo trail, with only our heads above the grass tops.

For a full two minutes the maddened elephant ran first in one direction, then in another, trying to locate us. We could have killed him half a dozen times with the heavy rifles, but knowing that he had received only a very slight wound from the arrow, we did not want to shoot him with the rifles unless forced to do so in order to save our own hides. Luckily, the beast stayed up-wind of us and was never able to get our scent. We stayed quiet and more or less out of sight, so that he could not locate us.

Finally he gave up, and turning towards the river forest again, was soon lost from sight. The old bull probably had a tooth-ache for a couple of days, but that was about all the damage the arrow had done. Had it gone into his chest cavity where I had aimed it, there would have been a different story to tell. A well-placed arrow in the chest cavity will kill an elephant just as quickly as if he were hit in the same place with a ·375 Magnum bullet. The fact is, an arrow-cut wound bleeds much faster than a bullet-torn wound.

On another occasion I shot a big tusker that came at me,

square in the brain region at less than thirty yards, and despite the fact that I was using a 110-pound split bamboo bow and a seventeen-hundred grain steel tipped dural arrow forty inches long, it lacked three inches of penetrating enough bone to reach the brain. From the angle at which the arrow struck, it would have had to cut almost fourteen inches of hide, muscle and bone to reach the brain. At almost the instant the arrow struck, Wayne Stotler hit the oncoming monster with a 300-grain full patch ·375 Magnum bullet and the fast-moving slug went through the brain, tearing it to shreds and passing out the back of the animal's head. The beast stopped as though hit by a giant sledge hammer.

The broadhead arrow has no impact, or what is commonly called in rifle ballistics, energy, and so gives an animal no shock to speak of. Therefore, when my arrow struck the bull in the centre of the head, about five or six inches above the line of his eyes, it had no more effect than the bite of a horsefly. I had doubted before this incident that an arrow would have enough penetrating power to go through sufficient bone to reach the brain. After that, I knew for sure.

During our stay in Africa our party killed seven elephants. three of which I got with the bow and arrow and one, with a rifle. Wayne killed two, and he and Ed. together killed another one. Of the seven, three charged, two after they had been wounded, and one without having even been scratched. While photographing them from jeeps, we had no less than half a dozen charges, but were able to outrun the beasts and we harmed none of those. I would say that in perhaps a dozen cases, individuals and herds ran away from us when they discovered we were near, but had we depended on them all to run away we would still be over there "pushing daisies from the roots up."

EPILOGUE

No man can explain the many and differing desires shut deep within the human heart. Down through the ages the mind, the heart and the soul of man have been influenced by an intangible force so strong as to be almost a compelling hand. It is doubtful that anyone has ever wholly controlled his own destiny. Ever since I came into the world the force that has guided me seems to have been the urge to *Go and See*.

The song of the birds, the voice of every living wild creature has lured me; the rolling plains, the swift-flowing rivers, the wild forest, the blue mountains, the mighty ocean have seemed to beckon me. The unknown wilderness has said to me: "Come sit in our green shade and commune with the Great Spirit in our leafy cathedrals while the choirs of bird-song fill your ears. Let the joy of living warm your heart as you walk beneath our branches and pit your skill against the cunning roebuck, the strong bear, the lordly moose, the wily jaguar, lion and leopard, the crafty buffalo and the mighty elephant."

For thirty years I have answered this call of the forest. I have walked under leafy branches and sat beneath their shade while my heart thrilled to the music of the birds. I have pitted my skill against that of many of the wild creatures in the untamed wilderness. From these experiences I have learned that no other song can rival the voice of the feathered choir, no other contest can give the satisfaction of trying my skill against the cunning of many beasts in a thrilling and dangerous game. I have come to realize that although nature in the raw may be beautiful, awe-inspiring, majestic and frightful, as the case may be, it is almost never mild. While beauty blooms on every side, mercy is unknown and death never sleeps in the wilds.

It has been my joy to sit for hours on end and watch the children of the forest as they played or made love or fought to the death. I have seen the eagle drop a thousand feet and snatch the innocent lamb from the side of a loving mother; spellbound,

I have stood and watched a Cooper's hawk pick a frightened teal in full flight out of the air. I have seen a lone coyote in a matter of moments kill twin fawns and their gentle mother with his deadly fangs; while I stood near, the mighty lion has ripped open with his cruel claws the belly of a full-grown wildebeeste. I have seen the strangling coils of the rock python holding within his deadly grip a half grown gerenuk. I have talked with men whose arm or leg or half of whose face had been torn away by the resistless jaws and snapping teeth of the hated hyena.

Although the face of nature is often breath-takingly lovely, beneath that exterior is a cruelty unmatched by mankind. To keep Mother Nature's children in balance, many must die that others may live. In my time, I have slain many of the strong to help the weak. Following the first law of survival, I have killed the innocent to appease my own hunger. I have shot thousands of feet of film, preserving the actions of animals encountered in the wilderness. These films, taking many persons into the wilds vicariously, have been seen and enjoyed by millions; no other work have I found to be so satisfying.

The idea of re-living his life if it were possible has occurred to almost everyone, I am sure. My own has been enjoyable, thrilling, frightening, and many times one false move would have caused sudden death, but I would not change my path if I had it to travel again, except I would perhaps spend even more time with nature than I have done. All over the world there are some who will understand, while others cannot.

There may be some who feel that man has no right to kill any living creature, yet I have noted that there are few vegetarians among human beings. In my own case, I have never slain for the pleasure of killing nor merely for trophies to hang on the wall and gloat over; I have killed for food, or to preserve the lives of innocent creatures, or on fairly numerous occasions, to save my own life; these have been my reasons. Some animals I have shot with the rifle, but most of them I have killed with the merciful broadhead arrow, which causes free hæmorrhage and quick death.

The Great Spirit gave us human beings no tusks nor fangs nor claws; rather, He provided us with a brain to invent and skilled hands to fashion weapons, by means of which we could obtain food and protect our families. My pioneer heritage or perhaps a trace of Indian blood—something—has caused me to choose the least destructive and most sporting weapon known to modern man, the long bow, but when used with skill and cunning accuracy, it is one before which no living creature can stand.

I love the bow above every other mechanical invention of man, yet it was his first invention before the dawn of history and was preceded only by the club in the hand of even earlier man.

Memories furnish the mind and warm or chill the cockles of the heart, as the case may be, but sharp, clear motion pictures of living creatures in their natural surroundings are the most durable and satisfying of all trophies.

Among all my experiences, however, the most valued have been the bonds of friendship forged with spirits akin to mine: strong and courageous Mike Osceola, a Seminole Indian; Charlie Snow, another of the same breed; crafty Ned Frost, perhaps the greatest living naturalist in America; skilled but reckless Frank Colcord, the phantom of the Tonto Rim country in Arizona, who hunts with dogs and the lariat, a man to whom fear is utterly unknown; Casumway, the black tracker of the Belgian Congo, who has spent most of his life along the jungle trails; Dave Coleman, another Indian; Wally Gravett, a Canadian Scotchman; these have taught me and been my friends. Besides them there are others, companions who are much like brothers to me, Ed. Hill, Wayne Stotler, Don Carson, Errol Flynn, Carl Mikule, Tod Oviatt, the late Glenn H. Curtiss, Arthur Phelps, Wally Opie, Smokey White, Rory Calhoun and Guy Madison. We have followed the trails together.

The future holds much of promise and interest to me: there are many places yet unseen, new animals to study, fresh acquaintances to be made, old friends to be enjoyed, more dangers to face and new thrills to be felt. I am not looking for the end of the trail. Adventure and the wilderness are calling me. I must *Go and See.*

CPSIA information can be obtained
at www.ICGtesting.com
Printed in the USA
FSHW022000190720
72294FS